HORSE CRAZY!

Horse Crazy!

1,001 Fun Facts, Craft Projects, Games, Activities, and Know-How for Horse-Loving Kids

JESSIE HAAS

Storey Publishing

The mission of Storey Publishing is to serve our customers by publishing practical information that encourages personal independence in harmony with the environment.

Edited by Lisa H. Hiley and Deborah Burns
Art direction by Jessica Armstrong
Book design by Sara Gillingham and Jessica Armstrong
Cover design by Sara Gillingham

Cover and interior color illustrations by © Galia Bernstein
Line drawings by © Elara Tanguy, except for pages 93 and 94
   (left) by Beverly Duncan, 94 (right) by Brigita Fuhrmann,
   155–161 by Melanie Powell, and 180–181 by Jim Dykeman
Maps by Ilona Sherratt

Indexed by Susan Olason

Be sure to read all instructions thoroughly before attempting any of the activities in this book, especially if you are inexperienced in handling horses. No book can replace the guidance of an expert horseman nor can it anticipate every situation that will arise. Always be cautious and vigilant when working with a large and unpredictable animal.

Printed in the United States by Versa Press
10 9 8 7 6 5 4 3

Library of Congress Cataloging-in-Publication Data

Haas, Jessie.
   Horse crazy! / by Jessie Haas.
      p. cm.
   Includes index.
   ISBN 978-1-60342-154-6 (pbk. : alk. paper)
   1. Horses—Juvenile literature. I. Title.
SF302.H33 2009
636.1—dc22
                    2009007848

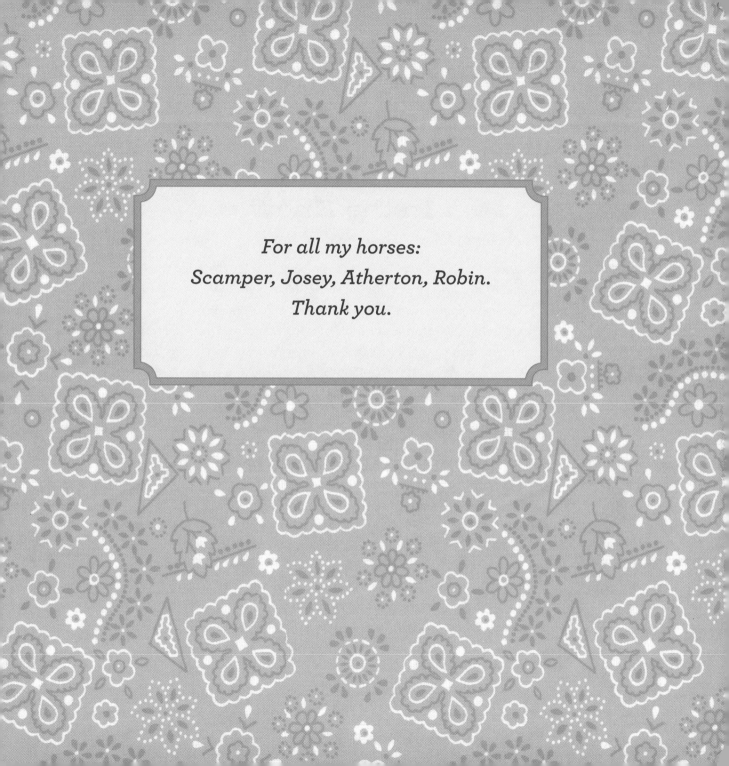

For all my horses:
Scamper, Josey, Atherton, Robin.
Thank you.

CONTENTS

Part 1
In the Know

Essential Equine Education for the Truly Obsessed

Part 2
In the Saddle

and in the Stall and in the Show Ring . . .

Part 3
In the Spotlight

The Arts, the Environment, and Some Equine Extras

The Tail End

More Good Stuff

Meet the Author

Horses have been an essential part of my life since early childhood. I've trained two and am starting with number three, my young Morgan, River Echo Red Robin. I love how horses look and sound and feel and smell. I love horse books and horse music. Horses are the only animal I can draw. I am certifiably Horse Crazy.

Are you horse crazy too? Then this book is for you. You'll find tons of great information, book and movie reviews all about horses, fun craft projects, and much more! You'll be able to:

✸ Make jewelry for your horse, your friends, and yourself.

✸ Practice tying useful knots.

✸ Jump into the show scene, even if your only horses (for now) are made of plastic.

✸ Read about unusual sports like jousting, Cowboy Mounted Shooting, and skijoring.

✸ Learn how to draw horses, photograph horses, write horse stories, and make horse music.

✸ Practice braiding your horse's mane.

✸ Have fun painting on your horse (it's okay, really!).

Take the quiz on the next page to find out just how horse crazy you are. Then saddle up and gallop into the future!

Jessie Haas

Jessie Haas

∽ WRITING ABOUT HORSES ∾

I'm lucky, because I've been able to turn my love of horses into a career of writing about them. Here are a few of the books I've written (I hope you've read some of them!):

✸ *Appaloosa Zebra, a Horse Lover's Alphabet*
✸ *Scamper and the Horse Show*
✸ *Runaway Radish*
✸ *Birthday Pony*
✸ *Jigsaw Pony*
✸ *Unbroken*
✸ *Shaper*
✸ *Chase*
✸ *Hoofprints: Horse Poems*

Learn more at my Web site: *www.jessiehaas.com*.

You're probably horse crazy if:

You'd rather muck out a stall than clean your room.

*

Your parents built an addition on the house
to make space for your Breyer models.

*

You've read every horse book in the library — how many times?

*

You secretly like the smell of horse manure.

*

You think every field would look better with a horse in it.

*

Your first word was "pony" and your second word was "faster"!

*

Your mom says "This room looks like a stable!"
and you take it as a compliment.

*

Your mom says "This room looks like a stable!" and you take it
as an insult. Your stable is much cleaner than your room!

*

You draw horses in the margins of your homework.

*

You can hear a carriage horse coming from five blocks away,
even during Friday rush hour.

*

When you grow up you're going to be an Olympic rider/
veterinarian/horse artist/horse breeder/horse trainer/groom —
oh heck, you're going to be a horse!

PART ONE

In the Know

Essential Equine Education for the Truly Obsessed

People have been obsessed with horses for thousands of years: painting them on cave walls, milking them, riding and driving them. It's easy to forget the importance of horses in human history, now that they are no longer necessary to run our world. But horses made us who we are — all of us, even people who never think about them.

One example of how horses changed the world is the impact they had on human language. This book is written in English, one of a family of languages called Indo-European. Languages from far apart places — India, Europe, Central Asia — share a common ancestor language, spoken about five thousand years ago in the area around the Caspian and Black Seas. Its descendant languages are spoken by roughly half the world's population. How did that happen? Well, it all started about 50 million years ago, with a little animal called *Eohippus*.

⚞ MO-OM! ⚟ THAT'S NOT HIS ANKLE!

If you are going to hang around with horses, or own one of your own, your mom and dad need to know a few things. Here's a list of basic information to start your parents off on the correct lead:

* The parts of a horse (next page)
* Horse colors (page 33)
* How to lead a horse (page 116)
* The importance of helmets (page 143)
* The difference between English and Western riding (page 126)
* How horses can help you in school (page 72)
* Ways to have fun with horses (page 242)
* How much horses mean to you (every page!)

PARTS OF THE HORSE

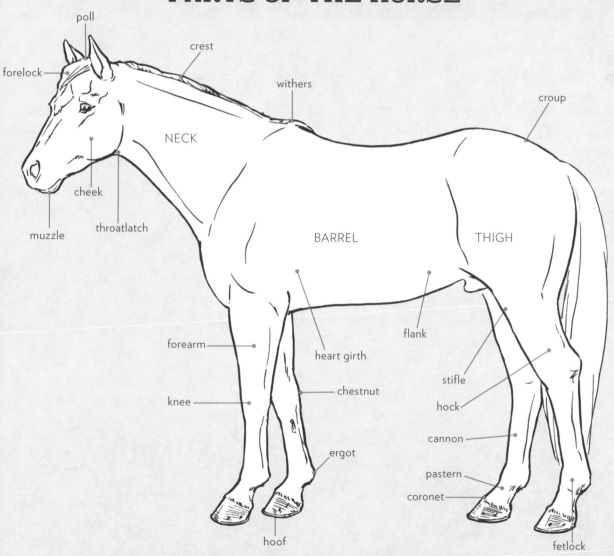

poll

crest

forelock

withers

croup

NECK

cheek

muzzle

throatlatch

BARREL

THIGH

forearm

flank

heart girth

chestnut

knee

stifle

hock

cannon

ergot

pastern

coronet

hoof

fetlock

PREHISTORIC HORSES

EOHIPPUS, the Dawn Horse

The first horse, *Eohippus*, lived 50 million years ago. She stood 14 inches high, about the size of a fox. *Eohippus* had four toes on each front foot, three on each back foot. Her foot had pads like a dog, good for walking on jungle floors.

Her eyes were set toward the front of her head, not on the side like a modern horse's. Her teeth were short, for eating soft leaves. To escape from predators, she could slip into the undergrowth.

MESOHIPPUS, the Next Step

Over the next 25 million years, a slightly different ancestor emerged called *Mesohippus*: she stood about 4 inches taller, now with only three, longer toes on each front foot.

Why did *Eohippus* become *Mesohippus*? As global temperatures climbed, jungles shrank. Unlike Grandma Eohippus, she couldn't hide in underbrush to escape predators. *Mesohippus* had to run from danger. The ground was drier and harder, and the longer leg and foot made *Mesohippus* faster.

14 INCHES

18 INCHES

MERYCHIPPUS,
the Ruminant Horse

By 25 to 30 million years ago, an even larger horse emerged. *Merychippus* was 30 inches high, about as big as a Shetland Pony. Her center toe was so big that the two outside toes hardly ever touched the ground.

Her neck was longer, which let her raise her head higher and see across longer distances. Her eyes were on the sides of her head, so she could watch for predators.

PLIOHIPPUS,
Equine Ancestor

About seven million years ago *Pliohippus* (roughly translated as "more horse") emerged; she stood about 48 inches at the withers (12 hands), the size of a Welsh Pony. She had a single toe and a leg shaped for speed. *Pliohippus* is the ancestor of modern horses; some of the more primitive breeds still look a bit like her.

48 INCHES

30 INCHES

HORSESHOE FRAME

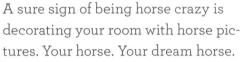

Materials Needed

1 horseshoe

Steel wool or wire brush

Paint (optional)

1 sheet of scrap paper

Pencil

Scissors

1 sheet clear plastic

Cardboard or thin rigid foam board

Slender knitting needle or nail

6 brass paper fasteners

A picture of your favorite horse

A picture hanger (optional)

A sure sign of being horse crazy is decorating your room with horse pictures. Your horse. Your dream horse. Your friends' horses — oh yeah, and your friends, too, if they're on or near their horses. Pictures from magazines. Pictures you've drawn or painted. Consider putting one, or a few, of these pictures in horseshoe frames; this is particularly cute if your horse is a small pony.

Directions

1. **Clean your horseshoe** with steel wool or a wire brush. Paint it if you like (spray painting should be done outdoors).

2. **Lay the horseshoe on the scrap paper** and trace around the entire outline. Draw a line between the inner and outer edges of the outline, where the nail groove is.

3. **Cut a solid horseshoe shape** out of the scrap paper following that center line — you want a piece that is slightly smaller than the outer edge of the horseshoe.

4. **Using the paper as a pattern** and holding the layers securely in place with a paper clip, trace around the paper. Cut the plastic and your picture the same size and shape as the pattern.

5. **Lay the horseshoe on the cardboard** and trace just the outside outline. Cut out the shape with scissors.

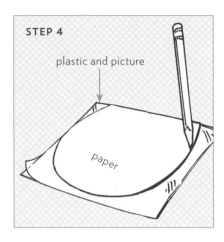

STEP 4

plastic and picture

paper

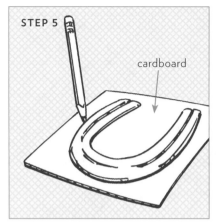

STEP 5

cardboard

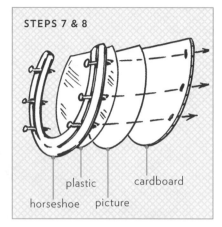

STEPS 7 & 8

horseshoe   plastic   picture   cardboard

6. **Place the shoe on top of the cardboard** and hold firmly together. Using the knitting needle, poke through the nail holes and through the cardboard.

7. **Slide the trimmed photo** and the plastic between the horseshoe and the cardboard (the plastic goes on top to protect your picture).

8. **Fasten all the layers together** with paper fasteners.

9. **Center and glue a picture hanger** to the back of the cardboard to hang your picture on the wall; or cut a rectangle of cardboard from the remnants of your project. Bend the top half inch, crimp, and glue to the center of the cardboard backing to make a freestanding frame.

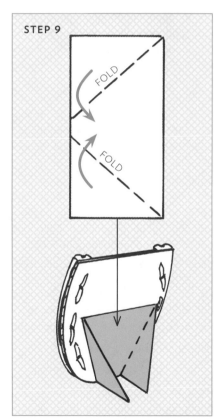

STEP 9

FOLD

FOLD

Horses and Humans: How It All Started

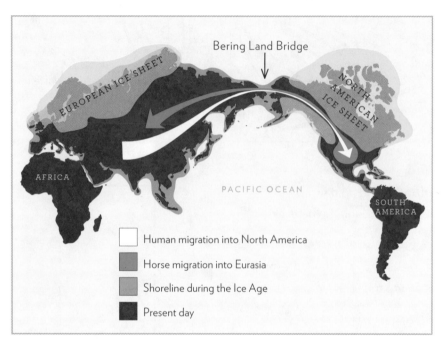

Bering Land Bridge

EUROPEAN ICE SHEET

NORTH AMERICAN ICE SHEET

AFRICA

PACIFIC OCEAN

SOUTH AMERICA

- Human migration into North America
- Horse migration into Eurasia
- Shoreline during the Ice Age
- Present day

About a million years ago, during the Ice Age, glaciers drove deep into the American continent, much farther south than they did in Europe. Grasslands and oceans shrank. Much of the world's water was locked up in ice. Horses had evolved on the plains of what is now North America, but when a land bridge was exposed between Alaska and Siberia, they crossed over it into Eurasia, where they met humans. At first the two species didn't interact much, but as people multiplied and became better hunters, horses multiplied and became wary of them. For 90,000 years, that was the relationship in Eurasia.

About 15,000 years ago, toward the end of the Ice Age, people crossed into North America. There, the horses had never seen humans and had no fear of them. The humans by now were excellent hunters and soon after their arrival, American horses (and most other large game species) became extinct.

Hunting for your meals is hard work. Around 10,000 BCE, humans figured out that keeping dinner nearby made more sense, and began to herd animals as well as hunting them. Sheep, goats, and cattle were the first herd animals to be domesticated.

Humans Become Horse Keepers

Until 4800 BCE (about 6,800 years ago), the only thing people did with horses was eat them and use their hides. On the central Asian steppe, horses were the most abundant game animal and people ate more horsemeat than anything else, even after they domesticated sheep and cattle.

The steppe was bitterly cold in winter. Sheep and cattle don't dig through snow with their hooves to find grass. They have to be fed through the winter. They don't break ice to get water, either.

Steppe people noticed that horses do both. They already knew there was a lot of good eating on a horse, so why not keep tame horse herds?

It wasn't easy. Horses are faster and harder to control than sheep and cows. The first tame horses may have been hobbled or deliberately crippled. But soon another possibility occurred to people. Somehow, somewhere, sometime around 4200 BCE, somebody trained a horse to be ridden. Now he (or maybe she) could keep up with the herd, and control them somewhat. Even better, riding was fun!

EQUINE GENES

DNA studies show that the female bloodlines of domestic horses are very diverse. At least 77 ancestral mares contributed their genes to produce the wide variety of modern horses. The male bloodline, however, is not diverse at all. In fact, all domestic horses may descend from a single stallion.

Wild stallions are fierce and hard to tame. This "Father of Horses" must have been gentle and controllable. Perhaps he had a hard time competing with other stallions in the wild and survived because he received special protection from humans who saw how useful he and his foals could be. There's a story there!

From that time on, horses were kept in stables or pens and used to hunt wild horses. Others were ridden to herd cattle and sheep. That changed life for everyone. A person on foot with a dog can herd about 200 sheep. A person on horseback with a dog can herd 500 sheep. When people started riding, they could own more livestock. Some of them became very rich.

Horses Change Everything

Larger herds need larger pastures. This started a migration. Riders and herders from the Caspian region pushed out in all directions, bringing their new way of life, and their language, with them.

Riding also led to conflict. Horses are easy to steal, and young tribesmen needed a certain amount of wealth before they could marry. It was tempting to ride a hundred miles away and steal horses from another village. They didn't know those people, their fathers didn't have treaties with them, and it was a good adventure. But that led to hard feelings among tribes.

Horses made fighting easier, too. Early warriors probably didn't fight from horseback; their bows were too long and clumsy. But they could ride to a village and dismount to fight then ride away quickly if it looked like they were losing. The ability to ride increased opportunities for violence; it also increased diplomacy, as responsible people looked for ways to prevent the killing.

Life became more complex — and probably more interesting.

❄ REINDEER PEOPLE ❄

In the Sayan Mountains of Mongolia, people tamed reindeer before they tamed horses. In some places reindeer pulled sleds; in other places, they were ridden. Wherever people drove reindeer, they also drove horses. Where they rode reindeer, they learned to ride horses. For many Central Asian tribesmen, horses and reindeer remained linked. Tombs contain ceremonial antler headdresses for horses.

The Invention of the Bit

When people started riding or driving horses, not just leading and tying them, they needed a better method of control than a rope halter. Horses' teeth have a handy gap at the back, known as "the bars." Anything put in the mouth there rests on bare gums, not on teeth.

Early riders and drivers of the Asian steppes may have used a cord around the jaw, as did the Native Americans. But eventually the bit was invented. Studies of equine teeth show that horses in Ukraine wore bits starting around 4000 BCE. The bits were probably made of twisted rawhide, the toughest material around.

As metalworking developed, people began to make bronze bits. Metal bits can be made in many shapes, but for countless years they were exact copies of the old rawhide bits, without any of the variety that we see today.

RUBBER SNAFFLE

EGGBUTT SNAFFLE

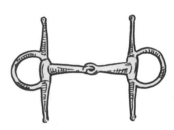

FULL CHEEK JOINTED SNAFFLE

CURB

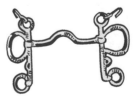

PELHAM

⮾ DON'T TRY THIS AT HOME ⮿

The Assyrians had strong, high-quality horses. Relief carvings from the ninth century BCE show them riding bareback or on ungirthed blankets. Reins were attached to a neck collar and decorated with a heavy tassel.

Historian J. Spruytte was intrigued by Assyrian tack, so he made some of his own and rode with it. He discovered that the tassel isn't just decoration. It weighs down the reins to keeps them from flopping. The horse can be steered by pulling the collar to the right or left.

Spruytte rode at full gallop on a saddle pad with no girth while shooting an arrow, just like an ancient Assyrian. Who says history is dry and dusty?

Horses as Pack Animals

The first animal-drawn vehicle, the *travois* or slide-car, was independently invented all over the world, designed first for dogs, then for reindeer, and finally horses. It's a frame of two poles that drag on the ground. A platform or animal skin slung between the poles carries goods or sometimes a sick or elderly person. These primitive vehicles were used in Europe and Asia until the invention of the wheel, and even later in poor areas such as 19th-century Ireland.

When horses arrived in North America, they were a perfect fit. Native Americans already used the travois (pulled by dogs). Their teepees were built on a frame of long poles, perfect for turning into a travois. Pulling a load, the horse could be either led or ridden. The teepee became a mobile home, and the tribes vastly expanded their territories. The travois is still used today in some cultures, still mostly pulled by dogs.

Horseshoe REVIEW

Spirit, Stallion of the Cimarron
(2002, rated G)

This animated feature of a mustang stallion's trials is handsome and horse-focused. Screenwriter John Fusco is a breeder of Choctaw and other American Indian horses, and his interest shines through in this movie. Realistic it ain't, but you don't necessarily expect that from an animated movie. Spirit is modeled on a Kiger Mustang — if only the animation artists had resisted giving him those silly eyebrows!

MYTHICAL HORSES OF THE SUN

Horses are associated with the gods in many ancient religions. Often the god of the sun drives across the sky in a fiery chariot.

GREECE

Seven horses pulled the chariot of the sun in Greek myth. Their names were Bronte (Thunder), Eos (Dawn), Ethiops (Flashing), Ethon (Fiery), Erythreios (Red-producer), Philogea (Earth-loving), and Pyrois (Fiery). They breathed fire from their nostrils, and it took the god Helios to control them.

Helios once promised his son Phaethon he would grant him any wish. Phaethon wished only to drive the sun chariot for one day. Though his father begged him to change his mind, he insisted. The horses bolted, and the chariot came too near the earth and caught it on fire. Zeus saved the world by striking Phaethon with a thunderbolt, killing him. Be careful what you wish for!

INDIA

In Indian mythology the sun chariot is also pulled by seven horses, either red or bay or golden. The sun god Surya is the only Hindu god that wears boots — and no wonder. That chariot is pretty hot! The god is driven by Aruna, a lame charioteer. The beautiful goddess Dawn goes ahead to herald him, and he travels with a retinue of hermits, celestial maidens, serpents, and giants.

The Sun Temple at Konarak recreates the Sun Chariot, with twelve wheels for the twelve months of the year. The seven horses represent the seven days of the week, and the seven colors of light.

SCANDINAVIA

Norse mythology gives the sun chariot only two horses, Arra'kur (Early Waker) and Alsvin (Rapid Goer). They were protected from the sun's hot rays by a shield attached to the front of the cart.

The chariot of the Norse God of Day, Dag, was pulled by a single white horse called Skin-faxi (Shining Mane). Golden light darted from his mane, lighting the world and bringing health, joy, and gladness.

AMERICAN SOUTHWEST

According to Navajo legend, the sun is carried across the sky on horseback by the god Johano-ai. Johano-ai has five horses — white, black, dun, bay, and chestnut — and rides them in turn throughout his daylong journey.

Inventing the Wheel

Around 3300 BCE, a new factor entered civilization: the horse-drawn vehicle. The wheel, which made vehicles much easier to pull, was invented in Mesopotamia (now Iraq) around 4000 BCE. Mesopotamian cities traded with the steppe tribes. Copper, gold, and a few horses flowed south. Cultural ideas, including the concept of the wheel, flowed north. Soon steppe people had developed wagons covered with felt panels (the covered wagon is ancient) and pulled by horses.

This development changed their lives even more than riding had. Now they could carry large supplies of food and water. That meant they could pasture their stock far out into the steppe instead of sticking close to the river valleys. Archaeologists studying the steppe have found that many settlements simply ended. Almost everyone took to wagons and began living in camps, not villages.

THE NOMADIC LIFE

Horse people moved often to find fresh grass. They owned little furniture, but what they had was elegantly simple. It folded or came apart, and

---

✸ AN ANCESTRAL HORSE ✸

The Tarpan, an ancestor of modern horses, lived in eastern Europe as recently as the early 1800s, when it became extinct after its native habitat was taken over by humans for farming. It had a shorter tail than modern horses, a short wavy mane, and was always dun, turning nearly white in winter. Described by one writer as having a loud, shrill voice and the general appearance of a vicious mule, it migrated north in summer, south in winter.

In the 1930s, two German scientists began experimenting with various horse and pony breeds in an effort to recreate this ancient breed. They used Polish Koniks, Icelandic Horses, Swedish Gotlands, and Polish Primitive Horses, which were descended from the last known Tarpans. The scientists also used genes from the Przewalski's Horse (see page 43), another ancient breed.

Today, there are only a few dozen Tarpans in the world, but their genes are behind the great endurance of breeds like the Trakehner, as well as the wavy coat of the American Curly (formerly called the Bashkir Curly). The people who know them say they are gentle and intelligent, but very stubborn and independent.

could be packed in a morning, loaded on a cart, and transported somewhere new. Their houses were tents (called *yurts* or *ghers*) made of heavy felt. Yurts were padded with colorful wool rugs. People sat on the floor to eat. The walls were hung with colorful felt fabrics that were beautiful and helped keep out the cold. Best of all, when you were ready to move to fresh pasture, you just folded up your house, loaded it into the wagon, and off you went.

Mare's milk was a staple food of the time. It was dried, turned into cheese, or made into an alcoholic drink called *koumiss*. People ate horsemeat, sang horse songs, sacrificed horses in ceremonies, and kept moving in search of new pastures. This was the way of life from the Black Sea to Mongolia, and was carried into Europe, India, and China by immigrants.

 MARE'S MILK

Mare's milk is great for foals — but did you know it's good for people, too? People on the Asian steppes have been drinking mare's milk for millennia. Now people in the West are slowly catching on. For example, mare's milk is very healthy for people with Crohn's disease, an agonizing intestinal disorder.

Mare's milk has 40 percent more lactose than cow's milk, with a protein structure closer to human milk, and more vitamin A and vitamin C. It's well tolerated by northern European people who tend to be lactose-tolerant.

What does it taste like? According to Virgil Buffington of Jamesport, Missouri, who has milked horses, "It's a little like skim milk and tastes sweeter than cow's milk." (*Draft Horse Journal*, Summer 2007)

Horses March Off to War, Part I

Sometime around 1800 BCE, a sleek wheeled cart — the chariot — was developed. The two-wheeled carts previously in use had solid wheels and a seat for the driver.

Chariots were different; they were designed for speed, with spoked wheels and a platform for a standing driver. His weapon was the javelin. He could throw it one-handed with the full force of his body, while driving with his free hand. Or he could switch to a bow, and steer by tying the reins around his hips. Chariots were a terrific weapon against foot soldiers and other chariots. But the advent of the mounted cavalry rapidly made them obsolete.

Charge of the Cavalry

Fighting from horseback became possible when the Scythians invented a short, powerful curved bow that could be fired on the move. Asian fighters were at their most dangerous when fleeing. Eager soldiers pursued, only to be met by a hail of arrows fired back over the horses' rumps.

Being on horseback, the invaders were more mobile and could fight on rougher terrain, while their technique of fighting while fleeing was shocking and highly effective. Wherever these invading tribes — called Huns in Europe, Hsiung-Nu in China — encountered chariot civilizations, they defeated them in battle.

Horseshoe REVIEW

Black Beauty

(1994, rated G)

In this version of a classic horse book, Black Beauty's voice narrates the story as it does the book. The movie is beautiful and well acted and the casting is fine — David Thewlis as Jerry Barker is especially good.

But the book is full of other equine voices — Beauty's mother, his friends — and it's full of social commentary. Too full, some think; it's a Victorian novel (from 1877) with a message, and the author had no qualms about pounding that message home. In those days, it was a matter of life or death for millions of horses. Some may miss that in this movie. No other horses speak, and the social commentary is muted. Still, the movie will help you visualize the book, especially the dark and crowded London street scenes.

After a while, chariots were abandoned everywhere and warriors took to the saddle.

From Persia to Greece to Rome

The Persian Empire rose on the strength of its warriors' riding skills. The Persians were famous for fine horses, which were used for hunting, racing, polo, and the postal system — the first known version of the Pony Express.

The Persians rode in collection, meaning they kept contact between their hands and the horse's mouth and used their legs to encourage their mounts to move forward in a rounded posture. They used an early form of the hackamore (a bitless bridle), called the *hakma*, to help achieve flexion (bend). Their skills impressed the Greek general Xenophon; he wrote about them in his famous book on horsemanship, *Per Hippikes*, which influences dressage riding to this day.

✹ A MIGHTY WARRIOR ✹ AND HIS FAITHFUL STEED

Alexander the Great came from Macedon, a tiny kingdom on the edge of Greece. He was the son of King Philip, who invented the massed cavalry charge in 340 BCE. (The name Philip means "horse-lover": *phil* means love and *hippus* means horse. Remember *Eohippus*, which means "dawn horse"?)

Alexander was only 12 when he tamed his great horse Bucephalus. The name means "ox head." Was this because of the shape of his head, as some writers suggest? Or was it an affectionate insult — as in, "Calm down, ya big meat head"? We'll never know.

King Philip had bought the stallion, paying a high price, only to find that the horse couldn't be ridden. Alexander noticed that the horse was afraid of his own shadow. He turned Bucephalus's face into the sun. Now his shadow was behind him. Alexander leaped on his back, galloped to the horizon, and galloped back. His father said, "You must look for a kingdom to match you, my son. Macedonia is not big enough for you."

Certainly it wasn't big enough for both of them. Eight years later, when Alexander was still a young man, Philip was killed by unknown assassins. Alexander rapidly conquered and united all of the Greek city-states, and then the rest of the known world. Bucephalus carried him in all his battles, until the horse died of wounds in India at age 30. Alexander founded a city in his honor, and named it Bucephalia. Alexander outlived his horse by only four years. After his death, his vast empire broke up.

CENTAURS

Centaurs in Greek myth were half-human, half-horse. The most honored centaur was Chiron, who had a school below Mount Pelion. He was accomplished at astronomy, music, hunting, medicine, surgery, botany, and justice.

Another part human, part horse was Mark, the legendary fifth-century King of Cornwall. His name in Welsh, March ap Meirchion, means "Stallion, Son of the Horses." He was said to have human form and the ears of a black horse. He always wore long hair and a hat, and the royal barbers were immediately assassinated after sweeping up the clippings.

His wife, Iseult, famously fell in love with another man, Tristan — looks like she may have had good reason! (A fun book with a centaur character is *Deep Secret* by Diana Wynne Jones.)

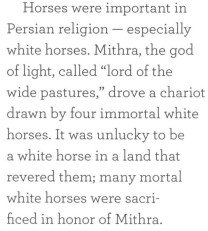

Horses were important in Persian religion — especially white horses. Mithra, the god of light, called "lord of the wide pastures," drove a chariot drawn by four immortal white horses. It was unlucky to be a white horse in a land that revered them; many mortal white horses were sacrificed in honor of Mithra.

The Persians were eventually defeated by Alexander the Great (see page 27). Alexander's empire was vast but short-lived. There was another power on the rise, centered in the city of Rome on the Italian peninsula.

Over the next few centuries, it became the dominant world power, mostly through the use of infantry soldiers to win battles. Cavalry and war chariots were less important, though you couldn't have a decent victory parade without chariots, and chariot racing had become an extremely important Roman sport.

Roman chariot racing was as highly organized as modern football and racing was a popular spectator sport. The cunning emperors used sports to keep commoners from rebelling against their autocratic rule. Charioteers were divided into four teams — Green, Red, Blue, and White, supported by Roman citizens and political parties. There was rioting in the streets after races, which was ideal for the Roman rulers because if chariot hooligans fought among themselves, they were less likely to band together to overthrow the government.

Divide et impera, "divide and rule," is an old Roman saying.

Along Come the Huns

The Roman Empire was already crumbling when challenged by the Huns, a horse-tribe from Eurasia. The Hun leader, Attila, assembled his warriors for a great battle with Rome at the Catalaunian Fields in the year 451 CE.

Before the battle began, he had all his men's saddles burned. His Huns could fight perfectly well bareback, but the other tribes he'd recruited weren't such good riders. Attila's move meant that they had to fight on foot. They couldn't mess up his highly drilled cavalry maneuvers, and they couldn't gallop off in a panic either.

The battle was essentially a draw. Afterward both the Hun and Roman empires went into decline.

∿ DO YOU RIDE A ∿ CHARIOT HORSE?

Chariots rapidly spread to Egypt, Mesopotamia, India, and China, where they were used for war and racing. Larger, stronger, faster horses were needed to pull them, so new breeds were developed. Chariot horses were handsome animals, standing 14 to 15 hands high, built like modern Barbs, but heavier and more broad-backed, with steeply sloping croups. They had distinctive heads with bony arches set above large eyes.

Chariot horses were bred and treasured by empire after empire (Hittite, Greek, Persian, Roman). As each empire collapsed in turn, the bloodstock was snapped up, eventually spreading around the world. Their genes show up today in Welsh and Connemara ponies, in the riding horses of Brittany and Normandy (ancestors of the Morgan), and in the Spanish breeds, which include many American breeds, most notably the Quarter Horse.

CENTAURS OF THE STEPPE

The Huns practically lived on horseback. Children who couldn't walk yet had horses to ride. It was said that the Huns didn't dismount even to "perform their natural functions," whatever that means! (Eating? Sleeping? Peeing?)

Each Hun fighter was accompanied by up to 30 loose horses — mares, foals, and extra riding horses. It made their armies look enormous. To fool the Romans, they some- times put dummy soldiers, like modern crash-test dummies, on the backs of spare horses. They also used the spare horses as a portable pantry, drinking horse milk and blood and eating horsemeat.

The Huns had stirrups, which they either introduced to the Chinese or acquired from them. No one in Europe had ever seen stirrups before. You can imagine the Romans slapping their foreheads and saying, "Why didn't *we* think of that?"

A Good Idea: The Stirrup

Before 300 CE, saddles had no stirrups. Riders' legs just dangled, and after many miles, they swelled painfully and developed sores. You'd think that would take the glamour out of riding, but probably fat legs and a funny way of walking became cool — a cavalryman's badge of honor.

Another problem was mounting. Horses were smaller in those days, but so were people. Riders either learned to vault on, or looked for a mounting block. Some people carried rope ladders, and braced them in one hand at the horse's

HORSE WORDS

Spur on: Encourage, urge on
Saddled with: Stuck with
Horse sense: Common sense
Beat a dead horse: Keep talking about an issue that's been decided

TOE RING

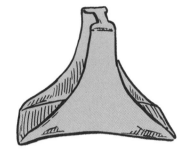

**SOUTHERN EUROPEAN
HAND-FORGED IRON**

MOROCCAN IRON

withers while they stepped onto them, like a stirrup.

Soldiers solved the problem by putting a short peg on the shaft of their spears. They jabbed the spear into the ground, stepped onto the peg, and then onto the horse. But mounting was dangerous for armed men. In 552 BCE, the Persian king Cambyses impaled himself on his own sword while trying to mount, one of many to die this way.

In India, riders girthed their saddles loosely and tucked their feet into the slack to stabilize themselves. (Don't try this at home!)

THE BEGINNING OF A BETTER IDEA

Safety concerns may have led to the next innovation, the toe stirrup, used in India in the second century BCE. It was a small loop of rope or leather that the rider stuck a couple of toes through. The good thing about this stirrup: You weren't apt to get dragged to death with only your toe in the stirrup. The bad thing: You had to

---

✳ ROMANS IN THE SADDLE ✳

Around the years 69 to 79 CE, Roman cavalrymen began mounting from the left, a habit we continue to this day. Cavalrymen wore heavy swords on their left hips, so it was easier to throw the right leg over a horse's back.

Stirrups didn't come along until very late in the Roman Empire, which is one reason why the Romans liked easy-gaited horses, called *gradiarus* or *ambulator*. Their trotting breeds had telling names: *concussator* (as in concussion) or *cruciator* (as in excruciating).

ride barefoot, which must have been tough in the winter. Brrr!

Chinese travelers may have seen these stirrup prototypes, or others from the tribal lands. Wherever the idea came from, Chinese riders were using a single stirrup for mounting by 302 CE. Shortly thereafter, by 322 CE, we have a depiction in Chinese art of a pair of riding stirrups.

You can't keep a good idea secret. The stirrup spread south to Korea and Japan, and north into central Asia. There it spread west, along trade routes and through barbarian invasions, and after a hundred years or so reached Europe. Riders' legs stopped swelling. People stopped stabbing themselves when they mounted. A new day dawned — and this being the Dark Ages, the main use for the discovery was war.

Horseshoe REVIEW

If you'd like to read more about the history of horses, I recommend the following books:

* *Conquerors* by Deb Bennett

* *The Encyclopedia of the Horse* by Elwyn Hartly Ellis

* *A History of British Native Ponies* by Anthony Dent and Daphne Machin Goodall

* *Horse Power* by Juliet Clutton-Brock

* *The Horse, the Wheel, and Language* by David W. Anthony

* *The Nature of Horses* by Stephen Budiansky

* *International Encyclopedia of Horse Breeds* by Bonnie Hendricks

* *Storey's Illustrated Guide to 96 Horse Breeds of North America* by Judith Dutson

* *They Rode into Europe* by Miklos Jankovich

* *Man on Horseback* by Glenn Vernam

* *The Mustangs* by J. Frank Dobie

* *The Horse Through Fifty Centuries of Civilization* by Anthony Dent

✺ HORSE COLORS ✺

- ✺ **Albino:** pure white with a pink skin
- ✺ **Bay:** brown body, black mane and tail. Red or "blood" bays are a deep ruby-red brown.
- ✺ **Black:** true black over entire body
- ✺ **Blue roan:** mixed white and black hairs over the entire body, possibly with a few red hairs mixed in; mane and tail usually darker
- ✺ **Buckskin:** yellow, golden, or tan, with black mane, tail, and lower legs. No dorsal stripe.
- ✺ **Chestnut:** golden or red-brown all over. Mane and tail may be the same color or lighter; a white mane and tail are called flaxen.
- ✺ **Chocolate:** very dark chestnut (nearly black) with white mane and tail
- ✺ **Cream:** light, medium, or dark cream color all over, with pink skin and light brown eyes
- ✺ **Cremello:** extremely pale yellow all over
- ✺ **Dapple-gray:** gray with an overlying darker mottled or spotted pattern
- ✺ **Dun:** yellow or golden body, dark mane and tail; usually a dorsal stripe down the middle of the back and zebra stripes on the lower legs, and sometimes over the withers
- ✺ **Gray:** born black or charcoal gray, but turns lighter with age, until coat appears nearly white
- ✺ **Grullo:** smoky-gray body; usually has a dorsal stripe and dark mane, tail, and lower legs. Coat does not lighten with age.
- ✺ **Liver chestnut:** dark brown all over; same color or lighter mane and tail
- ✺ **Medicine Hat:** a pinto with a white body, colored "bonnet" over the ears, and colored "shield" on the chest
- ✺ **Overo:** a pinto in which the dark color appears to be laid over the white. Overos rarely have white extending across the back. Legs tend to be colored, markings tend to be splashy and irregular.
- ✺ **Palomino:** golden coat, white mane and tail
- ✺ **Piebald:** black and white pinto
- ✺ **Pinto:** white splashed with brown or black (or vice versa!)
- ✺ **Red roan:** a mix of red and white hairs all over the body; black mane and tail
- ✺ **Skewbald:** any color of pinto other than black and white — chestnut, palomino, or roan
- ✺ **Sorrel:** a red chestnut; may or may not have lighter mane and tail
- ✺ **Strawberry roan:** a mix of red and white hairs all over; horse looks pinkish. Mane and tail may be red or flaxen.
- ✺ **Tobiano:** a pinto in which the white appears to be overlaid on the dark. Tobianos often have white across the back, and dark legs with white markings, like solid-colored horses.

Horses March Off to War, Part II

For a couple of centuries after the fall of Rome, no single great power dominated the world. But in the 600s, many Arabs became followers of the prophet Mohammed and converted to the new religion of Islam. Calling themselves Muslims, they believed they had a holy mandate to convert the rest of the world.

Arab lands lie south of the horse's natural range, and the Arabs had few horses at that time. To increase his army's effectiveness (and because he loved horses) Mohammed promoted horse breeding. His armies also acquired horses by conquest; when the Arabs defeated Persia, they got some of the best horses and riders in the world, and seemed unstoppable, conquering the world from India to Spain.

When they conquered Spain in 711, the Muslims (called Moors or Saracens by the Europeans) brought indoor plumbing, streetlights, the concept of zero, religious tolerance, and wonderful Barb horses. All the Europeans wanted were the horses.

The Beautiful Barb

European horses were heavy and slow compared to the swift Barb. Crossbreeding between heavy horses and Barbs would eventually allow Europeans to develop a strong horse that could carry an armored knight and move at speed, but that time was still to come.

In 732, the Moors and Franks (French) met at the Battle of Poitiers. The Moors charged repeatedly, but couldn't break through the wall of knights. When the knights counterattacked, their large chargers knocked the Moorish horses down.

The European cavalry couldn't follow up on this victory, however. Their horses were too slow to pursue the Moors, who retreated back to Spain and held it for the next 700 years. Europeans collected all the Barbs they could and began breeding lighter horses.

∽ WHO WEARS THE PANTS? ∽

In 334 CE, the north Chinese warlord Shi Hu formed a company of 10,000 mounted women guards for the capital city, Ye. They wore brocaded silk trousers and purple headdresses, and were well trained as riders and archers. These 10,000 armed women discovered the freedom, comfort, and good looks of a nice pair of pants and changed fashion in China forever. From that time forward, Chinese women were allowed to wear trousers.

Attack of the Viking Warriors

Europe also had the Vikings to deal with. For two centuries, these fierce raiders attacked Scotland, Ireland, England, France, and Russia. The Vikings were part-time warriors; the "Viking season" was summertime, between planting and harvest. Viking farmers used horses to pull their plows instead of slower oxen. Today's Norwegian Fjord is a close copy of the Viking plow horse.

In areas where the Vikings settled in coastal France and England, the native people also began to plow with horses. There, many of the big draft breeds developed, like the Ardennaise, Boulonnaise, Suffolk, and Clydesdale.

Squeezed by horse tribes — Moors, and Vikings — Western Europe focused on its own horsemanship, developing the system of chivalry.

Horseshoe REVIEW

Breed Books for All Ages

One of the great pleasures of being horse crazy is getting to know the different breeds — and there are more of them than most of us ever imagined. There are breed books for all ages, but I recommend starting with the youngest and working your way up.

✴ *The Encyclopedia of the Horse* by Elwyn Hartley Ellis; age 10 and up. Terrific color photographs of horses from all over the world; useful and user-friendly.

✴ *Storey's Illustrated Guide to 96 Horse Breeds of North America* by Judith Dutson, photography by Bob Langrish, and its small companion volume, *Horse Breeds of North America: 96 At-a-Glance Profiles*; age 10 and up. All these horses can be found in North America; it has lots of information and many fine photos.

✴ *International Encyclopedia of Horse Breeds* by Bonnie Hendricks; age 12 and up. This is a graduate-level breed book, global in scope, vast in historical sweep. The pictures are black and white, and small, but don't let that stop you!

FIVE BREEDS DESCENDED FROM SPANISH HORSES

Some of these horses have feral bloodlines. Others descend from ranches and missions that bred from Spanish bloodlines. Still others descend from Native American bloodlines. Spanish blood is the constant. Many were nearly lost and some are still quite rare, but dedicated horsemen are working to preserve them all.

AMERICAN INDIAN HORSE

THEIR STORY: This name is given to all Indian horses, from Florida to the Northwest. Many tribes bred their own specific strains of Spanish horse, which were lost when the tribes were conquered and displaced. The modern registry sweeps them all together, but some breeders still maintain specific tribal bloodlines. Class O horses can be traced back to original tribal lines. Other classes are for horses or ponies of Indian Horse type. Horses crossed with modern stock-horse breeds are allowed under Class M, but no draft breeding is allowed. The U. S. Army attempted to slow down Indian fighters by turning draft stallions loose to breed with their mares, to produce slower stock. This largely unsuccessful war tactic is still remembered.

DESCRIPTION: 13–16 hands; broad forehead that narrows quickly to a point between the ears, somewhat heavy neck; short back, sloping shoulder and croup; dense bone relative to its size; tough and durable.

GOOD AT: Endurance, American Indian games, which include events like Counting Coup (on potatoes, not enemy warriors), Firing the Prairie, and Indian Trail class, in which the horses are encouraged to look at and consider an obstacle before crossing it

CHICKASAW PONY (FLORIDA CRACKER)

THEIR STORY: Spanish horses came to Florida with Ponce De Leon in 1521 and have been there ever since; the Seminole and Chickasaw tribes used them, as did Florida cattle drivers. These small horses went out of favor in the 1930s when larger cattle were brought in from western states; Crackers were too small to handle the larger cattle and were replaced by Quarter Horses. They nearly disappeared, but are now making a bit of a comeback.

DESCRIPTION: 13.2–15 hands; straight head; narrow, strong back with sloping croup; comfortable to ride, quick, agile, good stamina

GOOD AT: Ranch work, endurance, trail, team penning

NOKOTA

THEIR STORY: Descended from Sitting Bull's herd of northern-type mustangs (influenced by Morgan and Canadian horses), the Nokota herd ran loose in North Dakota until the 1930s, when many wild horses were shot by cattle ranchers who wanted to eliminate competition for grazing lands. A small band was enclosed within the Theodore Roosevelt National Park. When the Park Service tried to eliminate them in the late 1970s, local horsemen bought some of the horses and have worked to preserve them. There are around a thousand of them registered.

(Nokota continued)

DESCRIPTION: Spanish head with ears slightly hooked at the tips; square frame with prominent withers, sloped croup, strong legs; two types — traditional, 14–14.3 hands; ranch type, 14.2–17 hands; the ranch type is larger and less refined.

GOOD AT: Pleasure, trail, endurance, ranch work, dressage, jumping

SPANISH BARB

THEIR STORY: A hot-blooded, high-quality cross between North African Barbs and Andalusians, brought to the New World by Spanish conquistadors. It was nearly lost in the vast American mix until the 1960s, when breeders began to preserve the strain.

DESCRIPTION: 13.3–14.3 hands; chiseled head with convex profile; powerful neck and shoulders; short back with rounded croup; well-muscled legs and exceptionally good hooves; smooth, long-strided gaits; great cow-sense

GOOD AT: Ranch and cattle work, western sports, trail, endurance, light carriage

LAC LA CROIX INDIAN PONY

THEIR STORY: These small horses of Spanish and preserved Canadian stock were used mostly in the winter by the Ojibwa Nation to pull logs and pack out furs. When no longer needed by the tribes, they were turned loose to forage for themselves in the woods of Minnesota and Ontario until the 1930s, when many were shot for dog meat. In 1977 the few remaining Canadian ponies were slated to be killed to eliminate a possible health risk when the Ojibwa, with the help of Fred Isham of Lac La Croix, decided to round them up and send them to private land across the border. Only four mares could be captured.

The ponies were used to eating grass, poplar buds, and bark; it was difficult for their systems to adjust to modern feeds, and one of them nearly starved to death on commercial grain and hay. A carefully selected Spanish Mustang stallion was brought in to cross with the mares. By now there are around a hundred of these ponies on 14 farms in Minnesota and Canada.

DESCRIPTION: 12–13.3 hands; a kite-shaped head with nostrils that close to keep out snow and rain; low withers, straight back, sloping croup; very sturdy legs; strong, sure-footed, with smooth, flowing gaits; intelligent and curious

GOOD AT: Driving, riding, light hauling, work with beginning and disabled riders, great family horses

HORSE WORDS

Feral: A formerly domesticated animal that has run away or been released and now lives in the wild. All horses in North America are descended from domesticated animals, so they are considered "feral," not "wild."

Stock horse: Any breed or type of horse used to work livestock. Stock horse classes are similar to reining, but with an emphasis on more flash and style in the performance.

37

A Knight in Shining Armor

The word *chivalry* comes from the French *chevalier,* which means "knight," and derives in turn from the Latin *caballarius,* meaning "horseman." The modern definition of chivalry is:

✳ the medieval institution of knighthood

✳ the principles and customs of this institution

✳ the qualities of the ideal knight, such as bravery, courtesy, honesty

Training for knighthood started young. Pages entered training at about age 12, serving a knight in his household and learning to care for hounds, falcons, and horses. At age 14 he might become a squire, attending a knight during travel and military campaigns. A squire could be knighted by the age of 21, and start acquiring honor and lands and his title — Sir Somebody of Somewhere.

Knights held their reins in the left hand, and carried a heavy shield on the left forearm. The right hand wielded a lance, sword, or mace. Their chargers were strong, though not as massive as today's draft horses. Saddles were heavy, with high cantles, so knights could brace against them. Armor was heavy, and became heavier as technology advanced. Horses needed armor too — *bardings* is the word for armor or decoration carried by a horse.

HORSE WORDS

On his high horse: Behaving in a lordly and overbearing manner

ARMOR IS EXPENSIVE

Sir Somebody protected the kingdom, but like all military technology, he was expensive. Equipping him cost the same as 20 oxen — the plow teams of 10 households. In peacetime, knights kept busy and in shape by jousting, a competition that continues today (see page 254).

A HORSE IN SHINING ARMOR

The most important horse for a knight was the *destrier*, the actual charger. The word looks a little like destroyer, but comes from the Latin word *dexter,* which means "right." The charger was only ridden in battle. Up until the knight mounted him, the squire led the charger with his right hand, and managed his own horse with his left.

The destrier was a fighting platform and weapon, trampling enemy foot soldiers and knocking down light cavalry. He was also a throne, allowing his master to

Horseshoe REVIEW

Fantasy Titles by Robin McKinley

If you love horses and fantasy, read Robin McKinley. *Beauty* is a retelling of *Beauty and the Beast* — it's about a girl who's not as beautiful as her older sisters, who likes working with her hands, and who loves animals, most of all her enormous horse, Greatheart. When her father brings home the fateful rose from the enchanted castle, Beauty insists on paying the Beast's ransom and going to his castle. Greatheart comes with her. His fear of the Beast, and Beauty's fears for her beloved horse heighten the tension of this magical tale.

Rose Daughter is a different take on the Sleeping Beauty story, more focused on roses than horses. But since this is Robin McKinley, she just can't leave horses out. Magical manure is important in this story — and how often is manure important in any book, let alone a fantasy?

In *The Blue Sword*, a misfit tomboy with magical powers she doesn't understand is kidnapped by a mysterious Arabian-sheik type, and falls in love with his hunting cats, his horses, and the man himself. But before she can hope for a happy ending, she has to use her powers to beat back an evil horde. Romantic, horsey, and deeply satisfying. It doesn't matter that the horses are all 18- and 19-hands high and any real person would need a stepladder to climb aboard — this is fantasy!

The sequel, *The Hero and the Crown*, is deeper and just as good — it won a Newbery Award.

see and be seen, and boosting his prestige. Other horses that played a role in the chivalric system included:

- **Sumpters:** pack and cart horses

- **Coursers:** fast hunters and racers

- **Rouncies or cobs:** multipurpose farm horses, not elegant enough to carry Sir Somebody

- **Hackneys:** all-purpose trotting horses that were ridden, not driven (roads weren't good enough for fast driving)

- **Palfreys:** elegant, gaited riding horses used for traveling, hunting, and falconry by Sir Somebody (until the moment of battle, when he switched to his destrier)

Horse PLAY

TRICK OR TREAT

Trick-or-treating on horseback is fun in the right circumstances, which include:

- Daylight. This is key! Never ride horses on a road after dark.
- Steady, reliable horses
- A quiet neighborhood with safe back roads
- A preplanned route
- A quiet bag for swag (cloth, not plastic)

Because your trick-or-treating will be a little earlier in the day than most, it's a good idea to call neighbors a few days ahead of time. Find out who's apt to be home. Do they mind horses coming up to the door? Will the dog be tied?

Make your costumes. The sky's the limit, but be sure that the costume doesn't include flapping, noisy elements that might scare your horse or the horses going with you. Your costume should allow you plenty of mobility, and unless you're leading your horse, every costume should include a safety helmet.

This is a good activity to include younger siblings in, as long as conditions are safe and you can lead them on a reliable horse or pony. Leave your own dog home to avoid unnecessary excitement on the trick-or-treat trail.

Costume ideas include knight, circus rider, headless horseman, super hero, Arabian rider, cowboy, Indian, princess, or sidesaddle equestrian if you have the equipment and the experience. You could turn your horse into a dog, a cat, even a cow (blow up a rubber glove to make an udder!).

Chatting with Horse Folks

Dr. D. Phillip Sponenberg, professor of pathology and genetics

Describe briefly your work/play with horses.
Most of my work is with conservation of rare breeds of horses. I usually get to look them over and evaluate them, and then make breeding recommendations so that the breeds do not go extinct. I don't actually have a horse of my own at the moment, which is fine with me.

What's cool about what you do?
I enjoy looking at good horses, and imagining what sort of foals they will produce. Good horses of any breed are a delight to see and to be around. I also enjoy the people I have met while doing the work — the rare breeds are fortunate to have a number of really interesting characters that are guarding them from extinction. I also enjoy putting the breeding programs together. It is something like working a puzzle, and I have always enjoyed that!

What's hard about what you do?
The work is most frustrating when a good horse is not being used to its maximum potential. It is frustrating to lose bloodlines because certain individual horses are not in the right place, at the right time, and made available to the right people. It is also frustrating when well-intentioned people do not fully understand the importance of traditional types of horses, and in some cases promote and sell horses that are not the right type as if they were something significant historically and genetically.

What could a kid be doing now to wind up with a career like yours?
A huge part of my day-to-day job is veterinary pathology, which is not really related to the breed conservation. But in either case, the recipe is to study hard and do well! I had a professor once tell the class that "there is always room at the top" and it is really true! If you do well, you will always have more options than the rest of the pack.

How did you choose this path in life?
Part of it was just long-term interest in animals and animal breeding, part of it was just providence of ending up in the right place at the right time. Fortunately many people appreciate what I do and the input I can bring to conservation programs.

What surprises you about your work?
My main surprise is how often we come across previously unknown or undocumented herds of horses that are really typey and worth conserving.

What's one thing you wish people understood about it?
I wish that people more adequately understood the importance of type in breeding horses, so that the breeds would remain distinct from one another — and that each would have a secure future based on using them for what they do best!

Meanwhile, in Mongolia

In Mongolia in the 1160s CE, a nomad boy named Temujin overcame childhood poverty and slavery to become the leader of his small clan and, later, leader of all the Mongols. He took a new name — Genghis Khan, which means "universal ruler" — organized his people, and crossed the Gobi desert to attack China.

Genghis was a brilliant tactician. He used nomadic fighting techniques on a large scale to conquer almost the entire known world, from China to Eastern Europe.

Horses made his success possible. The Mongol army was organized in units of 10 men and 50 horses. The Mongols triumphed through speed, mobility, and surprise — all thanks to their horses. But with five horses per man to feed, their army had to stick to the plains. Their drive to the west ended on the grasslands of Poland and Hungary, where they killed 100,000 soldiers in one brief season. It was European forests that stopped them, not European fighters.

PEACE, AT LEAST FOR A WHILE

After the initial bloodshed, Mongol rule brought peace. Borders were dissolved. Scholarship, craftsmanship, trade, and religious freedom all benefited. Along with musical instruments (see page 318), foods such as sorghum, sugar, citrus, and grapes spread far and wide, as did inventions like firearms, printing, and windmills. Merchants felt secure.

According to a Muslim historian, "a man might have journeyed from the land of sunrise to the land of sunset with a golden platter upon his head without suffering the least violence from anyone."

END OF AN ERA

Genghis Khan died of a wound received while hunting wild horses. His body was carried secretly into the vast forbidden zone of the Mongolian

---

✻ EATING ON THE HOOF ✻

The Mongols didn't just ride their horses; they ate them. When traveling in secrecy, the Mongols didn't even cook the meat. They put it under their saddles, where a long day's ride tenderized, salted, and warmed it. A large Mongol army could make camp without ever lighting a fire or sending up a single puff of telltale smoke. (On the other hand, legend has it that they could be smelled a long way off!) They also bled their horses, a little at a time, and drank the congealed blood. They carried powdered milk or yogurt, and mixed it into water for rations.

heartland known as the Great Taboo. For 800 years, no one was allowed to enter this area.

Even under the Soviets it was guarded. The Soviets murdered as many of his descendants as they could find and kept Mongolians out of the Great Taboo to prevent them from making it a rallying point. With the end of Soviet rule in 1991, Genghis is openly revered again, and some Mongolians have ventured into the Great Taboo. It remains a wild area, still marked with the stones of campfires built during Genghis's time.

PRZEWALSKI'S HORSE

Ignore the spelling; say, "sha-VAL-ski." Or better yet, call it by its Mongolian name, Taki.

Przewalski's Horse is the only true wild horse living today and most now live in captivity. It's a close relative of domestic horses but may be the last living equine ancestor.

This primitive equine once roamed a large swath of Eurasia and thrived in the harsh desert areas of Mongolia, where it survived conditions that would have killed a ruminant. It was a favorite prey of Asian hunters as the heavy body yielded lots of meat. (Genghis Khan died from an injury received hunting Takis.) After the breed was hunted to extinction in the wild, herds bred from zoo animals have been released on Mongolian reserves to return to their native land.

Przewalski's Horse stands around 13 hands and is always dun. The primitive mane stands upright and has no forelock. The head is long and heavy, and the neck short and thick. This horse was never domesticated and its temperament is aggressive.

It is probably the ancestor of the Mongolian pony and many other Asian breeds, such as the Tibetan Spiti and the Indonesian Sumba. These breeds may be rather ugly by our standards, with their large heavy heads, but they are tough and useful animals.

After a Long Absence, Horses Return to North America

*In fourteen hundred
and ninety-two
Columbus sailed
the ocean blue.*

And he brought horses with him, changing the course of history in the New World.

In 1492, after 700 years, the Spanish overthrew the Moors. Spain was eager to make a mark on the world, and ocean voyages of discovery were the hot, new thing. Ferdinand and Isabella took a chance on Columbus's idea of finding a faster route to India. Columbus brought at least 25 horses on his voyage, but they weren't the best that money could buy. Given funds to buy good warhorses, his men bought cheap nags instead and pocketed the extra cash.

Good or bad, these were the first horses to touch American soil in ten thousand years.

The native people, in this case the Arawak tribe, didn't know what to make of them. Were they animals or spirits? Their confusion gave the Spaniards a military advantage when

trouble began. Spaniards stole from the Arawaks. Arawaks ambushed and killed Spaniards. Then the Spaniards attacked Arawak villages with guns, dogs, and horses. In 1493 there was a full-fledged uprising.

In order to end the uprising, the Spaniards offered

☀ HORSE WORSHIPPERS ☀

El Morzillo (the Black One), the fine stallion ridden by the Spanish conquistador Cortés, became badly lame on an expedition in Honduras in 1524, and was left with friendly Indians. They treated him like a god, placing him in a temple and serving him strange fruits and chicken. El Morzillo soon died, probably of colic from his strange new diet.

El Morzillo's statue was eventually worshipped as a god of thunder and lightning. When Spaniards returned in 1697, more than 70 years after Cortés promised to come back for his horse, outraged priests destroyed El Morzillo's statue.

the Arawak cacique (chief), Cãonabo, a ride on a Spanish warhorse. Cãonabo was the first Native American to ride a horse, but he didn't enjoy it long. Columbus's men told him that handcuffs and leg irons would help him control the animal. How was he to know otherwise? Once they'd handcuffed him, the Spaniards killed his men and carried the chief off to prison — a rough first riding lesson.

Sailing the Ocean Blue

Once America had been discovered, more Spaniards came, looking for gold and bringing horses with them. Ocean travel was hard on horses. Many colicked and died. Others were thrown overboard when ships were stranded without wind or when water supplies ran low. The Atlantic tropics became known as the Horse Latitudes because so many horses were thrown overboard here. Closer to the Americas, some of these horses swam ashore to islands along the East Coast, where their descendants still live.

After a few years, Spain stopped exporting horses to the New World. They didn't want to lose all their good bloodstock. Fortunately, horses thrived and multiplied rapidly. Many escaped or were released when they became too much trouble to feed. By the 1550s, 10,000 horses grazed the area around Mexico City, and they began to spread north of their own accord.

HORSE SAYINGS

☀ *I'm so confused I don't know whether I'm afoot or on horseback.*
☀ *You can lead a horse to water, but you can't make him drink.*
☀ *Don't put the cart before the horse.*

Horses and Native Americans: A Natural Partnership

As the Spaniards fanned out into North and South America looking for gold, they came into contact with Plains Indian tribes, who soon figured out what horses were, and what to do with them. Then it was a matter of acquiring some. Once you have a few horses you can round up more, and suddenly everything changes. Now you can move faster than anyone ever dreamed possible. You can kill a buffalo to feed your family in the morning, raid that insulting tribe 50 miles away in the evening, and be back by suppertime the next day. Your life is faster and more exciting than your parents' lives were.

With horses, the Indians had a military advantage over the Spaniards. They'd always known the land better. Now they had speed, and the element of surprise. At that time, guns were inaccurate and slow to reload.

An Indian could fire many arrows while a Spaniard was getting off his second shot. With new horses and old weaponry, the Indians kept the Spanish Empire from expanding into the Great Plains.

Warfare among tribes became easier and more profitable. Horses helped warriors travel far and fast. They were valuable, easy to steal, and they carried themselves. Sneaking into an enemy's camp and stealing his prize horse was a way to gain honor and prestige. This was low-intensity warfare with relatively few deaths, but the arrival of horses did worsen relations among tribes and caused plenty of sorrow.

✳ TAKING A CHANCE ✳

Gambling and horse racing have always gone together. The American sport of barrel racing comes from an Indian game called the stake race, in which riders raced around poles stuck in the ground and spectators bet on the outcome.

The European Influence

English colonists reached America a hundred years after the Spanish. They came to farm and prospect, not to conquer. At a time when horses were mainly used for military purposes, they didn't seem important to early settlers, especially in New England.

But New Englanders soon found that horses were more useful than oxen in the deep snows of winter. They could dig through snow to find grass. Oxen can't. As well as being used in harness, horses could be ridden, at a time when roads were few and bad. As horses became more common, indentured servants from Ireland and Scotland contributed valuable horse-handling skills.

The Virginia colonists, disappointed in their early search for gold, discovered that they could prosper growing tobacco. Horses were useful in plowing and cultivating, and plantation owners could follow their upper-class, English passion of horse racing.

Conditions in the colonies dictated the kinds of horses colonists preferred. In the early days there was almost no carriage driving. The roads weren't good enough for wheeled vehicles. The Narragansett Pacer was popular for its easy gaits as a riding horse. (Later, when roads improved, many Pacers were exported to Canada, and absorbed into other breeds. No one needed the pure Pacer anymore, and the breed became extinct.)

Pony Tales

A ROYAL BEAST

The unicorn became part of the English royal coat of arms in 1603, when King James I united England and Scotland, which had long been bitter enemies. The Scottish coat of arms featured the unicorn, while the English symbol was the lion; now the coat of arms united them.

HORSES IN CANADA

French King Louis XIV sent many horses to New France (modern Canada). Forty had reached the colony by 1670, when imports ended. By 1698 there were 684; these horses were of Norman and Breton stock, some draft horses, some trotters. They ran loose in the woods in summer, when there was little use for a driving horse.

In winter, when horses could pull sleighs and sleds over the snow, they had little shelter and lived on straw. They worked hard, and were driven fast in blizzard conditions and left to stand uncovered. The colonists believed that exposure toughened them.

The Canadian horses strongly resembled the Morgan. They were solid and compact, with fine heads, bold eyes, excellent feet and legs, and an abundant, wavy mane and tail. They could both trot and pace, and were excellent road horses, very influential in the development of American breeds.

Many were taken to the western settlements around Detroit. Some escaped and ran wild, contributing to the northern Mustang. Others were shipped to the West Indies, where they influenced the Paso. Canadian horses flooded New England after the War of 1812, as roads became good enough for driving. They had a strong influence on the Morgan breed. Many people believe that Justin Morgan himself was a line bred Canadian horse.

Horses in the American Wars

Cavalry troops played an important role in the American Revolution, especially in the South. The American cavalry was organized in the winter of 1777. Generals Thomas Sumter, Andre Pickens, Harry "Light Horse" Lee, and Francis "The Swamp Fox" Marion drew their cavalrymen from the plantations of Virginia and the Carolinas. Young men there were racing-mad, and were raised to be fine horsemen.

Cavalry won the battle of King's Mountain in 1780, and Lee and Morgan saved the day at the Battle of Cowpens in 1781. That same year Marion gained the upper hand in a long-running guerrilla battle with the British general Banastre Tarleton.

THE WAR BETWEEN THE STATES

The Civil War broke out in 1860, over slavery and the constitutional issues it raised. At this time the North and South were very different cultures. The South was horse-focused, passionate about horse racing and breeding, and full of

✹ MILITARY MULES ✹

In 1899, the United States Military Academy adopted the mule as its mascot, a response to the Naval Academy's goat. The mule, valued for its toughness, shrewdness, and stamina, served as a pack animal in the Army through World War II. The Army deactivated its mule detachments in 1956.

The first official military mule was Mr. Jackson, who lived at West Point from 1936 until his death in 1961. The current mascots are named Raider, Ranger, and Scotty.

fine riders. With their superior horsemanship, men from the South dominated the United States Army through the 1800s. The North had its great horsemen, too, but was slower to develop an effective cavalry. Northerners tended to focus their horse passions on roadsters and trotting races; the North was also becoming industrialized and had less need for riding horses and fine horsemanship.

The war swallowed many thousands of horses to pull artillery and supply wagons, and to fight in massive battles. Countless numbers of the nation's finest Morgans, Saddlebreds, and Thoroughbreds were killed, and the suffering of horses was one of the great sorrows of the war for many soldiers. The clustering of large groups of horses caused diseases to spread; just as with humans, disease caused most of the casualties.

Ride Proud, Rebel! and Rebel Spurs
by Andre Norton (1961) and (1962)

Both of these books are thrilling and emotionally intense historical adventures on horseback; they're great reads for horse lovers from a classic science-fiction author.

Ride Proud, Rebel! follows horseman Drew Renny through the last years of the Civil War with the Confederate Army of Tennessee. The author reveals a lot about the heroism and suffering of horses in the Civil War. (*Ride Proud, Rebel!* is available for free download on the Internet.)

In *Rebel Spurs*, Drew discovers that his father isn't dead, as he had always been told, but is a rich rancher in Arizona. He rides west to find his dad, using a fake name because he is too proud to claim kinship with this wealthy man. Drew's deception becomes ever more complicated and dangerous until the deeply satisfying final scene.

THE MODERN CAVALRY

After the Civil War, the U.S. cavalry was involved in subduing the western Indians (see page 54). Horses and mules were used in World War I, but as the role of the horse diminished in the 20th century, the cavalry lost its horses and merged with the Armored divisions. The 1st Cavalry, however, still has a mounted drill team that demonstrates techniques from the Indian wars.

Donkeys and mules are adapted to working in the heat, but were slow to arrive in North America. George Washington was the first to breed and promote them, after receiving a jack named Royal Gift from the king of Spain.

Mules were first used in the army for pulling wagons. But when the cotton gin was invented in 1795, cotton growing exploded in the South. The mule was perfect for the heavy work of cultivating, harvest, and transport. It could take the heat, needed less care than a horse, and ate less. By 1860, 75 years after Royal Gift arrived, there were more than a million mules in the United States. They were the economic engine of the South until after World War II, when tractors took over.

When the slaves were freed after the Civil War, they were promised "40 acres and a mule" — enough land to make a living, and the ideal animal to help work it.

MULE   DONKEY

Chatting with Horse Folks

Yvonne Barteau, FEI trainer, rider, and instructor

Describe your work with horses.

I have been working with horses since I was in my early teens. Cleaning stalls, grooming, helping at shows, whatever I could do just to be able to spend time around horses. When I finished high school I went to work at the Standardbred racetrack, first as a groom and then eventually an assistant trainer. I stayed in that business for seven years and learned a lot about equine fitness and also lameness. From there I started retraining problem horses in central Florida, which led me to the Arabian Nights Dinner Theatre where I starred as a Principle Trainer and Performer in the show. I eventually became the Director of Entertainment Operations for the whole show.

Our family got out of the entertainment business and started KYB Dressage in 1997 and my husband and I run that business in Maple Park, Illinois, to this day. It is a family operation and we keep around 60 competition and sales horses in training at any one time. Each day I ride seven or eight horses, teach some lessons to our staff or students, and oversee the general business of our busy operation.

If a kid wanted to grow up to be you, what should she be doing now to get ready?

She should read and work. My passion and interest for horses was fueled by reading many books when I was young. I learned so much by reading that I was much more prepared than many other children my age to take on responsibility with horses because I had studied so extensively on the subject. I don't think the youth of today reads as much as they did when I was young, but I very strongly encourage knowledge through books.

Next, and equally as important, is that any aspiring horse person needs to be willing to work, and work hard, with a good attitude and great enthusiasm at anything that might lead you towards your riding goals. You never know who will be impressed with your attitude and abilities and give you the opportunity that you have been dreaming of. Everyone appreciates a hard worker who is humble and always wants to learn more.

What is one thing you wished people understood about your path in life?

I know I was meant to do exactly what I do each day, and each step of my life was necessary to bring me to this place. I didn't question my opportunities; I just embraced them and worked very hard, knowing that I was very lucky to be able to do what I most wanted in life to earn my living. I am sure I did not start out any more talented or smart than any other horse-crazy kid. I was just willing to do whatever it took to get good at and make my way in my chosen field, which has always been the horse industry.

MAKE A MURAL

Colonial homes often had murals that took up an entire wall. If you're a good artist (and you have adult permission) you could paint a horse mural on one wall of your room. Before you begin, sketch out your idea on large pieces of paper; tape them together if necessary. Then transfer the drawing to the wall by pencil so you can make corrections and add details until you have it just the way you want. If part of it doesn't come out right, you can just paint over it and start again!

Colonial murals were outdoor scenes, painted in light colors to give a sense of space. Consider a hunt scene, with lots of green fields and tiny riders in red coats. Or a cattle round-up. Or a beautiful plain with a herd of running mustangs. It's your wall. What kind of landscape would you like to wake up to every morning?

Make a 3-D Mural with Models

Do you have a herd of horses just standing around on a shelf, dresser, or tabletop? You can paint that shelf and the wall behind it and the bottom of the shelf above to create a landscape for your horses. The shelf they stand on is the ground. A brown shelf-edge will help create that idea. Give the horses a grass-green surface to stand on.

Keep the scene simple, keep it bold, and let the trees or fences get smaller as they recede into the background. Another way you could use your models decoratively is to arrange them on small acrylic shelves on the wall, as part of your mural.

52

❋ EQUINE QUOTATIONS ❋

"Lord Ronald said nothing; he flung himself out of the room, flung himself upon his horse and rode madly off in all directions."

—Stephen Butler Leacock
(from his short story "Gertrude the Governess")

. . . .

"God forbid that I should go to any heaven in which there are no horses."

—Robert Bontine Cunninghame-Graham

. . . .

"Far back, far back in our dark soul the horse prances . . ."

—D. H. Lawrence

. . . .

*"For want of a nail the shoe was lost;
For want of a shoe the horse was lost;
For want of a horse the rider was lost;
For want of a rider the battle was lost;
For want of a battle the kingdom was lost;
And all for the want of a horseshoe nail."*

—Traditional nursery rhyme

"A horse, a horse! My kingdom for a horse!"

—William Shakespeare, *Richard III*

. . . .

"Money is like manure; it's not worth a thing unless it's spread around encouraging young things to grow."

—Thornton Wilder

. . . .

"When I bestride him, I soar, I am a hawk; he trots the air; the earth shines when he touches it; the basest horn of his hoof is more musical than the pipe of Hermes."

—William Shakespeare, *Henry V*

. . . .

"Horse sense is the thing a horse has which keeps it from betting on people."

—W. C. Fields

. . . .

The best horse doesn't always win the race.

—Irish proverb

Westward Ho!

Horses were essential in the westward migration of European settlers of the United States. The Conestoga wagon was made near Lancaster, Pennsylvania, and the Conestoga horse — a medium-to-heavy draft horse with Friesian and English blood — was bred to pull it.

Six to eight horses pulled each wagon, and the teams were fitted with harness bells — soprano bells for the leaders, tenor bells for the middle pair, and a bass-toned bell for the right wheeler. The left wheeler wore no bell; he was ridden by the teamster, as the first Conestoga wagons had no seat.

Settlers heading west discovered Native Americans who were excellent horsemen, with large herds of horses to draw on. There was constant conflict between settlers and natives; each side felt desperate, but over time, the Indians were the losers.

Making War Against the Indians

After the Civil War the United States turned its military might on the western tribes. The settlers wanted free land and gold. It was time to sweep the Native Americans out of the way. Modern rifles and cavalry methods gave the United States government an advantage. The natives had few wins. Many "battles" were massacres, with old people, women, and children slaughtered along with the fighters.

But at the Sioux and Cheyenne encampment at Little Big Horn in 1876, an alert Indian gave warning that Custer's 7th Cavalry was approaching. The warriors poured out on their horses to confront him. As Custer had been warned, he was greatly outnumbered. The fight was fast and furious, the massacre complete. The Indians returned to a meal that had barely cooled, leaving a battlefield on which only one member of the 7th Cavalry remained alive: Comanche, the Morgan horse of Captain Myles Keogh.

The victory at Little Big Horn gained the Indians little. The United States continued its war until all tribes were driven onto reservations.

The cavalry made war against Indian horses, too. Previously, draft stallions had been released near wild bands in an effort to create larger, slower horses, but they didn't do well in prairie and desert conditions. So it became policy to slaughter Indian horses after the tribes surrendered. Horses of many tribes were killed, immobilizing the Indians and breaking their spirits.

HUNGARIAN COWBOYS

The Hungarian word *csikos* (pronounced CHI-kosh) means horse herder. The csikos also handles cattle and sheep, and embodies the dash and daring of the cowboy and gaucho.

He wears a shirt with wide, pleated midlength sleeves; pants with wide, pleated legs that end midcalf; and a broad-brimmed, black felt hat. He rides a girthless saddle, held in place by his own weight, and carries a whip with which he steers the cattle or "speaks" to his horse.

The csikos are famous trick-riders and horse trainers, and the horses learn to respond to the different sounds of the cracking whip as cues. These amazing riders specialize in the Hungarian Post, known in North America as Roman Riding. The rider stands on the backs of two horses wearing a harness that keeps them in step with each other. He rides at speed, balancing by bending his knees in rhythm to the horses.

Where did the Hungarians get their horse skills? They're descended from the Huns (see page 29), and the Magyars, another central-Asian horse tribe. Even today Hungarian breeders produce great horses that frequently win international competitions.

COWBOY ✳ LINGO ✳

During the 1800s, the United States expanded westward, seizing the Mexican (previously Spanish) lands that are now the states of California, Arizona, and New Mexico. Anglo cowboys and ranchers copied Mexican equipment, and adapted many of their words. Examples include: **cinch** (*cincha*), **hackamore** (*jaquima*), **lariat** (*la reata*), **lasso** (*lazo*), **mustang** (*mestano*), and **ranch** (*rancho*).

Some words, however, such as *latigo* and *sombrero*, remained in their original form.

The word **buckaroo** was an attempt at *vaquero*. "Buck" comes from it, though it was used mostly in the north. On the southern range, a horse was said to "pitch," not "buck."

HORSES AND GAUCHOS AND COWS, OH MY!

The plains and pampas of the Americas were perfect for raising cattle and sheep, and the Spanish had experience with that. So did their horses. Horses from Spain had innate cow-sense, from centuries of working cattle and fighting bulls. The Spanish inherited branding from their Roman overlords, and roping from the Moors and Arabs. In the New World, they became the *hidalgos* (meaning "masters") of large ranches and the *vaqueros* and *gauchos* (both words mean "cowboy") who worked the cattle.

However, conditions in America were wilder than

in Spain. So were the cattle. Roping became an important skill because the cows were harder to round up from horseback. Paraguayan gauchos became especially skilled. Using braided rawhide ropes up to 72 feet long, they made amazing catches in wooded country.

Argentine gauchos adopted an Indian device called the *bola*. This was a set of two or three heavy balls connected by leather cords. When forcefully thrown, the balls wrapped around an animal's legs, tripping it and holding it in place.

Hidalgo
(2004, rated PG-13)

John Fusco, the screenwriter for *Spirit, Stallion of the Cimarron* (see page 22), wrote this mustang movie as well. It claims to be the true story of a grueling endurance race, the Necklace of Fire, set in Arabia in the late 1800s.

Viggo Mortenson stars as Frank Hopkins, who accepts a challenge to ride his mustang, Hidalgo, in the great race, and on the way, perhaps will redeem himself from drink and the demons that haunt him. The story is suspenseful, but not as horse-oriented as a horse lover would wish. Hidalgo is the only equine character; the other horses are just part of the action.

Hopkins was a real person, but his autobiography, on which *Hidalgo* was based, was a tissue of lies and self-promotion. Disney and its writers seem to have taken it at face value; for a different view, go to the Long Riders' Guild Web site (see Resources, page 358).

This movie is worth seeing for some of the horse scenes, but be aware that the depiction of Arab people is negative and inaccurate. Horses were treasured among old-time Bedouin and Arabs. They were not ridden to death in a race like the Necklace of Fire. In fact, no such race existed.

FOUNDING FATHERS
A Few Breeds That Influenced Many Others

Some breeds, while famous in their own right, are equally important for the other breeds that sprang from them. Foundation breeds are always tough and easy to get along with. Many are also beautiful. People have always wanted a horse that can get the job done while looking terrific.

CANADIAN HORSE

THEIR STORY: Louis XIV sent horses to his Canadian colony between 1665 and 1670. They were small, active, all-purpose horses with some Andalusian and Friesian influence. The horses multiplied and became remarkably tough. Exported in large numbers and absorbed into other breeds, they approached extinction, but in recent years have become more popular.

DESCRIPTION: 14.3–16.1 hands; solid and well-proportioned, with a deep body, strong arched neck, and exceptionally sound legs and feet

GOOD AT: Pleasure driving and riding, dressage, jumping

BREEDS INFLUENCED: Large numbers of Canadians were exported to the Detroit area and to Illinois; escapees influenced the northern strains of mustangs. Justin Morgan may have been a Canadian; certainly many of the founding dams of the Morgan breed were. Canadians shipped to the Caribbean helped found the Paso Fino. The Canadian Pacer, developed from Canadian and Narragansett Pacer blood, was important in founding the Standardbred.

ANDALUSIAN

THEIR STORY: Cave paintings made in Spain dating to 15,000 BCE — 10,000 years before horses were officially domesticated — show horses apparently wearing halters. The slightly convex heads resemble Barbs and Sorraia horses. Celtic, Gothic, and North African invaders brought other horses, and the whole mix combined to create the Andalusian, admired for centuries as a warhorse.

DESCRIPTION: 15.1–15.3 hands; elegant head with straight or slightly convex profile, arched neck; short back, wide chest, rounded croup; strong, elegant legs

GOOD AT: Dressage, pleasure, ranch work, driving

BREEDS INFLUENCED: Friesian, Lipizzan, Kladruber, Morgan, Spanish Mustang and Spanish Colonial breeds, Paso Fino, Peruvian Paso, and many South American breeds

Horseshoe REVIEW

Justin Morgan Had a Horse
by Marguerite Henry (1954)

This is the story of a horse named Figure, who was given to Vermont singing teacher Justin Morgan to settle a debt. The small horse becomes legendary for his speed and strength, and the foals he sires become the Morgan breed. As in many of her books, Henry changed history a bit to make a better story. The changes Henry made allowed her to create a story with strong emotional appeal.

MONGOLIAN HORSE

THEIR STORY: Mongolian horses are one of the oldest known breeds; they helped spread the Mongol Empire from China to Europe, and crossbred with native horses all over the world. They've been bred pure in Mongolia for 4,000 years. Mongolian horses are raised in *taboons* — large herds raised on unfenced pasture with a mounted herdsman watching over them. They are quite wild before handling, and must be roped and "bucked out" like old-time western broncos.

DESCRIPTION: 12–14 hands; heavy head; short, thick neck; low withers; short, straight back; long, sloping croup; deep chest; and sturdy legs. Some Mongolian strains are gaited; the gait is a fast, four-beat gait very like the Icelandic tølt. They are quickly tamed and become very willing riding and driving horses. Mongolian Horses are tough and strong; a team of four can pull 4,000 pounds for 30 to 40 miles a day.

GOOD AT: Producing milk and meat, long distance carting and racing, children's horses

☀ NO FLEAS ☀

During the Middle Ages, the Black Death (or plague) spread over Asia and Europe and killed enormous numbers of people. The disease, curable today by antibiotics, is spread by fleas. Oddly enough the Mongols, with their traditional habit of living close to their horses, were somewhat protected. Fleas don't like horses.

BREEDS INFLUENCED: Indonesian breeds including the Sumba, Sumbawa, and Bali; many Chinese breeds including the Erlunchun; the Yakut from Siberia; and the Cheju from Korea

TURKOMAN

THEIR STORY: This ancient breed from central Asia has been neglected and misunderstood by historians, who see its slim, narrow, angular body as "weak." In fact these horses have extraordinary powers of endurance and have contributed to many modern breeds, most importantly the Thoroughbred. Many of the foundation sires of the Thoroughbred, mistakenly called Arabians or Barbs, were actually Turkoman-type horses — it is likely that the "Godolphin Arabian" was of Turkoman extraction.

Turkoman horses are raised in large herds until six months of age. Then the colts are staked out on long ropes and fed an extraordinary diet including alfalfa, straw, dates, and boiled chicken! They are heavily blanketed to sweat off all fat, ridden by a light rider at eight months, and raced as yearlings but they hardly ever break down!

DESCRIPTION: 15-16 hands; straight, wedge-shaped head; long, lean neck with prominent withers; long back and sloping croup; long slender legs with broad joints; thin skin and sparse coat

GOOD AT: Racing, endurance

BREEDS INFLUENCED: Akhal Teke, Thoroughbred, modern Turkmene, Yamud, Iomud

Horses in Farming

Horses became important in farming after the invention of the horse collar, which happened in China in the first century BCE. The Mongols brought the device to Europe.

A collar allows a horse to put his whole weight and power into pulling a load — and at the time of the collar's arrival, there were a lot of hefty warhorses looking for new jobs. The era of the knight in shining armor was over. Luckily for the big horses, the collar allowed their steeds to find new work. (Probably very few knights turned to farming, however!)

Horses work more quickly than oxen, a trait that became important as the feudal period ended. Farms were consolidated. Fields became larger. When the Europeans came to America and began spreading westward, they had not just fields to plow. They had prairies.

Inventors kept coming up with new equipment to meet new demands. After the Civil War, for example, the population of the United States grew rapidly, fueling an enormous demand for food. American machine companies like McCormick and John Deere invented new machines: the McCormick reaper and the enormous combine harvester pulled by a 40-horse team. Thousands of horses were put to work and millions of acres of virgin prairie were put to the plow.

Horses on the Road

Between 1750 and 1850, many countries set up a network of horse-drawn coaches to transport people and mail. The front wheels of coaches were smaller than the back wheels, allowing for tight turns, good stability, and light construction.

The Hungarians introduced a new system of springs that made the coach more comfortable, less likely to overturn, and easier for horses to pull. Axles were improved.

A surplus of horses had developed, especially in England, with its passion for racing and hunting. The improvement in coach technology meant there was something useful for the spare horses to do — carry passengers in coaches and light vehicles. Now there was a reason to improve the roads. The British rebuilt the old Roman roads and created others. In 1780, there were 5,000 miles of good roads; by 1830, that had increased to 20,000 miles.

Passenger coaches traveled at ten or fifteen miles an hour, with food and bathroom breaks at inns along the way. Coaching used vast numbers of horses. Only high-quality horses could reach and maintain the necessary speeds. Their life expectancy on the job was a mere three years.

In America, roads were also expanded and improved, and coaches ran everywhere. The Concord coach, made in Concord, New Hampshire, was the main vehicle. The long distances between towns in the West could only be served by coaches under heavy guard, to protect against Indian and outlaw attack.

HORSE WORDS

The word **coach** comes from the Hungarian *kocsi*, which is the name of a village where the vehicle was first introduced.

Horseshoe REVIEW

The Windy Foot series
by Frances Frost

Windy Foot is a great pony, the setting (a Vermont farm) is authentic, the writing is terrific, and the depiction of the 1937 flood, a major event in Vermont history, is memorably portrayed.

Books in the series are:

* *Windy Foot at the County Fair*
* *Sleigh Bells for Windy Foot*
* *Maple Sugar for Windy Foot*
* *Fireworks for Windy Foot*

A Horse for Every Household

Private driving also increased with improved roads. Amateur driving clubs held match races on the public roads, and the wealthy drove elegant rigs in city parks. A variety of vehicles evolved, including: dog carts with room for hunting dogs under the back seats; two-wheeled gigs for two people, pulled by a single horse; governess carts, which allowed a governess to drive several children; and the familiar doctor's buggy.

Driving horses were usually trotters. Comfortable gaits weren't important anymore. Now speed was the thing. Morgans ruled the American roads, replaced by Standardbreds when that even-speedier breed was established.

Besides pulling public and private passenger vehicles, horses delivered all the goods that came by canal or rail.

They pulled garbage wagons, fire engines, hearses, and the meat man's, iceman's, and milkman's wagons. Heavy horses pulled big loads. Vanners pulled lighter loads. Fast Cobs carried express parcels at a brisk 12-mph clip. Horses were used at mine pit heads to turn the hoist, operate other heavy machinery, and haul coal wagons.

✳ A HARD LIFE FOR A HORSE ✳

It sounds like a perfect world for a horse lover, but city horses created a lot of pollution; manure really piled up. In 1900, the 12,500 horses of Milwaukee produced 133 tons of manure a day. Powdered manure filled the air. Urine pooled in the streets. Streets were crowded and congested, and the life expectancy of the hardworking city horse was short.

Horses were often worked to death; in England it took an act of Parliament to prohibit mistreatment of animals, and the publication of *Black Beauty* to popularize the movement (see Horseshoe Review, page 289).

ATLANTIC ICE CO.

STARS OF STAGE AND SCREEN

For some of us, just watching horses out at pasture is entertainment enough. Others prefer something a little more elaborate, and horses have always risen to the occasion.

CIRCUS HORSES

Bareback riding and liberty acts have always been popular circus attractions. Both show off exceptional riding and training skills. In bareback riding, acrobats on draft horses perform somersaults, pyramids, and Roman riding. In liberty acts a number of horses — as few as 6 or 8 or as many as 24 — perform routines at the direction of a handler who has no physical contact with them. Often the horses are all stallions of the same breed and color.

Equine circus acts of the early 1800s were far more elaborate than they are today. Some of the more spectacular feats included a single horse leaping over the backs of three standing horses, a rider taking a jump while standing on the horse's back, and Roman riding (standing up) on as many as 17 very loosely connected horses at once!

Black Eagle, described as "The Horse of Beauty," appeared with the American Circus in London in 1858. He could waltz, polka, and stand upright on his hind legs. There are fewer circuses today, and they have less pull on our imaginations. But horse acts still tour the country; various Lipizzan and liberty troupes, and the French-Canadian Cavalia, which has been called an equine-human ballet. This superb liberty act features white Lusitano stallions as well as Quarter Horses, Belgians, and Percherons, performing to live music, without tack or whip.

TV AND MOVIE HORSES

The television show *Mr. Ed* ran from 1961 to 1966. Mr. Ed was a talking horse, played by a palomino Saddlebred gelding named Bamboo Harvester. The show was based on a short story by Walter R. Brooks, famous for his Freddy the Pig children's book series.

Another popular palomino was Trigger, the horse ridden by 1930s movie cowboy Roy Rogers. Trigger, a Thoroughbred cross, played Maid Marion's horse in *The Adventures of Robin Hood*, but after that he was leased to Rogers and was inseparable from the singing cowboy's image. Trigger's successor, Trigger Jr., was no relation; he was a Tennesee Walker. Trigger had his own Dell comic book.

Gene Autry, another famous movie cowboy, had a series of blaze-faced horses named Champion. One of them, Lindy Champion, was the first horse to fly from California to New York, in 1940.

The North American Horse Today

The horse lost its place in modern economies after World War II. During the Depression in the 1930s, few farmers could afford tractors. They already owned horse-drawn equipment and horses were cheap.

World War II, which started in 1939, took many young men away to fight. Farmers needed labor-saving machinery, and with a ready market for what they produced, they had enough money to buy it. The war industrialized the economy, and the end of the war created surpluses of petroleum to be turned into fertilizers and to run large tractors. Nearly every American farmer abandoned horses.

Many out-of-work horses were shipped to slaughterhouses. Luckier ones lived out their retirement years in a back pasture.

In 2008 over 9 million horses lived in the United States. Of those, 3.9 million are used for recreation — trail and pleasure — 2.7 million are show horses, 844,531 are race horses, and 1.7 million are "other," whatever that means! Quarter Horses are by far the most numerous breed at 3.2 million, with Thoroughbreds coming in second at 1.2 million.

The horse industry contributes, directly and indirectly, about $102 billion to the economy, and generates 1.4 million full-time jobs.

Horses began to feel the bite of hard economic times in 2009, though. Hay was scarce and expensive, many people lost their jobs and even their homes, and some found it impossible to keep their horses or to find buyers for them. In the western states especially, many horses were turned loose to fend for themselves. (See page 84 for more on unwanted horses.)

 TAKING THE PLUNGE

Diving horses and mules were hugely popular in the early 1900s. The animals were first trained to wade and swim in the ocean, then an artificial pool. Then they learned to jump into the pool, from progressively higher platforms up to 40 feet.

The shows were eventually shut down by animal rights activists, but this seems misguided. The animals worked at liberty and could have balked if afraid. Mules in particular can't be forced to do anything they consider dangerous. (See Horseshoe Review, *Wild Hearts Can't Be Broken*, page 194.)

Still Working with Horses

Some farmers, like the Amish, continue to prosper under the old model. Their overhead is lower, and their equipment is more versatile. An Amish farmer is often able to work his land with horses or mules, while his neighbor using a heavy tractor must wait for the ground to dry up.

The fuel a horse consumes — hay, grain, grass — can be grown on the farm. The waste a horse produces — manure — goes back onto the land as fertilizer. Big horses can help a farmer make money in other ways: by selling young stock, and by offering hay and sleigh rides to a public that still loves horses. In Amish country you'll see hitch-rails behind many businesses, and buggy traffic jams.

Horses for Fun

Some jobs can only be done on horseback; mounted police continue to be used and valued. National parks use mounted officers, as does the Royal Canadian Mounted Police. And the gasoline engine is still relatively useless at handling cattle on the range. Horses are needed and used in the American West.

The advent of a fossil fuel economy, which we have had for nearly 100 years, initially meant a steep decline in the horse population. However, as the need to work with horses was declining, the desire to play with horses was on the rise. Pleasure horses, bred for fun and sport, have become the majority of the horse population. Horses are a luxury for most people these days — a necessary luxury if you're horse crazy.

CREATE A DECORATIVE WALL BORDER

Instead of painting, create a horsey wall using stamps or stencils. With a stamp, you press the image onto the wall. With a stencil, you paint within the lines of an image that is cut out of a solid piece of plastic or cardboard.

Stamping a Horse-themed Border

Rubber stamps are usually too small for wall treatments, but you can make larger stamps out of art foam. Rather than having the detail that the smaller stamps do, these stamps should have a more bold, graphic design that shows up well from across the room. Horse silhouettes work well, as do simple shapes like horseshoes, bits, spurs, and the like.

Materials Needed

Paper and pencil

Scissors

Art foam sheets, ¹⁄₁₆ to ¹⁄₈ inch thick

Styrofoam blue board (from a hardware store, or use building scrap)

White glue

Latex or acrylic paint

DIRECTIONS

1. **Trace or draw your design** on paper and cut it out.

2. **Trace the pattern onto the art foam** and then cut around the shape with sharp scissors.

3. **Attach the shape onto the blue board** using a thin layer of glue. Let dry at least overnight.

4. **To use your stamp,** apply your chosen paint color evenly and not too thickly onto the stamp with a sponge brush.

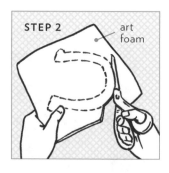

STEP 2 — art foam

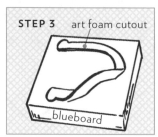

STEP 3 — art foam cutout
blueboard

5. **Align the stamp and press firmly.** Then lift the stamp, being careful not to smudge.

Stenciling a Horse Border

You can also decorate with stencils, either in a border design or dappled randomly on your walls. Horse stencils are available in lots of styles, sizes, and breeds, or make your own.

If you're doing a border near the ceiling, make sure an adult helps you set up a stepladder properly, and that someone knows you are working at a height.

DIRECTIONS

1. **Create a background** by painting or papering a solid strip where you want the border to be.

2. **Position the stencil** where you want it and mark the corners with your pencil; these are called register marks.

3. **Apply adhesive** or tape to the back of your stencil and stick it to the wall, within your register marks.

4. **Dip your brush into the paint,** and gently dab the excess paint off on newspaper or paper towel. Your brush should feel pretty dry.

5. **Apply the paint** in the open area of the stencil. You can use a swirling motion, starting in the middle and working toward the edges. Or tap the brush lightly on the surface to apply the paint.

6. **Remove stencil** from wall and repeat from Step 2.

Materials Needed

Stencils*

Pencil

Repositionable spray adhesive or drafting tape

Latex or acrylic paint

Stenciling brushes or sponges

Newspaper or paper towel

---

* To make your own stencil, make a simple drawing on a piece of cardboard. Poke a hole in the inside of the drawing and cut out the image from the inside, so that you have an open shape within a cardboard "frame." Give it a couple of coats of decoupage medium (see page 192) to stand up to repeated use.

Canvas shopping bag

Horse stencils

Masking tape

Fabric markers or fabric paint

Paint brushes

VARIATION: Trim a Tote

Canvas shopping bags save trees and reduce the number of plastic bags littering the planet. They can be handsome, too, and they're a good project to use those horse stencils nobody can resist buying. Paint makes a bolder, more color-saturated image, but can be messy and drippy. Markers are neater, but paler. (You can always use a mix on the same bag.)

DIRECTIONS

1. **Place the bag** on a firm, flat surface.

2. **Put the stencil where you want your design,** and hold or tape down firmly.

3. **Use your markers** or paint to trace the outline of the horse shape or to fill in the whole shape.

4. **Do it again** — the more horses the better!

⚞ LIGHT UP YOUR LIFE! ⚟

❋ Decorate a plain paper lampshade with stamps, stencils, or your own freehand design in paint or permanent marker.

❋ Get fancy with a fabric lampshade by appliquéing fusible pictures of you and your horse onto it (see page 210).

❋ Fasten a couple of winning ribbons to the top.

❋ Create a scene with your horse models around a taller lamp that could act as a "tree."

Smoky

by Will James (1926)

This story of a cowpony was meant to be a Western *Black Beauty*. Also written for adults, it won a Newbery Medal in the sixth year that award was given. You'll quickly get used to the cowboy dialect, and enjoy this fine story, illustrated with the author's own drawings.

In the story, Smoky is born wild, and after five years on the range is gentled by a cowboy named Clint. One day Smoky is lost in a storm and is captured by a cruel cowboy, whose rough methods turn him into a dangerous bucker.

After years on the rodeo circuit, his spirit apparently broken, Smoky and Clint are reunited. Smoky's nicker is gone, and the spark in his eye has dimmed. After healing him, Clint sadly turns him loose to run wild again, which is just the therapy Smoky needs. Grab a tissue in preparation for the touching ending.

TRY THESE, TOO

A lesser-known favorite from the 1920s is *Black Storm* by Thomas C. Hinkle. Black Storm will let only one man ride him, Joe Bain. The two are separated and Black Storm survives stampedes, fire, flood, infection from a flint wedged into his hoof, and wolves. Several kind people try to help, but Black Storm abandons them all in his quest to find his master.

Hinkle was a frontiersman who in his youth met Comanche, the horse who survived the Battle of Little Big Horn. He wrote a number of other books that are worth reading:

- ✺ *Blaze Face*
- ✺ *Buckskin*
- ✺ *Cinchfoot*
- ✺ *Hurricane Pinto*
- ✺ *Mustang*
- ✺ *Silver*
- ✺ *Tomahawk*
- ✺ *Tornado Boy*

OLDER THAN DIRT:
Five Ancient Northern Ponies

Ponies have been around a long time, and many have changed very little since the Ice Age. These ponies are similar to each other, because thousands of years ago, their homelands were connected by land bridges (see Doggerland on the map). They are tough and sturdy little animals, capable of a hard day's work but gentle and fun-loving enough for a child to handle.

DALES PONY

THEIR STORY: Originally bred in northern England as pack ponies for the lead-mining industry, as well as for work on small farms. They nearly died out several times due to crossbreeding to produce horses for transport and the military. By 1955 only four registered ponies remained, but with careful breeding and conservation the numbers have steadily increased.

❋ PIT PONIES ❋

Short and strong is best for underground work in cramped mining tunnels. Thousands of ponies lived and worked underground; the last only retired in 1994. Most pit ponies were Shetlands, and their export from the Shetland Isles almost caused the breed's extinction.

DESCRIPTION: 14–14.2 hands; broad head with short curving ears; muscular sloping shoulders, short body, deep chest and hindquarters; action is energetic and animated.
GOOD AT: Dressage, hunting, trail, driving; an excellent children's horse

DARTMOOR PONY

THEIR STORY: Originally used to transport tin from mines in southwest England, these ponies were allowed to run free when the industry dwindled. They were near extinction by the early 1900s, and many were lost to military service or were eaten during World Wars I and II. Careful breeding has increased their numbers.

DESCRIPTION: 12–12.2 hands; small head, strong but harmonious neck; sloping shoulders and medium-length back; strong, gentle, and sure-footed, with low, fluid action
GOOD AT: Children's pleasure and jumping, driving

EXMOOR PONY

THEIR STORY: The Exmoor descends from ponies that lived in Britain 100,000 years ago. In the harsh moorlands of southwest England they lived wild for many centuries. During World War II they were used for target practice, or were stolen and killed for food. By the end of the war only 50 remained. Today they are conserved on farms, but some continue to live wild on the moor.

DESCRIPTION: 11.2–12.3 hands; strong and stocky, with deep chest and large girth; very short ears; eyes have a fleshy hood known as "toad eyes." All are some shade of brown with a lighter muzzle; winter coat has two layers — short, wooly hairs underneath, topped by a longer, greasy coat that repels rain. The whorls of hair on the pony's body direct the drips away from sensitive parts of the body; the Exmoor also has an "ice tail," which is very thick with a fan-like growth at the top.

GOOD AT: Children's pleasure, endurance, driving

FELL PONY

THEIR STORY: Descended from native English ponies and from Friesians brought to Britain in 120 CE by the Romans, Fell Ponies were used as pack ponies and farm horses, and were ridden in trotting races. After cars became popular, the ponies' usefulness ended; many were slaughtered. They were rediscovered after World War II and have become pleasure horses.

DESCRIPTION: 13.2–14 hands; finely chiseled head, well-proportioned neck; sloping shoulders, long, straight back, rounded body, square quarters with a sloping croup; tough, athletic, and good-tempered with a long stride and good jumping ability

GOOD AT: Trail riding, driving

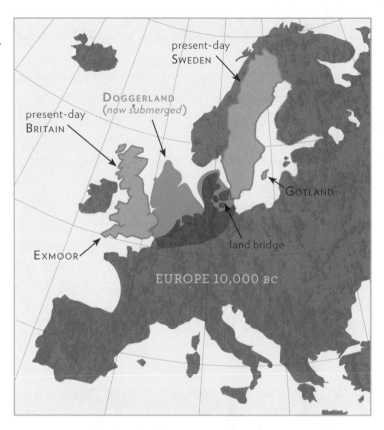

present-day SWEDEN

DOGGERLAND (now submerged)

present-day BRITAIN

GOTLAND

land bridge

EXMOOR

EUROPE 10,000 BC

GOTLAND PONY

THEIR STORY: Ponies similar to the Exmoor have lived on Gotland, an island off the coast of Sweden, since the Stone Age. The people who settled there, the Goths, used them to pull chariots, and the breed spread across northern Europe during wars and migrations. The Gotland influenced Spanish and Russian breeds, while thriving in its native Sweden until hungry Swedes were forced to shoot them for food during World War I. They were nearly extinct when a group of farmers created a 200-acre reserve for them, where a carefully managed herd still runs free. The local name for the Gotland Pony is Skogsruss, which means "little horse of the woods."

DESCRIPTION: 12–14 hands; broad forehead, small muzzle, short muscular neck; pronounced withers, deep chest, a long straight back and sloping croup; strong legs with well-defined tendons; an extremely dense winter coat; easy keepers and terrific movers, with good jumping ability

GOOD AT: Driving, children's pleasure and jumping

Bring Your Horse to School

School would be a lot more interesting if you could bring your horse — and maybe you can, if you live close enough and there's a nearby place to stable or pasture him. Your horse can be your school bus; if you drive him, he can be other people's school bus too.

Failing that, horses can give you great ideas for independent school projects. That's the secret to a happy life: figuring out how to earn credit or get paid for doing what you want. You can't learn this too early.

Am I encouraging you to be obsessive and to avoid learning about anything other than horses? Not at all. We all learn more when we're interested in a subject. If you write an essay about the Southern cavalry in the American Civil War, you'll learn things about the Civil War not covered in most textbooks.

Horse-related projects will not only help you learn more about your favorite animal, they'll help you become a

✷ EYE ✷ SEE YOU

Horses have the largest eyes of any land mammal!

SHOW and Tell

Today:

The United States

Periodic Table of the

better horseman, business person, or artist. Your apparently narrow focus will also broaden your knowledge of the world. It's one of the paradoxes of learning: deeper digging = broader knowledge.

English

Most English assignments can include horses. Are you supposed to write poems? Make them about horses. Stories? The same. (See page 282 for more on writing about horses.)

The standard five-paragraph essay — introduce your subject, make three points about it, and summarize — can be used for any horse topic, from a scientific look at how horses see, to a humorous essay on loading a horse into a trailer.

And there are always book reports! Use the Horseshoe Reviews scattered throughout this book to find a book you haven't already read; or ask your librarian for recommendations.

BREED ABC'S

Asturian (Spain)

Brumby (Australia)

Cheju (Korea)

Dongola (Cameroon)

Eleia (Greece)

Furioso (Hungary)

Garrano (Portugal)

Hirzai (Pakistan)

Israeli (Israel)

Java (Indonesia)

Karabair (Uzbekistan)

Llanero (Venezuela)

Miyako (Japan)

Nooitgedacht (South Africa)

Orlov Trotter, (Russia)

Persian Arab (Iran)

Quarter Pony (United States)

Rottal (Germany)

Shan (Burma)

Tibetan (Tibet)

Unmol (northeast Punjab, India)

Vyatka (Kirov and Udmurtia, former Soviet Union)

Wielkopolski (Poland)

Xilingol (Xilinggral Meng, Inner Mongolia, China)

Yakut (Siberia)

Zhemaichu (Lithuania)

History

Face it; for most of human history, the horse has been centrally important. In fact, here's a history question to ponder: In what times and places has the horse *not* been important to humans? Why not? Write an essay about that.

For a more specific assignment, here are a few topics that might be interesting:

✶ Great Horse Rescues of World War II

✶ Cavalry Tactics (if you're studying a period of warfare, which is usually the case in history!)

✶ Indo-European Migrations

✶ Horses in the American West

✶ Horses during the Industrial Revolution

Here's a general essay topic to think about: *What if the horse had gone extinct world-wide before it could be tamed? How would the world be different?* Look at how horses allowed people to cross vast land masses, encouraging cultures to mingle. *What if that hadn't happened? What would the world be like today?*

Use your research in a report, a poster, or a story. It could be about what really happened, or it could be speculative. How would life in the Americas have been different? Would the Indians have been better able to resist the European invasion?

PRESERVING ORAL HISTORY

History is made every day, but it often isn't written down.

Do a local oral-history project about the role of horses in your own town. Is there a racetrack or rodeo nearby? Do you live in an area where farming or ranching was, or still is, important? How are/were horses used? How has that changed, and why?

Find older people in your town with memories about the role of horses. Interview them, make recordings, and write a report. This is a good project to do with a partner. Make sure a teacher looks over your plan first and knows who you will be interviewing and when. She may be able to help you write up some useful questions ahead of time.

Horses as History

Many of the best horse stories published in recent years have been historical novels. Here are some good ones to try.

❉ *I Rode a Horse of Milk White Jade* by Diane Lee Wilson is the story of a lame Mongol girl in the time of Kublai Khan, who finds she must make her own luck.

❉ *To Ride the Gods' Own Stallion*, also by Diane Lee Wilson, tells of an enslaved Assyrian boy, and the prince and horse he serves. See also *Firehorse* and *Black Storm Comin'* set in more recent American periods.

❉ Alison Hart wrote a series about a black jockey in the Civil War era called the Racing to Freedom trilogy, which includes *Gabriel's Journey (Racing to Freedom)*, *Gabriel's Horses*, and *Gabriel's Triumph*.

  The story follows 12-year-old ex-slave Gabriel through a successful racing career, and then into the U.S. Army during the Civil War, as he becomes the personal groom to the white colonel's horse, Champion.

❉ K. M. Grant made a splash a few years ago with *The Blood-Red Horse* and its sequel, *Green Jasper*, about a pair of brothers, a young heiress, and a somewhat mystical horse named Hosanna.

  Set during the Crusades, these books have been welcomed for their antiwar stance and criticized for a lack of understanding of Islam and the history of the period. But there's no difference of opinion about Hosanna — readers love him!

❉ Deborah Savage is descended from the owner of the champion pacer, Dan Patch. She wrote about the horse and her family in *To Race a Dream*.

❉ The Horse Diaries series features stories from a horse's point of view, set in different periods of history, from Iceland around 1000 CE to Vermont in 1850. Nicely written, with informative extras at the back, and beautiful pictures by Ruth Sanderson, who really knows her horses.

BEWARE A GIFT HORSE

For 10 years, the Greeks laid siege to the city of Troy in an attempt to win back Helen, the queen of Sparta, who had been kidnapped by Paris. Tiring of war, Greek hero Odysseus built a massive wooden statue of a mare, and hid a band of soldiers inside her. He announced that he was abandoning the siege, and the Greeks sailed away out of sight.

Believing that such a prize would win them the favor of the goddess Minerva, the Trojans dragged the mare inside the walls of the city. In the night the soldiers came out, opened the city gates, and set the city on fire.

The Trojans were great horsemen and horse lovers, but horses were unlucky for that city. It fell three times because of them. First Hercules destroyed it when the king refused to give him six beautiful horses he had promised. After the Trojan horse incident, the city fell one more time when a horse standing in the way of the gate kept the Trojans from getting it shut in time to keep out the enemy.

Math

Math teachers are less likely to assign independent projects, but math is certainly useful for working with horses: If one horse eats half a bale of hay a day, how much hay will three horses eat in a week? How much hay do you need to get through the winter?

Calculating your carbon hoofprint is another math exercise (see page 330).

Betting at racetracks is a thrilling, high-stakes math game (like playing the stock market!) and one that can become addictive. Kids can play on paper, just as people play the virtual stock market and calculate whether they've won or lost money. This can be educational for both types of gamblers. It might be interesting to compare how well a stock market investor and a racetrack bettor do with their funds.

Science

Horses are our relatives, but they're as different from us as space aliens — lots of room for science reports there. Be sure any sources you use are scientifically valid; ask a biology teacher if you aren't sure. Here are a few ideas; you can probably think of many others.

Investigate horses' eyesight, sense of smell, or digestion. How do they work? How are they different from ours? How have horses adapted to their environment? How do they use their senses?

Investigate and report on horse evolution. Most books (including this one) give a very simplified picture. A detailed chart of horse evolution looks more like a bush than a ladder. It has many extinct branches, some of which were successful for millions of years. Ever heard of *Nannipus? Hipparion? Anchitherium?* What were they like and when did they branch out? When and why did they become extinct?

Try a training experiment in which you compare clicker training to another form of training. Which is quicker? Which establishes the behavior most firmly? How will you know? (To be objective and scientific you'll need to keep good records; work with a science teacher to design an experiment.)

✴ TO EAT LIKE A HORSE ✴

Horses have inefficient digestive systems. A horse gets only 70 percent of the energy from the same amount of food as a ruminant such as a cow, sheep, or goat does. Horses solve this problem by eating more and eating faster. So don't scold that pony for gobbling — he's just being true to his stomach!

Geography

What's in a name? In some cases, a whole geography lesson. Many breeds are named after their place of origin. Some of these names cover a lot of ground — Pony of the Americas and Canadian Horse, for example. Others refer to a place that's a small dot on any map — Exmoor Pony (England) and Kiger Mustang (United States).

WORLD WITHOUT HORSES

The only place in the inhabited world that doesn't have horses is equatorial Africa. The dreaded tsetse fly, common in many parts of that continent, carries sleeping sickness, which is deadly to most horses (see Pony Moussay, page 313).

Choose a good breed book (see page 35). Identify the breeds that are named after their place of origin. Percheron, for instance, is a familiar word, but did you know that this breed was developed in an old French province called Le Perche, in the district of Normandy? And the Fell Pony originally roamed hills called *fells* in northern England.

Locate these places on a map (first you may have to locate a map that's detailed enough to show them). Using a blank map, plot and label the places of origin of horse breeds. Are there clusters? What could explain this? Some possibilities include climate, soil, cultural and historical trends, ice ages, and human migration.

For instance, Austrian Archduke Charles chose Lipizza for his horse-breeding

Horseshoe REVIEW

Desert Storm
by Logan Forster (1955)

Logan Forster's series, beginning with *Desert Storm*, follows the classic model of the untamable Thoroughbred stallion who is nevertheless the fastest horse in the world. This story has a Southwest setting and an American Indian main character. Look for the rest of his titles too — the books are well written and gripping.

❋ *Anger in the Wind*

❋ *Mountain Stallion*

❋ *Revenge*

❋ *Run Fast, Run Far*

❋ *Tamarlane*

(Some of these books are available for free download on the Internet.)

program because of its limestone soil, which produces excellent grazing. Thus we get horses called Lipizzans. (The word Lipizza actually means "small lime," but refers to a lime tree, not limestone soil.) Limestone soils are also a factor in the Le Perche region, where Percherons are from, and Kentucky bluegrass country, where American horse breeding continues to thrive.

✳ PLACE NAMES ✳

Andalusian	*Andalusia in Spain*
Cleveland Bay	*Cleveland area of northeastern England*
Friesian	*Frisia, an area formerly covering parts of Germany, Denmark, and the Netherlands*
Haflinger	*Hafling, a village in Triol, Austria*
Percheron	*Le Perche, a province in the Normandy area of France*
Shetland Pony	*Shetland Islands*
Shire	*The English midlands — Cambridgeshire, Lincolnshire, Derbyshire, Leicestershire, and Staffordshire, collectively known as the shires*
Trakehner	*Trakehnen in East Prussia, now part of Lithuania*

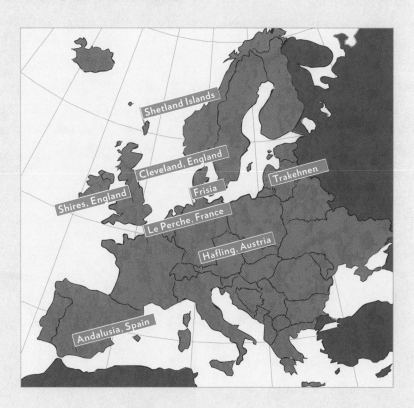

Art

This one is easy — you can always draw, paint, sculpt, or photograph horses. But you should also study horse anatomy (and lucky for you, to learn anatomy you don't have to do what the artist George Stubbs did in the 1700s — dissect dead horses and boil the meat off their bones). Use your knowledge to help create more realistic horses.

Do an art history report comparing the depiction of horses through time and in different cultures. A helpful and beautiful little book is *Horse: From Noble Steeds to Beasts of Burden* by Lorraine Harrison. It has an enormous range of artists and styles.

By studying the picture credits you can find out where each piece of art is located. If possible, go see a piece of art you've admired in a book. The impact of the real thing is usually much stronger.

A SKETCHPAD IN THE PASTURE

A good way to enjoy a horse without riding him is to take a pad and drawing instruments — pencil, pen, crayons, charcoal — out to the barn or pasture and spend some time sketching. This will make you really look at him, which sharpens your powers of observation. You'll see for the first time how often a horse shifts position. Just as you're really capturing that curve of his face, he'll sigh, snort, or turn his head, and everything will look different. This helps you learn to work *fast,* which loosens you up and makes your work more free. Here are some tips:

☀ Horses can be ridiculously curious. If you take out a jar of pencils, it will get tipped over. Try to keep all tools in a pocket.

☀ Set yourself up in a safe position — and if you're in a pasture with multiple horses, watch your back!

☀ Try not to get fixated on tiny details at first. Use a sweeping, scribbly method to capture the big picture — doodle tiny details in the margin. It worked for Leonardo!

☀ Old horses tend to be less fidgety; and sleeping horses are ideal. Keep your distance and don't wake them suddenly, especially out at pasture.

Music

Write a saddle song, one you could imagine singing on a long, long ride. Give it a rhythm that matches an easy-traveling gait, and a chorus that your riding companions could join in on.

Listen to some Tuuvan music (see Singing About Horses, page 316). Now listen to a few cowboy songs.

What similarities do you notice? How does the music suggest wide-open spaces? Describe the rhythm. Does it make you think of a horse's gait?

 JUST A RIDIN' AND A SINGIN'

Saddle songs often pick up the rhythm of a horse's gait. If you don't know the tune, just read them like a poem.

OLD CHISHOLM TRAIL

This very old cowboy song goes well to a Western jog. Here are a couple of verses out of hundreds — feel free to make up your own!

Come along boys
And listen to my tale,
And I'll tell you 'bout my troubles
On the old Chisholm Trail.

CHORUS:
Come a ti yi yippy yippy yi yi yi,
Coma a ti yi yippy yippy yay.

Cloudy in the west
And it's lookin' like rain,
And my danged old slicker's
In the wagon again

THE STRAWBERRY ROAN

This cowboy song about a bucking bronco goes along with a nice easy lope (just be sure you stay in the saddle!).

Down in the horse corral, standing alone,
Is an old caballo, a strawberry roan.
His legs are all spavined, he's got pigeon toes,
Little pig eyes and a big Roman nose,

Little pin ears that touch at the tip,
A big forty-four brand is on his left hip,
Ewe-necked and old with a long lower jaw,
I can see with one eye he's a regular outlaw.

He sure is a proud walker, he heaves a big sigh,
He only lacks wings for to be on the fly.
Turns his old belly right up to the sun,
Well he sure is a sunfishin' son of a gun.

He's about the worst bucker I've seen on the range,
He'll turn on a nickel and give you some change.
Hips on all fours and he rears up on high.
Leaves me a spinnin' up there in the sky.

BORN FREE:
A Few Breeds That Run Wild

What's the difference between "wild" and "feral"? Wild animals are those whose ancestors were never domesticated by humans. Feral animals are descendants of domesticated animals — they may have run free for a thousand years, but they're still not technically wild.

AMERICAN WEST: THE MUSTANG

THEIR STORY: The earliest mustangs in the American West strayed from herds belonging to the Spanish conquistadores in the early 1500s. Other breeds contributed, but Spanish blood still predominates. Numbers increased to around 10 million during the 1800s; today there are between 30,000 and 40,000. The Bureau of Land Management (BLM) captures hundreds each year and puts them up for adoption.

DESCRIPTION: 13.2–15 hands; tough and wiry; body types vary but most have sloping shoulders, short backs, narrow but deep bodies, sloping croups; extremely sound legs and feet. They are tough, intelligent, and often very trainable. Most mustangs are a mix of American breeds, but some herds, isolated in the mountains, are basically unchanged since the 1500s. Living wild has only made them tougher and more intelligent. Strains include:

❈ *The Cerbat* (northwest Arizona) has a straight head, narrow chest, sloping shoulders, a deep heart girth, and excellent legs. Many are gaited and they are easy to train. One of the purest Spanish strains, they seem to be descended from horses who spread into the Cerbat mountains in the 1600s.

❈ *The Kiger Mustang* (eastern Oregon) is descended from Andalusian and Sorraia horses. It has a small Spanish-type head, arched neck, pronounced withers, and a short back. The chest is narrow, but deep; the legs long and fairly fine with good bone. It is always some shade of dun.

❈ *The Pryor Mountain Mustang* (border of Montana and Wyoming) is an exceptionally handsome horse, with a deep, narrow body, short back, and sloping croup. It learns quickly and has excellent gaits.

❈ *The Shackleford Banker Pony* (Shackleford Island, North Carolina) is an East Coast mustang, descended from Spanish horses shipwrecked on the Outer Banks starting in 1585. It is a small Spanish horse with a narrow body, deep through the heart, low tail set, and a long, convex head. Like Chincoteague Ponies, Shackleford Bankers are rounded up each year for branding. Every four years about twenty are sold, to keep the population from getting too high.

VIRGINIA COAST: CHINCOTEAGUE PONY

THEIR STORY: After 1669, to avoid paying taxes and having to build fences, colonists in Virginia and Maryland transported their horses to the barrier islands for the summer, where they ran loose. Horses were rounded up annually and the colts branded. Currently the herd is owned by the Chincoteague Volunteer Fire Company, which rounds up and sells ponies to raise money for fire equipment. After the round-up, the ponies swim the channel between Assateague and Chincoteague Islands. Foals are auctioned off and adults returned to the island.

DESCRIPTION: 13.2–14.2 hands; attractive head, refined neck; well-angled shoulders, broad chest and loins; straight, sound legs; excellent children's ponies

AUSTRALIA: THE BRUMBY

THEIR STORY: Brumbies descend from horses brought by the European settlers, who brought all kinds of animals with them. In the drought-ridden bush, overgrazing by feral horses threatens native Australian wildlife with extinction. Brumbies are selectively culled; they are not highly regarded by most Australian horsemen.

DESCRIPTION: 14–15 hands; type varies. Many have heavy heads, short necks, short straight backs, straight shoulders, and sturdy legs. A few, reflecting Thoroughbred blood, are more refined and have excellent conformation.

ITALY: THE SANFRATELLO HORSE

THEIR STORY: Sicilian horses were admired before Roman times, but information on their history is contradictory or nonexistent. They live in a forested area of Sicily, in Italy.

DESCRIPTION: 15–16 hands; slightly heavy head, short, straight neck; medium-length back, muscular sloping croup, strong well-muscled legs. When tamed it makes a superb farm horse and mule progenitor, and shows potential as a sport horse.

AFRICA: THE NAMIB DESERT HORSE

THEIR STORY: The history of these beautiful African horses, which resemble Thoroughbreds or Akhal-Tekes, is unknown. They may be survivors from a cargo steamer loaded with Thoroughbreds, which ran aground on its way to Australia. They may be the remnants of a herd of horses owned by the German Baron von Wolf, killed in World War I. Whatever the bloodlines, this is an exceptionally hardy, high-quality horse.

DESCRIPTION: 14–14.3 hands; beautiful head; lean body with well-defined withers, sloping shoulders, deep chest, and dry, flat bone; thin skin, coat has a high sheen

Horseshoe REVIEW

Misty of Chincoteague
by Marguerite Henry (1947)

Misty is a Chincoteague Pony rounded up in the annual Pony Penning. She comes to live with the Beebe family and is befriended by the grandchildren, Paul and Maureen. This book is a must-read classic — though even as a little girl in the 1960s, when it seemed like boys got to do all the cool stuff, I thought Maureen could have ridden the climactic race just as well as her brother. Sequels include *Stormy, Misty's Foal* and *Sea Star: Orphan of Chincoteague*.

Every Horse a Wanted Horse

What is an "unwanted" horse? It's any horse that is no longer wanted by its current owner due to age, injury, behavior problems, illness, or inability to do the job needed. Unwanted horses come in all sizes, colors, and breeds. Some have serious health or behavior issues. Others are perfectly normal and healthy. All are in trouble.

Vast numbers of horses in the United States are not wanted, far more than can be taken care of by rescue groups. Basic care for a horse costs $1,800 to $2,400 yearly. Funding resources, volunteers, and placement opportunities are not in place to handle the need. Horse slaughter has been outlawed in the United States, but that only means unwanted horses are being shipped to slaughter in Canada and Mexico. Also, many unwanted horses are simply abandoned or turned loose to fend for themselves when their owners move.

The Unwanted Horse Coalition

The Unwanted Horse Coalition (UHC) has a mission to educate and guide horsemen on what it means to "own responsibly." UHC is an alliance of horse organizations that have joined under the American Horse Council. The mission of UHC is to reduce the number of unwanted horses and improve their welfare.

UHC asks facilities that will accept and/or place horses to list themselves on the UHC Web site. This will allow the Web site to become a bridge between owners seeking homes for their horses, and facilities that will use or

house them, such as rescue, retirement, and retraining facilities, therapeutic riding programs, college riding programs, police organizations, public stables, and government and park service programs. If you know of such a facility, talk with the owners about listing with UHC. It could save a horse's life.

The Adoption Option

Why adopt a horse? To save a life, to rescue an animal, or to get a horse you can afford. Adoptable horses include mustangs, retired racehorses, horses who've been abused or abandoned by their owners, and Premarin mares and their foals (Premarin is a hormone replacement drug; it is made from PREgnant MARe urINe).

However, in many cases, taking on these horses is a job for experienced riders and trainers only, or for someone who can commit to working

with a professional. Many rescue horses come to their new homes with little handling or training. They need retraining, conditioning, and in some

cases, a lot of vet care before they can become solid citizens. If you want to adopt or rescue a horse, have him evaluated by an experienced horseman first.

⤙ STAND UP ⤚ FOR STANDARDBREDS

Calm, level-headed retired Standardbreds often make terrific pleasure horses. Only 10 percent of adopted Standardbreds are used for driving. Their new jobs include trail, endurance, showing, drillteams, gymkhanas, dressage, and police work — anything you could do with another breed. As an added bonus, many Standardbreds have a running walk gait. In their racing life it's not useful, but for a rider this can be a terrific plus.

Be prepared to spend some time retraining your Standardbred, however. He'll know all about being handled, tied, and loaded, and zero about being ridden. Get some experienced help teaching him his new job; for example, your Standardbred can certainly canter — he will out at pasture. But he's been trained not to break into a canter when trotting and pacing; maybe he's been punished for it. You'll have to overcome his conditioning and, again, you may need experienced help.

Many trainers care about the fate of their horses, and are happy to help local organizations to place them. The American Standardbred Adoption Program screens adopters based on their experience and expectations of the horse, as well as veterinary and farrier references. Regular inoculations and farrier care are requirements of adoption.

Horsemen Helping Horses

Even if you don't have room for a rescue horse, you can still support horses in need. Charities, shelters, and horse rescue organizations can always use money, supplies, and the gift of your time.

After Hurricanes Katrina and Rita, many Americans focused on holes in our social support network, including support for animals. The United States Equestrian Federation (USEF) is establishing a permanent Equine Disaster Relief Fund to help with future catastrophes. Donated funds will help prepare for natural disasters and assist equine victims. The National Reined Cow Horse Association has its own crisis fund that assists NRCHA members facing hardships due to natural disasters, personal tragedies, or health crises — all of which can leave horses uncared for.

When disaster strikes, it's easy to sit mesmerized by television footage, feeling helpless. It's great to know there's something you can do. Buy from retailers like SmartPak and State Line Tack, which donate substantial sums to disaster relief; make a donation yourself; or raise awareness by doing some fundraising.

Making a Difference Yourself

Fundraising can be as simple as holding a bake sale, or set-

Horseshoe REVIEW

Horses of the Storm
by Ky Evan Mortensen (2008)

This is the story of Louisiana State University's Equine Rescue Team, which helped save hundreds of horses after Hurricane Katrina. Along with moving rescue stories, this book includes many practical tips to help horse owners prepare before a disaster.

Molly the Pony
by Pam Kastner (2008)

Molly waits patiently in the barn while Hurricane Katrina sweeps across the farm and she gets hungrier and thirstier. She is rescued and finds a new home, but is badly injured by a dog. Molly's leg must be amputated; find out how she fares in this moving and inspiring true tale.

ting up a table at the feed store on Saturday morning. Print some pictures of the disaster and the affected horses, and explain that you'll be sending all donations to the USEF disaster fund. People feel better about giving when they know their money will go to a responsible organization.

You could hold a sponsored ride for disaster relief. Pick a safe route, print out forms, and ask people to sponsor you and other riders (enlist some adults to help make sure you've covered details like permission slips). Your charity ride could become an annual event, making it fun for riders who come to look forward to it and making your fundraising more effective, as riders work to beat their own fundraising records.

Even saving all your change in a jar and donating it annually to a reputable charity will make a difference. It may not seem like much, but it can really add up.

Horseshoe Review

Books by Glenn Balch

Glenn Balch grew up on an Idaho ranch, a boy who loved dogs and horses. He became a forest ranger, a newspaper writer, and then a successful author of children's books and articles for adults. My favorites of his books are *Christmas Horse*, about a boy catching and training his own horse, Inky, and taking him to a cutting horse championship, and *Indian Paint*, a story about an Indian pony.

Balch's own favorite of his books was *Tiger Roan*, about an abused rodeo horse who finds happiness with a kind rider. His other titles include:

- *The Brave Riders*
- *Buck, Wild*
- *The Flaxy Mare*
- *Horse in Danger*
- *Horse of Two Colors*
- *Indian Fur*
- *Indian Saddle-Up*
- *Keeping Horse*
- *Little Hawk and the Free Horses*
- *Lost Horse*
- *The Midnight Colt*
- *The Runaways*
- *Spotted Horse*
- *The Stallion King*
- *Stallion's Foe*
- *Wild Horse*
- *Wild Horse Tamer*
- *Winter Horse*

PONY-THEMED PILLOWCASES

❧ BASIC ❧ SEWING TIPS

- ❋ **Measure twice** and cut once.

- ❋ **Run the sewing machine** backward and forward for about a quarter inch at the start and finish of every seam, so the thread won't come out.

- ❋ **Practice makes perfect.** Take a piece of scrap fabric and practice making straight lines, rounded curves, and sharp corners. Pretend you're riding a dressage or reining test, and bring that smoothness and precision to your work.

- ❋ **Don't get your finger too close** to that flashing needle — getting sewed hurts!

This easy project can make a big horse impact in your room — and maybe even influence your dreams. Choose smooth cotton fabrics for these, or experiment with unusual fabrics like fleece. You can make them to match your curtains (see page 106).

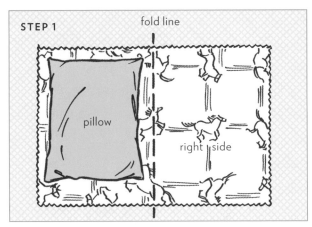

STEP 1

fold line

pillow

right side

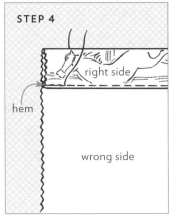

STEP 4

right side

hem

wrong side

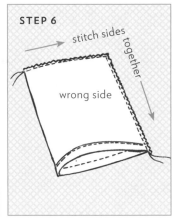

STEP 6

stitch sides together

wrong side

Materials Needed

Yardstick or measuring tape

Horse-themed fabric

Sewing shears

Iron

Matching thread

Sewing machine

DIRECTIONS

1. **Measure a piece of fabric** that's 3 inches longer than your pillow and twice as wide, plus an inch for the seam.

2. **Fold one of the long sides** over ¼ inch and iron, wrong sides together.

3. **Fold and iron that edge again**, about 1 inch deep.

4. **Sew along the bottom edge** of this fold to make a hem for your pillowcase.

5. **Fold your fabric lengthwise,** right sides together this time.

6. **Sew along the bottom,** turn the corner, and sew along the side, using a ⅜ -inch seam.

7. **Turn right side out** and you're done!

Sharing Treats with Your Horse

Everyone knows horses love carrots and apples, but many horses also like things you wouldn't imagine. I've known them to eat bologna sandwiches (I don't know how healthy this is!) and Fudgsicles, and to drink wine, beer, tea, and soda; I had a Belgian buddy who enjoyed the hot pepper spray I put on the barn door to stop him from chewing it!

Horses have individual tastes, so offer a selection of healthy treats and see which ones different horses go for. Most veggies are fine, so the next time you visit the barn, raid the fridge and bring along some broccoli, cabbage, celery, lettuce, or whatever you have on hand.

Here are some other treats that are safe to share:

* Bananas (peels, too)
* Watermelon
* Oranges
* Cornhusks
* Fruit Popsicles
* Hard mint candies and candy canes
* Cough drops
* Butter cookies and gingersnaps
* Bread and pretzels

WARNING!

The following should *not* be fed to any horse:

* Any part of a tomato or potato plant (toxic to horses and many other animals)
* Fruit with pits, such as peaches, plums, cherries (okay if you take pits out)
* Yard and shrub clippings (may include toxic plants)
* Lawn trimmings (may be moldy)

The following should not be fed to show horses because they may result in a positive drug test:

* Caffeinated drinks
* Cinnamon
* Chocolate
* Nutmeg
* Persimmon
* Sassafras
* Soda
* Willow leaves

Giving Treats Safely

The safest way to give a treat is to drop it into your horse's feed bucket; that way nobody gets nipped. But many of us enjoy feeding our horses by hand. That can be safe, too, if you do it right. The rules are simple:

Hold smaller treats like an apple, cough drop, or small amount of grain on the flat of your hand. Stretch your thumb and fingers back out of the way.

Give stalky treats, such as goldenrod, flower-end first, and let go as soon as he's got hold.

Discourage begging for more by stepping back again. Or offer a different kind of treat, such as a nice neck scratch.

Never reward bad behavior. Shoving you with his nose, poking at your pocket, or otherwise bullying, is a signal for you to step out of reach and ignore him for 30 seconds. When he's standing still and looking sweet, reach out your hand.

 Horse PLAY

A PONY PICNIC

One of the best noncompetitive ways to trail ride is to take your horse on a picnic. You can do this alone, but it's even more fun in a group, with someone as a leader who knows a new trail to explore.

✻ **Fill up your saddlebags** with a halter and rope, extra rope for emergencies, a hoof pick, a sharp knife (for making repairs, cutting rope if a tied horse gets into trouble, slicing cheese, whittling), and a small first-aid kit.

✻ **Choose "durable" food**, like sturdy sandwiches, hardboiled eggs, apples, granola bars, and so on. Pack it safely in your saddlebags with ice packs.

✻ **Plan a route that offers water for horses:** either a stream along the way or a water source at the picnic site.

✻ **Watch the weather.** Modify your plans if excess heat, storms, or other adverse weather threatens.

✻ **Always tell an adult** where you are going and when you expect to return.

✻ **Pay attention to the details of tying horses safely:** Tie high and short, tie horses a safe distance apart, tie to sturdy trees with thick bark that won't be damaged, tie with quick release knots (see page 119).

Make sure your horses are secure and comfortable first. Then settle down, eat, and enjoy before heading safely home again.

Mildly Medicinal Treats

Ever had a stomachache and been given flat ginger ale? That's an herbal remedy. Ginger prevents and eases nausea, reduces gas, and stimulates the lining of the stomach. Ginger ale is a good drink to choose if you feel a little queasy or dizzy — like after a day at the amusement park.

Horses get stomachaches just like we do. But they can't throw up, so any digestive upset can become serious. There are a lot of herbal remedies we can give our horses that are similar to ginger ale. They aren't as powerful as a tube of bute or bana-

mine, but a lot of times your horse doesn't need something that strong. He just needs a mild and appropriate tonic for what ails him.

Try the remedies below when your horse is well. They'll tone his system and you'll find out which ones he likes. If he refuses a favorite treat later on, that can be a sign that he's feeling sick.

COUGH DROPS FOR COLIC

When my mare Josey had a stubborn colic, the only thing that would bring her ears forward was the rustle of a cough drop wrapper. She went through almost a bagful

of herbal cough drops before she got better. The cough drops gave her something to look forward to, and they gave her a small dose of eight different herbs, almost all of which are good for digestion.

I'm not saying that you can cure colic this way, but naturally flavored cough drops like Ricola are an herbal remedy. (Check labels for ingredients; many brands have more sugar than herbs.) Most contain mint, one of the classic herbs for easing indigestion. As horses crunch them down, they deliver a strong dose of mint to the stomach, where it soothes spasms, decreases gas, and increases digestive activity (it also makes your horse's breath smell great!). Hard peppermint candies do the same thing. Before you invest in a giant bag, grab an extra mint at a pizza restaurant and let your horse try it. Some horses like mint and some don't.

✲ ON-THE-HOOF ✲ HORSE HERBS

Horses on pasture eat herbs all the time. Pasture plants have many benefits, and good hay is full of dried pasture herbs that benefit your horse all winter. For example, clover is good for lungs and skin. Dandelion is a liver tonic. Plantain soothes coughs.

GOLDENROD FOR GAS

Look along the edge of your field. You'll likely find goldenrod growing there. It's one of America's most common weeds. If you break off a stalk you'll notice a sweet herbal scent, which indicates the presence of the essential oils and other components that make this lovely plant a good medicine. The leaves get rid of gas in the digestive tract and the flowers act as a laxative.

Josey first showed me the medicinal value of goldenrod when I noticed her grazing on it at the edge of a lush field when she was colicky. A check of my herb books told me she was right — again! If you watch what your horses choose when grazing freely, they'll teach you a lot.

DIGESTIVE CAKES

These digestive cakes contain fennel, which helps reduce intestinal gas and soothes coughs. You can find chamomile and fennel in bulk at your local co-op or natural food store. You'll need the following ingredients:

1 cup sweet feed	1 grated apple or carrot
½ cup applesauce	¼ cup dried chamomile flowers
½ cup flour	2 tablespoons corn oil
½ cup rolled oats	2 tablespoons fennel seed

Making these treats is easy:

1. Preheat oven to 375°F.
2. Oil 12 muffin cups.
3. In a medium-sized bowl, combine all ingredients and mix to make a sticky dough that holds together. (If it's too dry, add a little more applesauce. If it's too soupy, add a little more flour or oats.)
4. Divide the dough evenly among the muffin cups.
5. Bake for 20 minutes.
6. Remove from oven and cool on a rack for 5 to 10 minutes.
7. Loosen with a knife and turn out onto the rack. (They may be a little crumbly.)
8. Cool before serving.

Feed one or two in the morning and evening, or more if they are all your ailing horse will eat.

Offer goldenrod when a horse seems dumpy or mildly colicky, or if you think they've overeaten. They enjoy it, you'll enjoy the smell of it being picked and munched, and when our horses perk up, we're all happy.

CHAMOMILE FOR CALMING DOWN

Chamomile is a gentle but powerful herb that benefits the digestion and relaxes the nerves. It also cools inflammation and soothes aches and pains. The effects are cumulative, meaning it builds up in the system, and horses enjoy the mild, sweet flavor, which makes chamomile great for treats.

FENNEL FOR FLATULENCE

Fennel seeds are good to chew when you have gas pains, and they freshen the breath, too. For a refreshing treat, buy a fennel bulb (also called anise) the next time you're in a grocery store. Look for them in the produce cooler near the celery. The bulb is delicious raw, and horses love the stalks and fronds.

Disguising Disgusting Meds

Every horse owner dreams of finding a way to administer medications that's as easy as feeding grain. Not every medicine can be disguised, but many can. Here are a few tricks:

Use food supplements: If you feed a flavor supplement to coax finicky eaters (I've never had a horse who didn't wolf down all feed offered, but I understand they exist), then you can use that for medicating, as well as mixing it into your horse's cookies.

People who regularly feed a strong-smelling supplement like CocoSoya or powdered garlic have an advantage when it comes to slipping in medications. The strong flavors of these supplements mask the odor and bitterness of medicines.

Horseshoe REVIEW

For many more recipes for horse treats, read these books, both by June V. Evers.

☀ *The Original Book of Horse Treats* (1994)

☀ *The Ultimate Guide to Pampering Your Horse* (1997)

Use an added flavor: Add a strong-tasting homemade additive to disguise the offending medicine. Try out the new flavor without added medicine first, to be sure your horse will eat it. You can mix powdered meds with crushed peppermints, applesauce, molasses, grated carrots or apples. Or mix the medication with sugar or fruit-flavored gelatin powder and stir into the feed.

Use a special treat: After Josey's prolonged colic, I was advised by my vet to give her Milk of Magnesia twice a day for a couple of days. I had a vivid memory from childhood of how terrible that stuff tastes. Josey was a big, strong-minded mare, how was I going to get this dreadful substance into her? The answer: oat balls! I mixed the recommended amount of Milk of Magnesia with molasses and instant rolled oats until I had a consistency that could be rolled into balls.

✵ A GREAT IDEA ✵ I Have Never Tried

Teach your horse to love deworming syringes. Fill a used syringe with applesauce or a similar squishy treat, and administer as you would a dewormer. Picture your horse's surprise when a wonderful flavor hits the back of his tongue. Do this every day or so; on deworming day he should accept his dose eagerly — but make sure you have a syringe full of the good stuff ready for a chaser.

A Bad Idea I *Have* Tried. Core an apple and fill the hole with a dose of dewormer. Feed it to your horse. Guess what? Your horse will notice, and you may put him off apples for a long time. It was two or three years before Josey would take another apple from my hand. Teach your horse to take his wormer by trying the applesauce technique above.

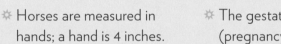

SOME HORSE NUMBERS

✵ Horses are measured in hands; a hand is 4 inches. A horse that is 15.2 hands stands 62 inches at the withers, or 5 feet, 2 inches.

✵ Male horses typically have 40 teeth, while mares have 36.

✵ The gestation period (pregnancy) of a mare can range from 305 to 395 days, with the average being 340.

✵ A horse can live for 30 years, though the oldest horse on record, born in 1760, lived to be 62!

JUST HORSING AROUND

I bet you've hopped on your bike and zoomed around the block, feeling the wind in your face while you dream that you're galloping on your favorite horse (or any horse, for that matter!). Kids have loved their imaginary and toy horses for thousands of years. Here are some old favorites — how many of these have you ridden?

Stick Horses

Stick horses are the oldest toy horse around. They likely go back to the day after somebody first rode a horse; his or her kid must have picked up a crooked branch, noticed a squiggle that looked like a horse's head, and mounted up. Stick horse heads can be wooden, leather, or stuffed fabric. Some models have handles on the upper end of the stick; some have wheels on the bottom.

Rocking Horses

The first true rocking horses, on semicircular rockers, were built in the 1600s — King Charles I of England had one — and they became more popular in the 1700s. In 1880 a Cincinnati company invented a swing horse that glided back and forth instead of rocking. It took up less space and was safer and quieter. Queen Victoria tried out a dapple-gray rocking horse and gave one to her children, making dapple-gray the color of choice for rocking horses all over England. Rocking horses remained popular until World War I, and are still loved by many today. A Web search will lead you to do-it-yourself sites with directions to build your own.

Carousel Horses

The Italian word *garosello* means "little war," and believe it or not, early carousels were a training tool for mounted soldiers. Seventeenth-century French riders practiced spearing rings while they circled on legless wooden horses, attached by wooden arms to a central pole. Recreational carousels became popular in the 1870s with the advent of steam power.

There are two styles of American carousel horse. **Philadelphia-style** horses are realistic and regal, and wear military trappings. **Coney Island–style** horses are more lively and fanciful, and sport circus ornaments and jewels.

Spring Horses

Spring horses are a direct descendant of rocking horses. Instead of gliding or rocking back and forth, riders bounce and jounce on four sturdy springs, suspended within a metal frame. Kids can spend hours bouncing on these large toys. They come in hard plastic or plush.

Coin-Operated Horses

Nowadays, these guys are hard to find, but they were popular at amusement parks in the 1950s. (There were cars and space ships too, but who cares about those?) They also found a place outside of grocery and department stores as a potential reward for a horse-crazy child who behaved herself. Put in your money and the horse gallops, but for all too short a time.

LEAPING THROUGH HISTORY:
The Lovely Lipizzan

The white stallions that perform their beautiful dance in the Baroque hall of the Spanish Riding School in Vienna are some of the best-known horses in the world. But those stallions, and the red-coated riders on their backs, are just the tip of the iceberg. The stallions have impressive pedigrees and a long, fascinating history.

It began in the midsixteenth century, when the Austrian royal family began to improve a strain of sturdy white native horses. They imported excellent Arabian and Spanish stock (early Andalusians) and established a stud farm at Lipizza, which was then in Austria and is now in Slovenia. There the white mares grazed mountain pastures and raised their foals, which are born dark. At age three, already turning white, the best young stallions were taken to Vienna, to be trained in high-level classical dressage. The mares stayed in Lipizza, and the stallions returned there for breeding.

During World War II bombing threatened the School. The stallions were moved to a castle in upper Austria. When American general George Patton occupied the area, the riding master of the School, Colonel Alois Podhajsky, put on a formal dressage demonstration and begged for his help. Patton put the Spanish Riding School under the protection of the U.S. Army. However, the mares and young stock were in an area about to be captured by the Russians. Without the mares, the breed

AIRS ABOVE THE GROUND

It takes many years of rigorous training before a stallion is ready to perform all of the intricate maneuvers listed below.

* *Ballotade:* A leap into the air from a rearing position, with the hind legs tucked up
* *Capriole:* A leap forward into the air, with the hind legs kicked out behind before landing
* *Courbette:* A series of leaps performed from a rearing position
* *Levade:* A stationary crouch with the hind legs at a 45-degree angle
* *Passage:* A slow, measured trot with high-stepping knees and fetlocks
* *Piaffe:* A high, collected trot performed in place

Literature about Lipizzans (and one classic film)

Many wonderful books have been written about the amazing Lipizzan. Here are a few:

* *My Dancing White Horses* by Colonel Alois Podhajsky (1965). Podhajsky was the director of the Spanish Riding School during World War II. This book details his education, how he restored the School to excellence after a period of decline, and the dramatic World War II rescue by Colonel Patton.

* *The White Stallion of Lipizza* by Marguerite Henry (1964). This wonderful book tells the modern story of the Lipizzan stallions of Vienna, focusing on one stallion of particular character, Maestoso Borina.

* *The Emperor's White Horse* by Vernon Bowen (1956). This story follows a boy who becomes an apprentice rider at the Spanish Riding School during World War II.

* *The Miracle of the White Stallions* (1963, rated G). Filmed in Austria with the assistance of its hero, Colonel Alois Podhajsky, this is a fairly faithful rendering of the real-life evacuation of the Lipizzan stallions from World War II Vienna, the performance for the American General Patton, and the raid behind enemy lines to rescue the Lipizzan mares. There are beautiful scenes of the young horses playing in the fields, and the performances of the stallions are simply wonderful.

would be lost. Patton undertook a raid and was able to bring most of the mares into the area controlled by the United States, thus saving a great cultural treasure. What would have happened without Patton? The Lipizzan mares might have been driven back to Russia, to enrich Russian bloodlines. Or they might have been eaten by hungry Russian troops.

The Lipizzan is still a rare breed. There are only about 3,000 worldwide, with 1,200 Lipizzans in the United States and 30 to 40 new foals registered each year. The breed has never been numerous and probably never will be, but it will remain secure as long as horse-lovers value the artistry of the Spanish Riding School.

LOOKING AT LIPIZZANS

Lipizzans are a compact breed, standing 15 to 15.3 hands high. They have distinctive heads, with a convex profile; long, strong backs; broad sloped croups; a high tail-set, and strong, muscular legs. Though most turn white or gray as they age, the occasional bay is seen. These extremely intelligent animals tend to be one-man horses.

Click, Treat, Train

Clicker training is a wonderful way to have fun with a horse and to develop a strong and positive relationship. This positive training method feels more like play than work, and it's based on food treats — horses' favorite thing.

Clicker training grew out of training dolphins to do tricks. You can't put a choke chain on a dolphin. You can't soar with him as he jumps and stuff a fish into his mouth in mid-air. You have to find a way to explain what you want from a distance, without using force.

Karen Pryor, the clicker-training pioneer, applied behaviorist principles to figure out how to signal — with a clicking sound or whistle — when a dolphin was doing something she wanted. When the dolphin heard the signal he knew he'd performed the correct task, and that the fish he got a few seconds later was because of that particular jump or spin.

These training methods are even easier to use with cats, dogs, and horses. Clicker trainers love the difference they see in their animals. With clicker training, the animal has a feeling of control. There's a "Helen Keller moment" early in the process, when the animal realizes that his actions caused the trainer to give him a treat. "Can I make her do it again? Whoopee! I've got the key to the cookie jar!"

Yes, you *can* create a monster this way, so it's important to study clicker training before you start: learn the principles, establish a goal, break it down into steps, and understand how you'll take each one.

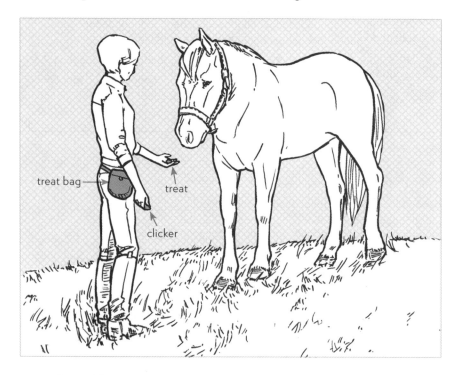

treat bag

treat

clicker

"Charging" the Clicker

The first step in clicker training is teaching your horse what the click means. Click, then immediately give him a small treat, following the rules below. Step out of reach of that mugging nose, wait for a moment when he's not begging, and do it again.

Soon the light will dawn. At the click, his ears will snap forward. Click means treat! Congratulations. Your clicker is now charged and you are ready to teach. However, it's important to be able to give treats and still be treated with respect. Every time we interact with our horses we're training them, even if it's just giving them an apple or sugar cube.

Your horse needs to do something to earn the treat. *Never* reward him for mugging or frisking you. If your horse nudges your pockets or nips at your hands, simply step out of reach and briefly ignore him. Teach him that pestering you for treats never works.

When he does what you want, give him his reinforcement. Never let him put his nose into your personal space to get it. That is bad manners and can lead to nipping and other pushy behavior. Hold the treat out, close to *his* body, not yours to reinforce politeness.

WHAT'S A CLICKER?

A clicker is a little plastic box with a flexible piece of metal mounted in the top. You press it with your thumb, it makes a crisp, clear *click*, and magic happens.

Once it's established as a signal that means "Yes! You've done it!" the click bypasses the thinking centers of the brain and goes straight to the pleasure center. A well-timed click is faster and clearer than verbal praise because the behavior, the click, and the brain response are virtually simultaneous, with the treat following closely behind.

Yes, you can make a click sound with your mouth, but it's not quite as effective. The slight delay while you get your tongue curled, and the variation in sound make this a less precise form of communication. But if you don't have a clicker or your hands are too full, it can work. Clicker training is a very forgiving method.

THE RIGHT KIND OF TREATS

Giving treats properly is an important part of clicker training. The treat should be something your horse likes, of course, and it should be small — a teaspoon of grain, a slice of carrot or apple, a tiny peppermint — you don't want him to spend a lot of time chewing. Leave him looking for more!

Hitting the Target

Once your horse understands the concept of the click, you can start shaping his behavior by reinforcing actions that you want and ignoring ones that you don't. The easiest behavior to start with is targeting: Hold out an object — try a cone or the handle of your whip. When your horse touches it with his nose, click and treat.

To make this easier, put your horse in his stall with the door closed or with a stall guard across the doorway. Hold your target in front of his face. The target should be close enough that it catches his interest. He may touch it with his nose, or he may only put his nose toward it and sniff. Whichever behavior you get, click and treat.

Do it again. And again.

In the beginning your horse will touch the target randomly. You may have to put it very close to his nose to make him notice it. But as the treats start rolling in, at some point it will "click" (sorry!) and the next time he touches the target it will be in a different way — maybe more tentative and experimental, maybe more boldly and strongly. This is the moment when he makes the connection between his behavior and your response.

REINFORCING THE RIGHT BEHAVIOR

Repeat the sequence a few more times. If your horse is learning quickly, experiment with holding the target high, low, off to the side. Move it around and see if he'll follow with his nose. End with a good clear touch, and give a jackpot — a big handful of grain or half an apple.

Stop for the day, or at least for several hours, with plenty of praise. You two have just accomplished something big. It's important to end on a good note and not to try to do too much at once.

Once your horse has mastered targeting, you can teach him to follow his target while walking. Trainers have used a target to teach horses to back up, lower the head, enter trailers, roll balls, bow, or lie down. You are limited only by your imagination, and the physical abilities of your horse.

 SOME BOOKS TO READ

* *Don't Shoot the Dog* by Karen Pryor (1999)
* *Clicker Training for Your Horse* by Alexandra Kurland (1998)
* *The Click That Teaches* by Alexandra Kurland (2003)
* *Getting to Yes* by Sharon Foley (2007)
* *You Can Train Your Horse to Do Anything* by Shawna and Vinton Karrash (2006)

The Endless Possibilities of Clicker Training

What can you do with clicker training? Practically anything: You can teach your horse to pose for pictures, teach him to bow, teach him to lie down on cue, teach him to raise his back and poll, as required in dressage, while on the lunge line or even at liberty, like a circus act.

You can also use the clicker to overcome countless fears. Once I'd taught my horse Atherton that going toward a scary object would be rewarded, he often made me laugh by approaching large barking dogs or other threats and then glancing back quickly at me. "See, I'm brave. Treat please!"

It's a bit disturbing to discover how negative our habits of mind are. We continually notice behaviors we *don't* want in our animals, and ignore behaviors we *do* want. Turning that mind-set

around feels powerful and revolutionary. That change is reflected in the soft, intelligent look in a clicker-trained horse's eyes. He's no longer bored, confused, and muddling through. He's your partner, figuring things out with you.

If you don't have a horse to train yet, you're still in luck. Clicker training works on dogs, cats, rabbits, goldfish, canaries, and even little brothers! By the time you have access to a horse, you can be an expert clicker trainer.

✹ GROWN-UPS ARE TALKING ✹

If you don't want to create a spoiled monster with clicker training, which you surely don't, then teach your horse a lesson that trainer Alexandra Kurland calls "the grown-ups are talking." It's a lesson we've all had to learn and it's especially important for clicker trainers.

You're standing there with a pocketful of treats. Your horse, with his practically supernatural sense of smell, knows that. How do you keep him from mugging you? You don't. By that, I mean, you don't push his head away, correct him for nuzzling, or do any of the other things that seem natural to most of us.

Instead, you watch, very alertly, for even the beginnings of the behavior you want. Your horse moves his head away from you, even for a second. Click and treat — in his personal space, not yours. Wait for him to do it again, and reinforce it again.

Horses quickly catch on to this game, and it's funny to see them standing still and being good just as hard as they can. Once he's learned, don't fall back on the old habit of ignoring him if he's good and paying attention if he's bad. Continue to reward the behavior of standing still and not mugging you — not every time, but often.

THE AMERICAN MINIATURE HORSE
Good Things in Small Packages

The affectionately nicknamed "Mini" is one of the fastest growing breeds in North America, in terms of numbers, if not size. Over 300,000 are currently registered, with around 9,000 foals born per year in the United States. It's not hard to figure out why they're so popular — they have the beauty and temperament of a full-sized horse, yet can be kept in a suburban backyard.

Developed in the United States from English stock, mainly Shetland ponies, the Mini is not considered a pony breed. It is proportioned like a full-sized horse; while some do look more like Shetlands, many resemble Arabians. Unlike other breeds, Minis are measured in inches, not hands. The breed standard recognizes two heights: 34 inches and under for Division A; 38 inches and under for Division B.

Minis aren't good riding horses, as you can imagine. Fifty pounds is the weight limit, and most children that size don't ride well enough to control a real horse with a mind of its own. But Minis can pull three to five times their own weight; a cart with two adults is fine on easy terrain and you can certainly haul firewood with them. They are also shown in hand and they make wonderful companions and pets. Some people even let them in their houses!

FUN FACT: The Falabella is a miniature breed developed in Argentina.

MINIATURE HORSE TURNS INTO SEEING-EYE DOG

No, it's not a headline from one of those newspapers at the grocery store checkout. It's a new trend in the field of service animals. One example is a little black-and-white mare named Panda.

Panda was chosen to be the seeing-eye horse of Ann Edie, a horsewoman who's been legally blind since birth. Ann's work with clicker trainer Alexandra Kurland, and the sensitivity of her riding horses, made her want to try a seeing-eye horse.

Panda was chosen for her small size, sociability, and intelligence. She entered training with Alexandra Kurland at age nine months, and was turned over to Ann Edie at age two and a half. She lives in the house during the day — has never had an accident! — and does most of the jobs that a guide dog does. She travels in cars, climbing readily into the backseat of a subcompact, and has even attended a John Lyons clinic as a well-behaved member of the audience.

✲ HORSE HEALTH: Signs of Trouble ✲

There are some signs that obviously spell trouble for your horse's health and should send you straight to the phone to call the vet — flowing blood, more than slight lameness, a nail in a hoof. Other signs are less definitive. Knowing when to call for help is essential for your horse's well-being, especially when dealing with colic.

Colic is one of the worst health troubles a horse can have. Horses can't vomit. You may not think of barfing as a blessing, but it rids your system of what's upsetting your stomach. Without this ability, horses have to wait till it emerges at the other end, and lots of things can go wrong in between. Colic is a problem for a vet to deal with. Your job is to recognize when something serious is going on. Here are some signs:

- **Not eating.** This is a big deal for most horses. If your horse refuses a meal, and especially if he refuses a treat, take notice.
- **Absence of manure in the stall.** This means nothing is passing through.
- **Rolling.** All horses roll to scratch an itchy back. But if a horse rolls repeatedly, in odd places, and seems distressed, this is another strong sign of colic.
- **Kicking the belly.** Again, all horses kick at flies. Watch closely. If flies are involved, you'll be able to tell. If not, and especially if he turns to look back at his side, he's in pain.

Opinions differ, but many vets will have you walk the horse. This keeps him from rolling and hurting himself. The action of walking can also ease out and sometimes even cure a minor colic by getting that intestinal gas moving on out. (Here's a case where farts are good!)

Talk with your vet. Some recommend keeping a tube of Banamine on hand to help with minor colic cases until help can arrive. Don't give medications until you've talked to the vet and gotten his okay. You don't want to mask your horse's symptoms.

Respiratory illnesses usually show themselves the same way they do in humans — nasal discharge or difficulty breathing. Fever usually shows up as listlessness and lack of interest in food. Other odd signs may include standing in an unusual place in the pasture and refusing to move, lying down for long periods of time, or just looking kind of miserable.

It's important to know your horse. Then you'll know when he's behaving in an unusual way, and when he may need help.

COOL CUSTOMIZED CURTAINS

Curtains are simple to make and have a big impact. There are lots of fabrics out there with horses or horse themes. Choose materials that complement the colors in your room. Make a set for every season. Cotton is light and airy for the summer. Fleece — an unusual choice — has a heavy, velvety impact, and will help keep the winter chill out.

Materials Needed

Yardstick or measuring tape

Curtain rod

Horse-themed fabric
(you need twice as much fabric
as the width of your windows)

Sewing shears

Iron

Matching thread

Sewing machine

DIRECTIONS

1. **Measure the width of your windows.** To create curtains with ample folds, each curtain should be twice the width of the window plus a couple of inches.

2. **Measure the length of your windows.** Your curtains should reach at least the bottom of the window trim, and may be longer.

3. **Measure the diameter of your curtain rod** and multiply by 2. You will be making a channel for the rod to fit through. When calculating your total amount of fabric, add that measurement, plus an inch for the top hem, plus enough fabric (about 4 inches) to make the bottom hem, to the measurement from step 2.

4. **Measure and cut your fabric** with the shears.

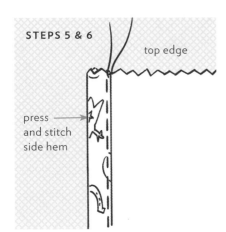

STEPS 5 & 6

top edge

press
and stitch
side hem

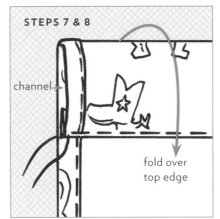

STEPS 7 & 8

channel

fold over
top edge

5. **Turn under a ½ inch of fabric** along the sides of the curtains (wrong sides together). Press with the iron.

6. **Finish the sides of the curtains** by folding this edge under again, pressing the fold, and sewing along the edge.

7. **Fold a half-inch of the curtain's top edge down** (wrong sides together) and press. Then measure (again!) the size of your curtain rod, and fold this edge down the necessary amount to make the channel. It should be slightly wider than the rod.

8. **Sew the channel,** keeping the sewing machine needle about ¼ inch from the folded and pressed edge of the fabric.

9. **To create a finished hem,** fold a half-inch of the curtain's bottom edge up (wrong sides together) and press. Then fold this edge up again until the curtain is the desired length. Press again and stitch as you did in step 8.

10. **Hang and admire your curtains.**

TOTALLY "TACK-Y" TIEBACKS

Now, what about some interesting tiebacks? Depending on how rustic your theme is, you might consider:

✻ Baling twine

✻ Creatively macraméed baling twine

✻ Creatively dyed baling twine

✻ Leather latigo, with or without conchos

✻ Lengths of rein

✻ Stirrup leathers

✻ Snaffle bits (you can attach them to the wall or window frame with screw-in hooks, but first get permission to make holes in the wall!)

✻ Spurs with leather straps

✻ Horseshoes

Chatting with Horse Folk

Lesley Ward, magazine editor, writer, and photographer

Describe briefly your work/play with horses.
I'm the founder and editor of *Young Rider* magazine and editor in chief of *Horse Illustrated*. I decide what goes in each issue. I write features and instructional articles for *Young Rider* and I take nearly all of the photos. I have four horses on my farm in Kentucky. I do a lot of trail riding and sometimes I compete in lower level eventing and dressage.

What's cool about what you do?
I love having a job that involves my passion — horses! I write about horses and take pictures of horses. I go to big shows and events. I'm around horses all the time. And I get to meet and talk to lots of enthusiastic young riders (readers of my magazine) who are keen to learn as much as they can about horse care and riding.

What's hard about what you do?
Office work! There's a lot of paperwork that comes with running two successful magazines. I hate sitting inside at a desk when it's sunny outside. Luckily, I consider riding and taking lessons an important part of my job. I can always learn something when I'm on the back of a horse!

What could a kid be doing now to wind up with a career like yours?
Buy the best digital camera you can afford and go out and take tons of pictures of horses and people riding.

Don't expect to become a great photographer overnight — it takes a lot of practice. Take writing and journalism classes in high school and college and volunteer to write articles and shoot pictures for the school paper. Volunteer to cover shows for local horse magazines and clubs.

How did you choose this path in life?
I've been riding since I was 11. I've always owned horses, and I started out by reporting on horse shows for a local magazine as a freelancer. I was working in retail when I saw an ad for an editorial assistant for a horse magazine and even though I didn't have a ton of writing experience, the magazine hired me because of my horsey knowledge. When someone left, I was promoted to section editor. Eventually I decided to start my own magazine, and *Young Rider* was born.

What surprises you about your work?
That I get paid for writing about horses and riding!

What's one thing you wish people understood about it?
That you have to pay your dues and start at the bottom. In my first job, I had to answer phones and get my editor lunch! I didn't go on photo shoots or cover horse shows. But it wasn't long before I was promoted and got to do more fun stuff.

PART TWO

In the Saddle

and in the Stall and in the Show Ring...

Yep, you're horse crazy. It's an established fact. So the thing you want most of all is to get your hands on a horse. Here's how to do it the right way, so you and the horse feel relaxed, confident, and safe. Approaching, haltering, leading, and grooming horses; tacking up and riding basics; a short course on knots — it isn't everything you'll need to know, but it's a start.

Approaching a Horse

Around 20 percent of horse-related injuries happen to people on the ground. You can prevent many accidents by taking simple precautions, thinking ahead, and knowing the correct techniques.

Safety around horses starts with manners. If you are walking into a stable or up to a fence with a horse owner, always ask if you can pat the horses. Not all horses are pattable. Some nip. Some are skittish. Some owners are just nervous about people approaching their horses.

If it's okay, approach from the left shoulder/neck area, not head-on, because the horse has a blind spot directly in front of him. Speak his name in a clear, calm voice. Watch the horse's reaction. If he lays his ears back, don't go close. If the ears point forward with a pleasant expression, you may continue. You want to pat him low on the side of the neck, or on the shoulder.

Horse Sense

I'm sure you already know this: never approach a horse from the rear, even one you know well. If you must come up on a horse from behind, speak to him and wait for him to turn and face you, or circle around so he can see you.

If he walks away, don't follow directly behind; circle around to get in front of him again.

No Nipping

If he's friendly and curious, the horse may intercept your hand with his nose. This is fine as long as he doesn't nip. If his lips open, step back and ignore him for a moment. A friendly horse wants contact with people. If being mouthy makes people ignore him, he'll soon experiment with not being mouthy. This behavior should be rewarded with a pat.

Nose to Nose

Some horses may want to sniff noses with you. This is a natural way that horses get to know each other — but it's risky for you if a nip occurs. That's your face up there beside those big, yellow teeth!

You want to be polite. You want to make friends. What should you do if a horse wants to sniff noses? It depends on the horse. If the owner is reluctant, don't do it. She knows the animal better than you do. If the owner says the horse won't bite, I'd allow a brief sniff. Don't let it go on too long. Just puff your breath at each other, and then step back.

If the horse is a youngster, however, it's best not to sniff

noses. Young horses find nipping irresistible. They want to sample the whole world. If something's not good to eat, it might be good to play with. I repeat: that's your face!

HALTERING A HORSE

You've approached his front left side. You have a halter and lead rope, maybe carried openly, maybe hidden behind your back. (Some horses will go the other way if they see you carrying a halter. Halters usually mean it's time to work!)

Here are two ways to put on a buckled halter. (Find out how to make an emergency halter and how to put on a rope halter on page 114.)

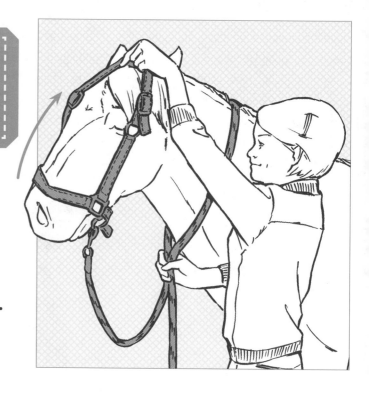

1 **Walk up to the left side.** Loop the rope around the horse's neck, and hold it closed with your right hand. With your left hand, ease the halter up over the horse's head, guiding the horse's left (near) ear into the halter.

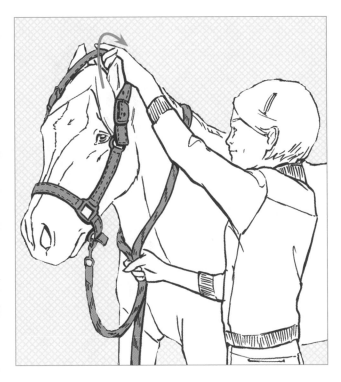
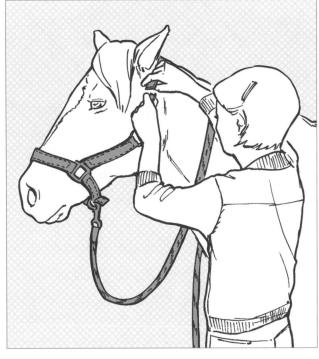

2 **Still holding the rope** in your right hand, reach your left hand over the horse's head and guide the right ear in. Fasten the throat snap, and withdraw the rope from around the horse's neck. Be sure not to whip it off and startle him.

3 **If you prefer,** you can fasten and unfasten your halter using the buckle. To halter this way, loop the rope around the neck. Slip the halter onto his nose. Now reach under his neck, put the strap over his neck, behind the ears, and buckle.

TYING AN EMERGENCY HALTER

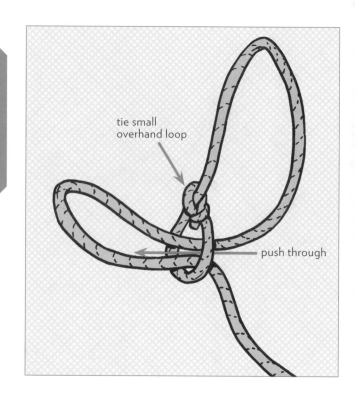

tie small
overhand loop

push through

Learning this trick will come in handy if you ever find yourself chasing a loose horse down the road or around the barnyard.

Horse Sense

TIP: Practice making this halter with yarn for your model horses; that way when a real emergency with a real horse happens, you'll be able to make a halter quickly.

1 **Tie a small overhand loop** in one end of your rope.

2 **Catch your horse** by putting the other end of the rope over his neck. Make a loop in the rope, and push it through the small loop.

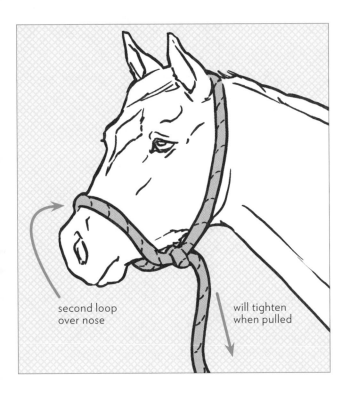

second loop
over nose

will tighten
when pulled

3 **Put the second loop** over the horse's nose. This will tighten if you or the horse pulls, and if you're catching a stray horse you won't mind having that extra degree of control.

Credit: *Stable Smarts* by Heather Smith Thomas (2005)

❋ WESTERN ❋ ROPE HALTERS

Rope halters are most popular with Western riders but plenty of other horse people use them too. Rope halters are put together with knots instead of metal hardware. They are very strong, and many trainers feel they give a more precise signal to the horse. Because they're slender, they also show off a beautiful head.

Leading a Horse

Most horses are trained to lead from their left side. To lead safely and effectively, stand at the horse's left shoulder. Hold the rope in your right hand, about level with the halter ring, leaving a short loop of slack. Hold the rest of the rope in your left hand. Never wrap any part of the rope around either hand. Fold the end (called the bight) of the rope in flat loops, to keep it from dragging on the ground. If you're carrying a whip, hold it in your left hand.

Say *walk on* and step forward decisively. Walk about even with the horse's head. If the horse doesn't step off when you do, you can reach back and tap lightly with the whip. If he's really "stuck to the ground," try turning his head to one side or the other and leading him off slightly to one side rather than moving straight ahead.

If the horse crowds your personal space, use the butt of the whip to poke him in the neck or shoulder. (Extending your arm and straightening your elbow a bit can help prevent a pushy horse from stepping into you.)

When you want to stop, say *whoa*. Stop, turning your left shoulder slightly toward the horse. Horses respond to our body signals — sometimes before we know we're giving them! The turn tells him, "You can't come through here."

GROOMING EQUIPMENT

A good grooming kit includes a currycomb, body brushes, a grooming glove, a mane comb, and a hoof pick. Collect all your gear in a bucket or tool box.

CURRYCOMB

BODY BRUSH
(STIFF BRISTLES)

 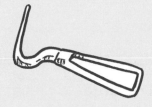

BODY BRUSH
(SOFT BRISTLES)

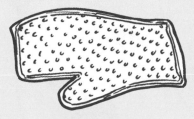

GROOMING GLOVE

MANE COMB

HOOF PICK

* **Currycombs** are used in a circular motion to loosen dirt and hair.
* **Body brushes** move in the direction the hair grows, to sweep the loosened dirt off (stiff bristles) and to polish the horse's coat (soft bristles).
* **A grooming glove,** with its gentle nubs, gives a final polish to a clean coat.
* **Mane combs** are used to gently untangle mane and tail. A regular hairbrush with coated wire bristles is also useful.
* **Hoof picks** remove dirt from the horse's hooves. Use the pointed end and work from heel to toe.

PLAYING WITH ROPE

Learning knots can be a pleasant pastime on a winter's evening. Scouts, sailors, cowboys, and farmers all know their knots; they know how to make them quickly and what they're good for. There are many useful knots that horsemen should know too.

Once you master a few you'll know how to tie a horse safely, put a loop in the middle of a rope for hanging up coiled hose, tie down a load of bales or a tarp, or hitch two ropes together. I prefer quick release knots for most purposes because they're easy to untie.

QUICK-RELEASE CLOVE HITCH

A simple way to tie your horse

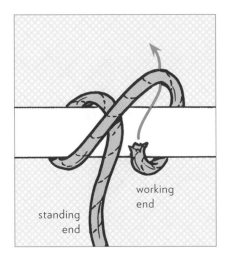

standing end

working end

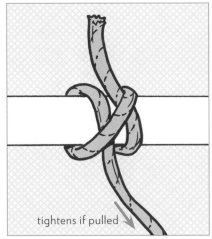

tightens if pulled

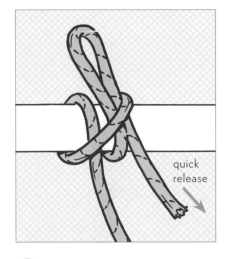

quick release

1 **Wrap the working end of the rope once** around the pole. Start around again, poking the working end up under itself as in the illustration.

NOTE: When using a halter rope, the "working end" is the free end. The "standing end" has the horse attached to it.

2 **Now you have a standard clove hitch.** It will tighten if pulled. Do not tie a horse using this knot!

3 **For a quick-release clove hitch,** fold the working end, and push the loop under the second wrap. This knot will tighten if the horse pulls, but can be released quickly by pulling on the free end.

MANGER KNOT

A secure knot that unties easily

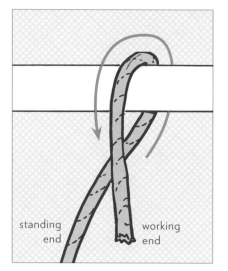 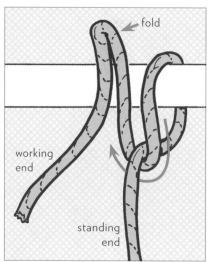 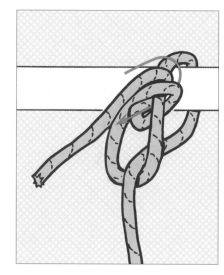

1 **Bring the working end up** and around the pole or ring.

2 **Loop the working end** below the standing end and fold as shown.

3 **Slip the folded part of the working end** through the first loop and then into the second loop that you've created.

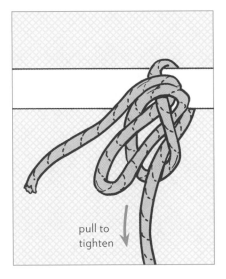

pull to
tighten

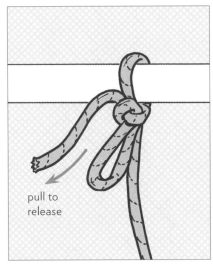

pull to
release

4 **Pull the standing end** until the knot tightens.

5 **To release,** pull on the free end.

NOTE: To prevent your horse from pulling it loose, run the working end back through the loop.

Mig o' the Moor

by Nancy Caffery (1953)

This is the story of a mysterious white stallion, discovered on the Irish moors on a memorably foggy evening by Sean Flynn, an Irish horseman visiting from his new home in America.

Sean imports the stallion to a racing stable in his new homeland, where the horse forms a bond with his nephew, a horse trainer's son who has become afraid of riding. Mig seems to be some sort of pooka (a mischievous spirit) and in the end disappears as mysteriously as he emerged from the mists.

This stirring book has fine illustrations by Jeanne Mellin.

RING KNOT

A quick-release knot for tying a horse to a ring

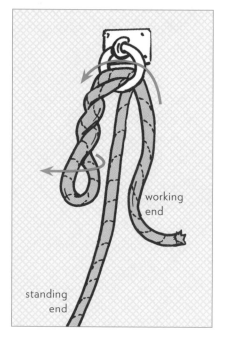

working
end

standing
end

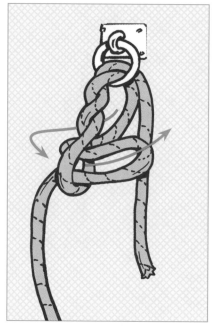

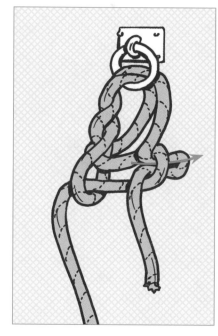

1 Double the rope and pass the loop through the ring from behind. You need to create a longish loop here. Twist the loop two or three times.

2 Bring a short loop of the standing end through from behind.

3 Put a loop of the working end through the loop in the standing end. Pull the standing end to snug the knot up.

NOTE: You can untie this knot with one pull, but so can a clever horse! To prevent that, run the free end of the rope back through the last loop. You'll have to pull it free before untying the knot, which is something even a pretty smart horse won't be able to figure out.

SQUARE KNOT

Fix a broken rope or tie a gate shut

1 **Cross the two ropes.** Bring the working end of the upper rope behind and around the lower rope.

2 **Cross the ropes again.** The same rope should be on top each time. Bring the working end of the upper rope behind and around the lower rope.

3 **Pull from both ends to tighten.** This knot tightens when pulled, so never use it to tie a horse.

BOWLINE KNOT

A nonslip knot handy for catching a loose horse with just a lead line

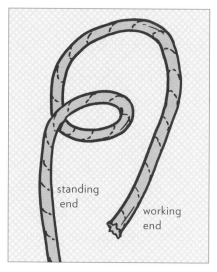

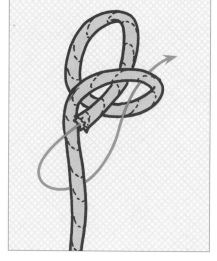

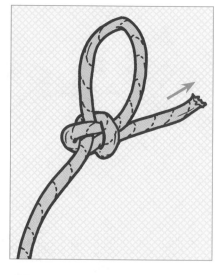

1 **Form a loop by passing the working end** over the standing end, and pinching together the spot where the rope crosses.

2 **Bring the working end** through the loop from behind. Pass it in front of the standing end, then behind the standing end, and back through the loop from the front.

3 **Pull tight.** Control the size of the knot by holding the loop as you snug it up. The loop should not tighten if the rope is pulled, making it the safest knot to tie around a horse's neck.

SAFETY TIP

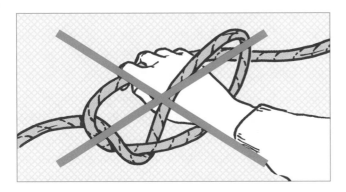

When tying any sort of knot, don't stick your hand or even a finger through a loop to pull the rope through. If your horse suddenly pulls back, you could be hurt. Instead, push the rope through the loop before grabbing it.

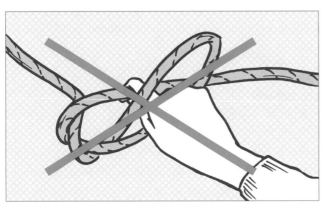

HORSE WORDS

Horse feathers! — Nonsense!
Dark horse — A surprise winner
Horsing around — Rowdy play
Horse laugh — Loud raucous guffaw

Pony up — Pay your money
Dog-and-pony show — An elaborately staged event or presentation
One-horse town — A small town with few amenities

Learning How to Ride

You can't learn to ride from a book. You can learn a lot about riding from reading, though, and refine your techniques once you have gained some experience. Real life is different from a book. Horses and ponies have wills of their own. The unexpected happens. The expected often doesn't. To learn riding you need: a) lessons, b) experience, and c) some good books to help you understand what's going on.

Finding a Good Teacher

Start by deciding if you want to learn English or Western. The basics are the same — one leg on each side of the horse, bottom in the saddle. But there are some key differences.

English riders hold the reins in both hands; Western riders use only one hand and neck-rein. The speed of the gaits is also different. English horses are expected to trot briskly; Western horses to jog slowly.

There's a lot more to learn besides getting on and staying on. Once you decide what kind of riding you want to do — English, Western, jumping, dressage — find a teacher who specializes in it.

Take lessons from an experienced teacher. Find a good one by asking riders you admire — the calm, happy, successful ones — who they would recommend. A good riding teacher will have happy, healthy school horses and a safe facility. She'll require helmets and boots.

She'll likely help you get comfortable with horses by having you tack up, and maybe do some gymnastic exercises

Horseshoe REVIEW

Sylvester
(1985, rated PG)

This is the movie that hooked Will Faudree — 2002 Young Rider of the Year and frequent high-placing event rider — on three-day eventing. Faudree's from Texas, where most of this movie takes place. Charlie Railsberg, played by Melissa Gilbert, is raising her two orphaned brothers and working in a stockyard when she spots a special horse among the broncs.

The horse-breaking scenes are pretty realistic, and the movie is unsentimental and gritty in a way that merits a PG-13 rating, in my opinion. It's also gripping and satisfying, with a lot of thrilling horse scenes.

on horseback. A good teacher won't push you if you're fearful, but she'll have a lot of ways of helping you past your concerns.

HAVING REASONABLE EXPECTATIONS

Riding's harder than it looks, and learning to ride well takes time. Don't expect to canter and jump after just a few lessons — actually, once you're up on a horse for the first time, cantering and jumping will probably be the last thing you'll want to do!

You need to learn to steer, stop, and balance yourself. You need to learn what the different gaits feel like, and how to read a horse's expression when all you can see are his ears.

You'll also need to learn to be firm yet patient with school horses. These hardworking animals teach many novice riders in the course of a week, and put up with a lot of pulling on their mouths and thumping on their sides. In self-defense,

many try to ignore their riders. They know how to do things right, but they also know you are still learning, they're probably bored silly, and they're going to make you work!

Don't get mad — get better at riding. You'll be amazed at how light and responsive a school horse can become when your skills match his.

TACKING UP

Paying attention to details as you tack up will make the ride more pleasant, and safer, for you and your horse.

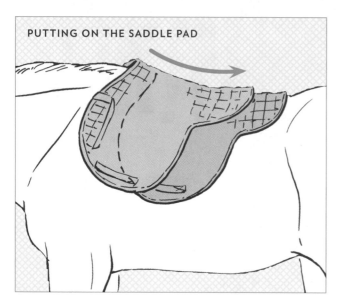

PUTTING ON THE SADDLE PAD

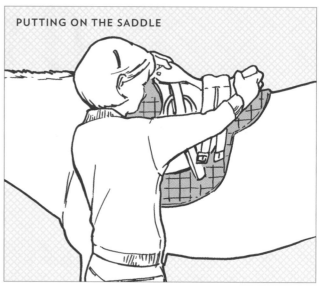

PUTTING ON THE SADDLE

1 **Check both sides of the pad** for sticks, pebbles, or burrs. Set the pad slightly ahead of your horse's withers and slide it back into place, smoothing down the hairs.

2 **Swing the saddle up and over the horse's back in one smooth movement.** Settle the saddle onto the pad lightly — don't bounce it onto the horse's back.

FASTENING AN ENGLISH GIRTH

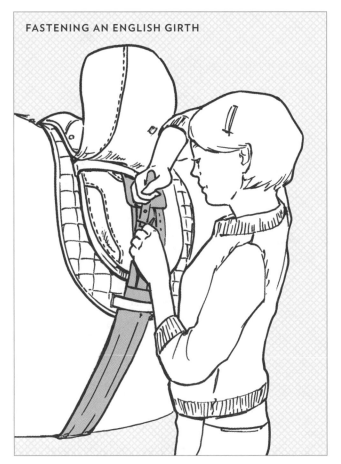

FASTENING A WESTERN CINCH

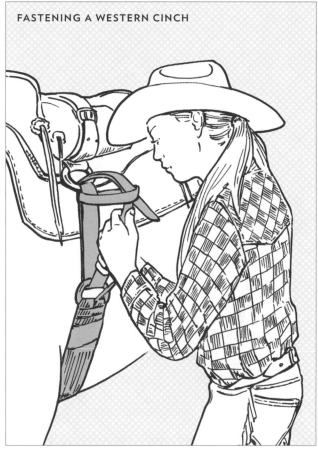

3 **For an English girth,** fasten the buckles on the right side and then the left, using the lowest holes. Girth up gradually, not all in one squeeze.

For a Western cinch, tighten the cinch knot, wait for several seconds, and then tighten it further.

NOTE: Be sure to check the girth or cinch again after a few minutes of riding. You'll usually find you can tighten it a bit more.

(continued on next page)

PUTTING REINS OVER HEAD

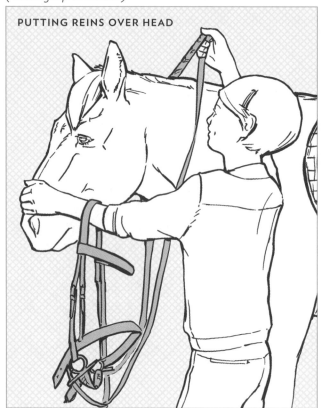

SLIDING BIT INTO MOUTH

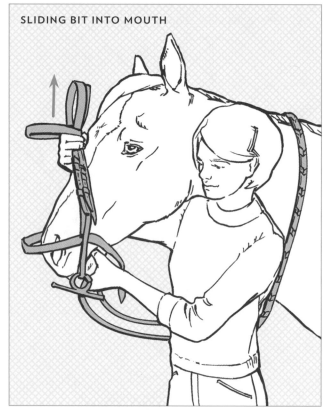

4 **Slip the reins over the horse's head.** Hold the top of the bridle in your right hand, with your arm over the horse's neck and between his ears. (If your horse is tall, pass your right arm under his jaw and hold the bridle above his face by the cheekpieces as shown in Step 5.)

5 **Cradle the bit in your left hand.** Put your thumb into the corner of his mouth. Press down on the gum if needed. When he opens his mouth, slide the bit into his mouth by pulling up gently on the bridle with your right hand.

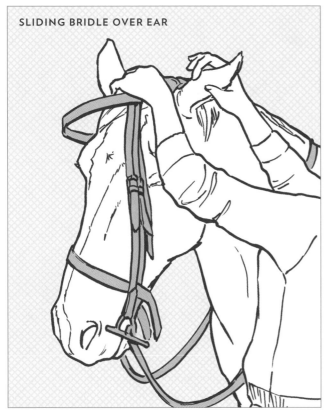

SLIDING BRIDLE OVER EAR

6 **Now slide the bridle** gently past his eyes. Handle his ears carefully. Buckle all buckles and make sure his mane and forelock are neat and not being pulled by the straps. Adjust the browband.

Phar Lap
(1984, rated PG)

These movies about real racehorses of the 1930s have some thrilling race scenes, but both are really more about the people affected by a great horse than about the horse himself.

Phar Lap is horsier, but sadder. Most of the people surrounding this extraordinary animal seem motivated by money-lust and the movie ends with Phar Lap's mysterious death. But there's a groom who loves this horse, and the scenes where he unlocks Phar Lap's speed are excellent, as are the races themselves.

Seabiscuit
(2003, rated PG-13)

Seabiscuit was a quirky horse whose personality is mostly absent from the movie that bears his name. The people are fascinating, yes, but so was the horse. You wouldn't know that from this movie. Read *Come On, Seabiscuit* (see page 133) to really meet this funny, opinionated horse.

Also, the races in this movie seem to go on for an eternity, unlike real Thoroughbred races. Still, the last two are thrilling.

THE THOROUGHBRED
Racing Royalty

Thoroughbred racing is called "The Sport of Kings," and Thoroughbreds are equine royalty. They can run farther at greater speed than any other breed of horse. They're elegant, beautiful, and full of the courage and determination horsemen call "heart." And don't they know it? Many Thoroughbreds have a haughty, imperious attitude, akin to the attitude of old-time English nobility. When displeased they're apt to throw an equine temper tantrum.

The Thoroughbred was developed specifically for racing in the 1600s and 1700s by the English royal family and the upper classes. Noblemen and soldiers collected excellent stallions from Turkey, Arabia, Morocco, and even farther afield. The famous trio of Founding Fathers were the Byerly Turk (probably an Akhal Teke), the Darley Arabian, and the Godolphin Arabian, who was almost certainly a Turkmene horse. Arabians were the prestige breed in 1700s England, and lots of horses that were called Arabian were really something else. (For more about the Godolphin Arabian see the Horseshoe Review on page 191.)

These stallions get all the glory, and today's Thoroughbreds trace back to them. But what about the mares? Many of them were Hobbies, an Irish breed that was very fast over short distances. Almost every modern Thoroughbred traces back to a Hobby mare named Old Bald Peg. The Running Horse, an English sprinting breed, also played a key role. The Hobby and Running Horse bloodlines have been carried on by the female lines of the Thoroughbred breed.

GOING THE DISTANCE

Thoroughbreds were bred to run over distance. The original races were often four miles long, and run in three or four heats. There was a reason for this. After King Charles I was deposed and beheaded due to the superiority of Cromwell's cavalry, Charles II wanted to be sure his soldiers had horses that could run fast over long distances while carrying weight!

When Thoroughbreds came to America, the distances dropped. Today a long race is 1¾ miles. But those grueling English races are the source of the Thoroughbred's toughness and heart. Thoroughbred racing is America's most popular spectator sport, but Thoroughbreds excel in many other sports, including steeplechasing, foxhunting, eventing, and show jumping.

LOOKING AT THOROUGHBREDS

Thoroughbreds are long and elegant, with prominent withers, well-sloped muscular shoulders, slim legs, and a fine coat. All colors are allowed, including pintos, which do occur in the breed, though rarely. Thoroughbreds range between 15 and 17 hands and weigh 1,000–1,250 pounds.

GREAT THOROUGHBREDS

☀ *Man O' War,* foaled in 1917, is considered America's greatest racehorse. He was only defeated once, in a race that started with him facing the wrong way of the track. Even so, he managed to catch the leaders and nearly win.

☀ *Seabiscuit,* a grandson of Man O' War, under-performed as a two-year-old. But one trainer saw promise in him, and eventually Seabiscuit lived up to that promise. Most racehorses give up if another horse catches them in the stretch, but Seabiscuit put on a fresh burst of speed and typically won "going away," increasing his lead as he crossed the finish line.

☀ *Secretariat* won the Triple Crown in 1973, setting records in the Derby and Belmont (and probably the Preakness too, but the official time clock malfunctioned). Most horses slow down over distance; in the Derby, Secretariat was still accelerating when he crossed the finish line.

TRIPLE CROWN WINNERS

In over 130 years, only 11 horses have won all three races that make up America's coveted Triple Crown: the Kentucky Derby, the Preakness Stakes, and the Belmont Stakes.

☀ 1919 Sir Barton
☀ 1930 Gallant Fox
☀ 1935 Omaha
☀ 1937 War Admiral
☀ 1941 Whirlaway
☀ 1943 Count Fleet
☀ 1946 Assault
☀ 1948 Citation
☀ 1973 Secretariat
☀ 1977 Seattle Slew
☀ 1978 Affirmed

Horseshoe REVIEW

Man O' War
by Walter Farley (1962)

A real-life horse as amazing as The Black Stallion? That would be Man O' War, the horse who captured the American public's imagination. Farley follows the great horse (known as "Red" to his friends) from birth to death, and is mostly true to historical detail.

The one major departure is his creation of Danny, a boy who is Red's groom in the story. In real life Red's groom was an African American man named Will Harbut.

Come On, Seabiscuit
by Ralph Moody (1963)

This is still the best book about Seabiscuit. He had a strong, quirky personality, and Moody gets it all down on the page in lively, engrossing writing. You'll be rooting for this underdog all the way.

Another great read is *Seabiscuit, An American Legend* by Laura Hillenbrand. Hillenbrand focuses more on the people in Seabiscuit's life than on the horse himself, but they were certainly a fascinating bunch.

BASIC RULES OF RIDING

Mounting

Hold the reins in your left hand, braced against the horse's withers. Put your left foot in the stirrup, and swing up.

Avoid the following: digging the horse's side with your left toe; hitting him in the butt with your right foot as you swing over; tugging on the reins.

Land lightly in the saddle — no thumping! Slide your right foot into the stirrup (it's okay to look first, but pretty soon you'll be able to find it with your eyes shut). Take a moment to organize your reins, your seat, and your thoughts. Then ask your horse to walk.

English Seat

Your hips should be above your heels, with your weight on the balls of your feet. If an unseen hand whisked your horse out from under you,

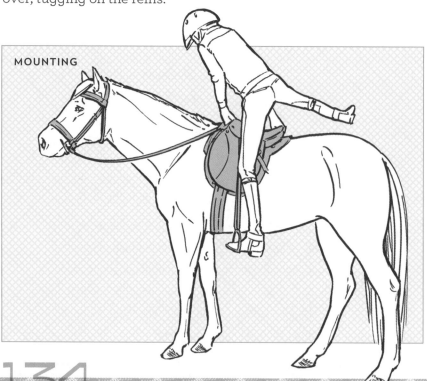

MOUNTING

SITTING, ENGLISH-STYLE

you should be left standing upright like a toy plastic rider.

Think of your head, torso, hips, and legs as a set of building blocks, and stack them so they don't tumble — head high, shoulders back and relaxed, upper arms loosely against your ribcage. Your heels should be lower than your toes. This is called "balanced seat."

English Reins

Hold your reins in both hands. The rein should pass between your third and fourth fingers (ring finger and pinkie). The buckle end is held between your thumb and forefinger.

Close your fist gently and keep your thumbs up. You can communicate with your horse by squeezing your third finger, two fingers, or all three.

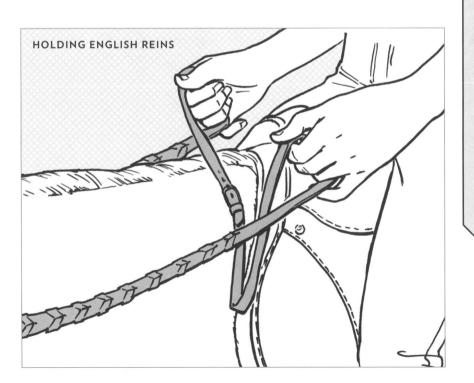

HOLDING ENGLISH REINS

Horseshoe REVIEW

Lucy and Danae: Something Silly This Way Comes
by Wiley Miller (2005)

In this collection from the comic strip *Non Sequitur*, the main character Danae wears black with skull motifs, has a razor-sharp mind, and sports the wickedest grin since Calvin. Lucy is the sweet-with-attitude pony Danae falls in love with at camp.

From acting as guide pony to the blind to having an adventure at Santa's Workshop, this pair will make you laugh, and think.

Western Seat

Stack your building blocks — head, torso, hips, legs — just like an English rider in balanced seat. Heels down, body relaxed yet upright. Your free hand may rest on your thigh, hang at your side, or, with elbow bent and fist lightly clenched, be held in front of your stomach.

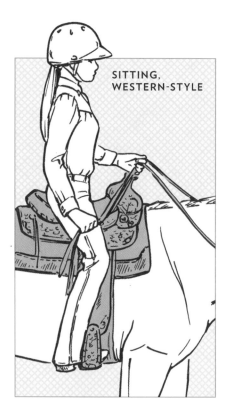

SITTING,
WESTERN-STYLE

Western Reins

Hold your reins in one hand — your left if you are right-handed, your right if you are left-handed. This leaves your handiest hand free for work.

Split reins are held in a closed fist, with your forefinger between the reins to keep them separate. Closed reins are held in a closed fist. Your free hand holds the romal (the piece that joins the reins and can be used as a quirt), on your right thigh.

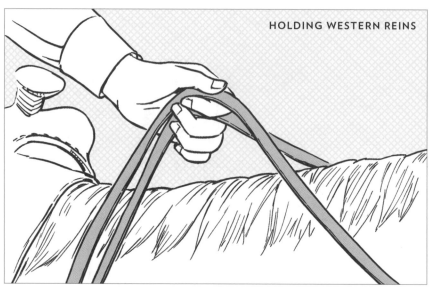

HOLDING WESTERN REINS

RIDING IS
✹ RISKY ✹

One in five riders will suffer serious injury in their lifetime. Novice riders are at three times higher risk than intermediate riders and five times greater risk than experienced riders. But pros are at risk, too. Pros and instructors have a 94 percent chance of injury during their career, compared with a 54 percent risk for novices.

THE AMERICAN QUARTER HORSE
Most Popular Horse in the World

Out of 9.2 million horses in the United States, 3.2 million of them are Quarter Horses. What makes them so popular? Think "boy next door" — the clean-cut high school athlete with the good grades, the job, and the pick-up truck. Quarter Horses get the work done, and if it involves speed and cows, they're that much happier.

It all began on the east coast of colonial America. From Rhode Island south, the English settlers were crazy about horse racing. But it's hard work clearing a racetrack in the wilderness. So the settlers smoothed out quarter-mile tracks, or raced their horses down the main street of town.

When distance racing became popular in America in the 1850s, Thoroughbreds replaced Quarter Horses on the racetracks. Many Eastern settlers took their Quarter Horses west, and with the rise of cattle ranching, their other great talent was discovered. Bigger than mustangs, level headed and kind tempered, they were the perfect all-around ranch horse. Many still do ranch work today.

Mostly, though, Quarter Horses rule the world of Western sports and games. They dominate reining, cutting, barrel racing, and Cowboy Mounted Shooting. Quarter Horses also compete in English sports like jumping, eventing, and dressage.

Quarter Horses still race, too. No more dirt paths or main streets, though; you have to go to a racetrack to see them. But the distance is still a quarter of a mile, and they're still unbeatable at that distance.

LOOKING AT A QUARTER HORSE
Racing strains look more Thoroughbred-y, and halter strains have more of a muscular, "bulldog" look, but your basic working Quarter Horse is compact, short-legged, powerful, and balanced. The breed is fairly level from head to tail, with powerful haunches, a deep broad chest, and a short, straight head. The muscles are powerful and well defined, and often "cut" like the muscles of a body builder.

All colors are allowed, but a horse with white above the knee or hock, or white body patches, can't be registered. Quarter Horses range between 14.2 and 17 hands and weigh 1,000–1,500 pounds.

A FAMOUS QUARTER HORSE
Zanaton, known as "the Mexican Man O' War," was starved, abused, and then jogged for miles to the racetrack, where he was ridden by a 140-pound man in a heavy stock saddle. In spite of those handicaps, he still ran 300 yards in 15.4 seconds, a blazing pace.

BRUSH EARRINGS

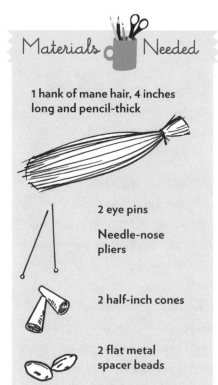

1 hank of mane hair, 4 inches long and pencil-thick

2 eye pins

Needle-nose pliers

2 half-inch cones

2 flat metal spacer beads

2 decorative beads

1 pair French hooks

Nail clippers or wire snips

Scissors

There are hundreds of artists who, for a fee, will make a piece of jewelry out of your horse's hair. But you can make beautiful horsehair jewelry yourself, too. It costs a lot less, and it's very satisfying.

Brush earrings use mane hair from your own horse, your favorite camp horse, or a friend's horse. Make sure you have permission from the owner before you start snipping.

For a splashier effect, mix hair from a couple of horses: streaky hair makes gorgeous earrings. Jewelry-making supplies, called findings, are not necessarily expensive. Sterling silver costs more but is easier to twist than what is called "base metal."

For some of these steps four hands are handier than two. This is a fun project to do with a friend or your mom.

Directions

1. **Divide the hair** into two even bunches.

2. **Open one eye pin with pliers.** Fold one bunch of hair in half and hook the fold into the eye pin. Squeeze the eye pin shut.

3. **Push a cone down over the hair and the eye.** Make sure it's pushed down as far as it will go.

4. **Thread a flat spacer bead** onto the eye pin.

STEP 2	STEP 5	STEP 6	STEP 7	STEP 10

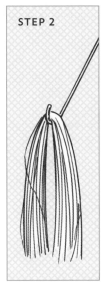   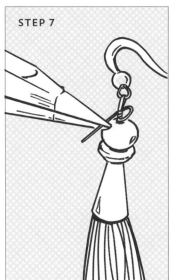 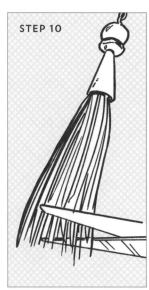

5. **Thread a decorative bead** onto the eye pin.

6. **Thread a French hook** onto the eye pin. Push beads and hook firmly down.

7. **Twist eye pin shank** into a firm and decorative coil around the loop of the French hook.

8. **Snip off the extra wire** with nail clippers.

9. **Repeat Steps 1 through 8** to create the second earring.

10. **Hold earrings level with one another.** Using scissors, trim hair to the desired length or leave tapered for a more natural look.

Wear with pride!

HORSEHAIR JEWELRY

Horsehair is often used to make jewelry for horses, too. Western outfitters sell horsehair bridle tassels. Spanish and Portuguese bridles are often decorated with elaborate sets of horsehair tassels.

Horsehair can also be braided to make jewelry, or it can be "hitched," a different kind of craft that uses knots to create beautiful and complex patterns out of tail hairs.

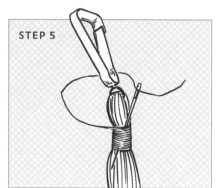

STEP 1

STEP 5

STEP 7

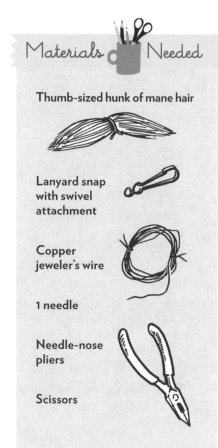

Materials Needed

Thumb-sized hunk of mane hair

Lanyard snap with swivel attachment

Copper jeweler's wire

1 needle

Needle-nose pliers

Scissors

VARIATION: Zipper Pull

If you don't have pierced ears, or have made a few pairs and want to try something different, here's another option for using hair from your favorite equine.

Directions

1. **Fold hair in half and insert** through swivel attachment.

2. **Make a slipknot** in the wire.

3. **Pull knot over hair** and draw tight.

4. **Wind the wire tightly** around the folded hair several times, making sure to cover the knot. Snip from coil, leaving a 3- to 4-inch tail.

5. **Thread the tail through the needle;** draw the needle under one of the wrapped wire strands and wrap once or twice in the opposite direction.

6. **Make a slipknot.** Draw wire through the wrapped coil and snip it off very short with scissors.

7. **Trim hair** to desired length.

Books about "The Black"

The Black Stallion is the ultimate horse fantasy. A boy and a magnificent untamed horse are marooned on a desert island. They become friends, they're rescued, the incredible speed of the horse is discovered, and then there's the match race against the greatest Thoroughbred racehorses of the day.

Could it happen? A horse so fast that the speed of his running rips his rider's shirt to shreds? Whose speed makes his rider black out? No — but who cares? Walter Farley makes it all seem real. The Black is a dream horse and he expands Alec, bringing him into the adult world, but also into a larger world where he becomes half-man, half-animal. *The Black Stallion* gives readers that experience as well. This book will feed your imagination for years to come.

Farley began writing *The Black Stallion* when he was a high school kid like Alec, and published it in his twenties. The nephew of a not-very-good horse trainer, he knew horses well.

The Black's adventures continued through the many titles in the series:

* *The Black Stallion and Flame*
* *The Black Stallion and the Girl*
* *The Black Stallion and Satan*
* *The Black Stallion Challenged*
* *The Black Stallion Legend*
* *The Black Stallion Mystery*
* *The Black Stallion Returns*

* *The Black Stallion Revolts*
* *The Black Stallion's Courage*
* *The Black Stallion's Filly*
* *The Black Stallion's Fury*
* *The Black Stallion's Ghost*
* *The Black Stallion's Sulky Colt*
* *The Blood Bay Colt*

* *The Horse Tamer*
* *The Horse That Swam Away*
* *Son of the Black Stallion*
* *The Young Black Stallion* (with Steven Farley, his son)

If you love the *Black Stallion* books, try these other books by Walter Farley:

* *Island Stallion*
* *Island Stallion Races*
* *Island Stallion's Fury*

* *Little Black: A Pony*
* *Little Black and Big Red*
* *Little Black at the Races*

* *Little Black Goes to the Circus*
* *Man O' War* (see page 133)

Chatting with Horse Folks

Cheryl Rivers, trainer and breeder of Morgans

Describe briefly your work/play with horses.
I breed, raise, and train Morgan horses at my farm in Vermont, River Echo Morgans. I also give riding and driving instruction.

What's cool about what you do?
Getting to know special horses and making lifelong friends. Being able to learn something new every day about horse nature or human nature.

What's hard about what you do?
I become emotionally attached to every horse I raise and train, and it's hard to say goodbye even when they are going to a wonderful home. I love it when they come back for a training refresher or a lesson with their owner.

It is also physically demanding and sometimes dangerous dealing with a horse who does not respect or trust humans. At 5 feet tall and 57 years old, I use more finesse than strength, but sometimes strength, agility, and quickness are important.

What could a kid be doing now to wind up with a career like yours?
Take lessons from knowledgeable people. Look for every opportunity to gain horse experience. Find a mentor and learn what they have to offer. Read everything you can. Observe at competitions and learn from brilliant performances and from mistakes. It is difficult to make enough money in the horse business, so have a backup plan. Knowing you have an alternative will help free you to develop your passion.

How did you choose this path in life?
Hm. Did I choose it? I was lucky enough to grow up on a horse farm. I have always breathed horses and sought their companionship. It's like drinking water. I need them to be happy. I have done many other things in my life, but I always come back to horses.

What surprises you about your work?
One would think that after over 50 years working with horses in one capacity or another, it would seem routine or even boring. It never does. There is something to be learned every day, and each new horse has something special to offer if I am open to it.

What's one thing you wish people understood about working with horses?
I wish people understood if they want to be successful with horses they need to be committed to lifelong learning for both themselves and their horse. I wish people understood that working with horses is part science, but more an art. I wish people understood that horses need clear boundaries and kind but consistent and firm guidance.

Helmets: Absolutely, Completely, Totally Required

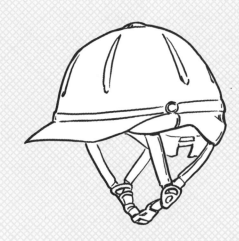

English Helmet

Western Helmet

Wear a helmet whenever you ride. Period. Why? So you can tell stories about your spectacular accident, instead of lying there in a coma or a coffin. If you think that sounds harsh, keep reading.

Hardheaded Helmet Facts

Horses' eyes are different from ours, their ears are different from ours, and their brains are way different from ours. Things scare them that we don't even see.

A horse is hard wired to jump first and look second. If that sound is a puma, not a crinkling candy wrapper, jumping first can save a horse's life. But what about *your* life?

The most common reason for hospitalization and equestrian-related death is head injury. Here are some other facts you should know:

❋ Most riding accidents happen during pleasure riding, when the horse is randomly spooked.

❋ According to the Equestrian Medical Safety Association, a fall from a mere 2 feet can cause permanent brain damage. On a horse, you're a lot higher up than 2 feet!

* The human skull can be shattered by an impact of 1 to 6 miles per hour (mph). Horses can gallop at 40 mph.

* Death isn't the only serious outcome. Survivors of head injuries may suffer epilepsy, mental impairment, and personality changes.

TEA TIME

Taking a cup of tea (use a plastic or paper cup) out to the barn in the evening, sitting on a hay bale, and listening to the sound of crunching hay is a great way to enjoy some peace and quiet. You'll learn what the normal sounds are in your barn at that time of day. It takes you out of your ordinary frame of mind and lets you spend time just being in the proximity of horses.

Offer your horse a palmful of whatever you're drinking. Many horses enjoy tea, and cider's just another form of apple.

Don't be afraid; be smart. Wear a helmet. Every time. Every ride. Even if you go out bareback in a meadow or are just fooling around in the ring. It could make the difference between bouncing back and maybe never riding again.

❋ BUYING THE RIGHT HELMET ❋

All helmets should be ASTM/SEI certified for equestrian use. Helmets used in other sports are not good enough. (And "cowboy hard hats," construction helmets shaped like Stetsons, are worse than not good enough. The hard brim can dig into the ground during a fall, and break your neck.)

Certified helmets are highly effective. One good thing to know — high cost and prestige brand names don't equal increased safety. All certified helmets meet the same standards. An inexpensive certified helmet is just as safe as an expensive one.

HELMETS AND WESTERN RIDING

Western riders have always had a problem with helmets. They just don't look Western. This is cowboy riding, and the right hat to wear is a cowboy hat. (It's not just a Western problem, though. Dressage riders at Grand Prix level, saddle seat riders, drivers, and competitors in costume classes rarely wear helmets either.)

But ideas about helmets are changing. Western riders are becoming much more interested in safety. Rodeos now require helmets for bull riders. The legendary barrel racer Martha Josey became an advocate of head protection after she suffered a head injury. Delores Toole, another professional barrel racer, made headlines in 2004 when she wore a helmet while competing at the Wrangler National Finals Rodeo.

Helmet makers are helping. Troxel has brought out several versions of its Western Helmet, a close-fitting low-profile helmet covered in stitched leather and ornamented Western-style with studs and rhinestones.

They don't look like cowboy hats, though. They look like polo helmets. To remedy this, Troxel has introduced a helmet that does look right to Westerners, a premium wool felt hat fitted over an ultra-low-profile helmet.

If you drive or ride saddle seat, Troxel makes a handsome felt derby fitted over an ultra-low-profile safety helmet.

Horseshoe REVIEW

Books by C. W. Anderson

Besides the Billy and Blaze books for young readers, C. W. Anderson wrote profiles of famous horses and novels. *Afraid to Ride* is one of his best. In it, a girl is injured in a riding accident and becomes afraid to ride horses, once her greatest passion. A mare who's been abused by another rider comes into her life, and when an emergency arises, the two teach each other courage.

If you like that one, try these other titles:

- ❋ *Another Man O' War*
- ❋ *The Blind Connemara*
- ❋ *Bobcat*
- ❋ *C. W. Anderson's Favorite Horse Stories*
- ❋ *The Complete Book of Horses and Horsemanship*
- ❋ *The Crooked Colt*
- ❋ *Deep Through the Heart*
- ❋ *A Filly for Joan*
- ❋ *Great Heart*
- ❋ *Heads Up, Heels Down!*
- ❋ *High Courage*
- ❋ *Horse of the Century, Man O' War*
- ❋ *The Horse of Hurricane Hill*
- ❋ *The Lonesome Little Colt*
- ❋ *The Outlaw*
- ❋ *Phantom, Son of the Gray Ghost*
- ❋ *A Pony for Linda*
- ❋ *Pony for Three*
- ❋ *The Rumble Seat Pony*
- ❋ *Salute*
- ❋ *Sketchbook*
- ❋ *Twenty Gallant Horses*
- ❋ *The World of Horses*

Be a Helmet Pioneer

Many Western junior shows require helmet use. Some open competitions allow helmets in the ring without penalty. But do the officials at your particular show know that? Many riders don't think so, and feel like they have to wear a Stetson in order to be fairly placed by a judge. Find out what the regulations are before you sign up.

You may have to be a pioneer on this one, and that takes courage. But you wouldn't ride at all if you didn't have guts. Sure, you could wear a helmet everywhere but the competition arena; that would cut your risk, as most riding accidents happen during pleasure riding. But what kind of example are you setting? If you're successful, younger kids will look up to you. If you wear a helmet, they'll think helmets are cool.

✻ ALL HORSES MUST WEAR PANTS ✻ IN FOUNTAIN INN, SOUTH CAROLINA

The following silly horse laws come from *Horse Trivia: A Hippofile's Delight* by Deborah Eve Rubin (Half Halt Press). This fun book also has a ton of great equine facts and figures of every variety.

✻ No Fishing: Colorado bans fishing from horseback, as do Washington, DC, and Utah. Knoxville, Tennessee, prohibits riders from lassoing fish. Norfolk, Virginia, says that horses aren't allowed in the Chesapeake Bay.

✻ No Shorts: Human females weighing over 200 pounds, when attired in shorts, may not legally ride a horse in Markanville, Illinois. In Raton, New Mexico, it's women wearing kimonos who can't ride horseback down a public street.

✻ No Acrobats: Denver doesn't allow acrobats on the sidewalk, as they might scare the horses. In Fairbanks, Alaska, acrobats are probably safe on the sidewalks, but it's a misdemeanor to ride a horse or mule there. In Philip, South Dakota, it's illegal to have a horse or mule on the sidewalk whether they are ridden, driven, or led.

✻ No Sneezing: In Leahy, Washington, and Waterville, Maine, blowing your nose around horses is a no-no.

✻ No Sense: Ada, Oklahoma, ordinance 235: it shall be unlawful for any person or persons to leave, keep, or permit any horse, mule or mules, vehicles, wagons, buggy, automobile, except if same is provided with a grease pan. (Huh?)

UNICORNS

Unicorns have been creatures of myth and legend for many, many centuries. Greek historian Ctesias described one found in ancient India as being the size of a horse with a white body, purple head, and dark blue eyes. Its horn was colored red, white, and black. It was a fierce fighter and the horn had many healing properties. Another Indian unicorn was described as dun-colored with a sharp black horn, broad hooves like an elephant's, and a curly pig's tail!

China also had a unicorn, a heavenly messenger that came to our world to bring good news. The Ki-Lin, as it was called, had the body of a deer, the tail of an ox, and the hooves of a horse. Its horn was 12 feet long, with a soft tip. On its back were the sacred colors black, white, red, blue, and yellow. Its belly was brown or yellow. The Ki-Lin was so gentle it wouldn't even step on a bug. It wouldn't eat living grass, only dry hay.

So Many Ways to Show a Horse

Horse shows come in hundreds of stripes. There are local, state, regional, and national shows, as well as special youth shows and shows for every conceivable discipline and every breed under the sun.

The central resource for finding out about showing nationwide is the United States Equestrian Foundation (USEF). USEF rates and provides rules for nearly three thousand shows each year in English and Western disciplines, driving, vaulting, parades, and para-Equestrian for disabled riders. On the USEF Web site you can find shows near you, get contact information, and find out more about the benefits of membership. If you do join, USEF keeps track of the points you've accumulated throughout the year.

Enjoying a Show Even If You Don't Own a Horse

Showing is one way to enjoy your horse; for some people, it's the whole reason for owning a horse. But what if you don't have a horse? Showing can still be for you. Consider volunteering at a show.

Shows are a huge amount of work, and there's always a job for a willing body to do. Volunteering puts you behind the scenes, close to horses and with a ringside view of the competition.

You can learn a lot, make valuable horse contacts, and earn a lot of points with hard-working show officials that may help you achieve your

TRY SOME NEW TREATS

Feeding a horse vegetable scraps from your kitchen is a great way to give him some variety, to find out what he likes besides apples and carrots. To find out what he doesn't like, watch him make some funny faces as he tells you! You'll enjoy the fresh-crunched aroma of fennel, celery, or broccoli stems, and you'll get maximum use and enjoyment out of the veggies your family buys.

Cabbage leaves, broccoli stems, fennel stalks and fronds, apple and carrot peelings, celery, citrus peels, and even bananas — these are enjoyed by many horses and are safe to try. You can also experiment with cornhusks, melon rinds, beets and turnips and their greens.

Avoid green potatoes, potato leaves and stems, tomatoes, peppers, and any fruit with pits, like cherries, plums, and peaches, unless you remove the pits first.

horse goals. And you'll be part of making everybody's fun day possible, which is a good thing all in itself.

Volunteer opportunities vary depending on the size and type of show. You may be able to help at the secretary's booth; open and close gates; assist a ground crew in replacing jump poles; be a runner for a judge.

In fact, being a runner is your most likely role. A horse show is a long day and people's feet get tired. The people in charge will be grateful to anyone who can save them a few steps by bringing a drink or delivering messages across the show grounds.

Another option for the horse-less horseman is to become involved in driving (see page 236). In many driving sports, grooms or navigators are needed to ride along with the driver. This is a good opportunity for a horseless, but knowledgeable person, or for two friends or family members to share showing a single horse.

What Kind of Show Is Right for You?

There are as many kinds of shows as there are kinds of horses, maybe more. As a spectator, you can enjoy them all. As an exhibitor you'll need to go to the kind of show that matches your horse's breed or discipline and your own skill level.

* **Open shows** are the most common kind to be found. Any breed of horse can enter, and you don't need to belong to the sponsoring organization to compete. Open shows offer a range of classes, and competitors are divided by age.

   The youngest riders compete in walk-trot classes; no cantering allowed. Youth competitors are divided between juniors and seniors. Adults compete separately, as do English and Western riders. In a large, open show the English riders may be divided between hunt seat and saddle seat.

* **Breed shows** may include many disciplines, but the only horses allowed to compete are horses belonging to the specific breed, such as Quarter

Horse or Morgan. Some breeds with small numbers may combine; in the Northeast the so-called Baroque breeds — Friesians, Andalusians, Lusitanos, and the Gypsy cluster of breeds — combine their shows.

* **Gymkhanas** are more casual shows that are all about games. Some have a Western emphasis — barrel races, pole bending. Others feature Pony Club games.

* **Performance shows** allow you and your horse to compete in specific disciplines like dressage, hunter-jumper, three-day eventing, cutting, or reining.

Figuring Out Types of Classes

Within each show you can enter a variety of different types of classes. Some are based on the rider's performance, while others focus on the horse. Classes are often divided by age and level of experience as well.

Though most riders compete in either English or Western, there are many classes that are common to both disciplines. The following classes take place in both English and Western shows, and at most breed shows.

* **Pleasure classes** judge the horse's suitability for pleasure riding; gaits, manners, and looks are considered.

 BREED ORGANIZATIONS

Many breed associations have youth organizations that offer education, competitive opportunities, and sometimes cash scholarships. If you own a purebred horse, find out what's available through the breed association. If you don't, check out the associations of breeds you're interested in. Many offer programs and competitions for the horseless horseman, including a chance to try for scholarships. Let your love of horses help you through college. That'll show the people who say horses aren't practical!

For example, the American Quarter Horse Youth Association (AQHYA) offers several programs. Junior Master Horsemen (JMH) is an educational program with a great Web site, and is available to the horse lover with no horse (yet). You can earn recognition and awards as you work through the program. AQHYA also runs art, photo, caption, and essay contests in which you can win points, and it holds an international youth event, the American Quarter Horse Youth World Cup, every two years at varying locations around the world, which is a mix of competitive and leadership activities.

Dressage is all about the relationship between horse and rider. You and your horse enter the arena alone and complete a test that includes all three gaits, transitions, halting, backing, and lateral movements. There are many levels to these tests. You begin at the bottom, preelementary, and rise up through the levels as you and your horse become more accomplished.

Working Hunter judges the horse's jumping ability and manners, as well as the rider's skill. The horse needs to have steady paces and a good mouth. The rider's turnout is important, and in hunter equitation you'll be judged on your own form, both on the flat and over jumps. Hunter courses are simpler than jumper courses, and have a low-key, natural look.

Jumper classes are more about the horse's jumping

Equitation classes judge the rider's form in the saddle and her ability to handle the horse.

Halter classes, also called Fitting and Showing, judge the condition and cleanliness of the horse and tack, and the handler's ability to show the horse to best advantage.

Trail classes include obstacles and judge the horse's suitability for trail riding.

Horse shows can get serious, all too serious. One class where you can let loose and be silly is **costume class**, where you and your horse dress up. Your imagination and the tolerance of your horse are the only things limiting you here. Have a ball!

CLASSES IN ENGLISH COMPETITION

Some classes are only seen in English competition. These include the following:

ability, focusing on time and points. A clear round in the shortest amount of time wins, no matter how your horse looks or how hard it was to keep him under control. Jumper courses are tough and twisty, with brightly patterned jumps of many different types.

* **Short-Stirrup** jumping classes are for riders ages 12 and under. Fences may be up to 2 feet, 3 inches high, with verticals, walls, and spreads. The rider's style is important here — taking off

BAD DREAMS

In some northern European traditions, a hag stone, or holy stone — a stone with a hole through it — will ward off Marë, the Nightmare, if suspended over the house door or tied to the key.

☀ GAITED HORSES ☀

If you thought three-phase eventing was something you couldn't do with your gaited horse, check out Three Phase Event, Inc. This annual event, held in Kentucky, features a dressage test, a stadium obstacle course, and a cross-country endurance ride.

at the right point, landing on the correct lead, and looking good at all times.

* **Three-Phase Event** is a test of overall skill that includes dressage, arena jumping, and cross-country jumping, all on the same horse. The three disciplines have very different requirements, and it's a rare horse that excels at all three.

CLASSES IN WESTERN COMPETITION

Western shows include the following classes:

* **Reining** is often called Western dressage. Horse and rider lope and gallop through a pattern of circles,

spins, and sliding stops. As in English dressage, they are judged on smoothness, flow, and invisibility of aids.

* **Cutting** classes test a horse and rider's ability to select and move individual cows out of a larger group.

* **Working Cow Horse** is the Western equivalent of the Three-Phase Event. It includes reining, cutting, and fence work, which involves controlling a cow's movements at speed along the long side of the arena.

* **Barrel Racing** sends rider and horse in a cloverleaf pattern around three barrels at top speed.

THE APPALOOSA
Seeing Spots (Lots of Spots)

Appaloosas have plenty of other things going for them, but since time immemorial people have liked virtue best when it's wrapped up in a pretty package — in this case, a polka-dot package. Spotted horses have been popular forever. We have Egyptian art depicting them in 1400 BCE. The ancient Altai horse of Siberia is often spotted. So is the Knabstrub, a Danish riding horse. During the mid-1700s Appaloosa-patterned horses were extremely popular in Europe. Even some Lipizzans and Andalusians were spotted.

But fashions change, and sometime around 1760, spots went out of vogue. The market became bloated with spotted horses no one wanted, and hundreds of them were shipped off to the New World where the Ni Mee Poo (better known as the Nez Percé) used them to produce beautiful and tough warhorses. The name of the breed comes from the Palouse River region in western Washington State and eastern Idaho where the Nez Percé lived.

In its war against Native Americans, the United States government nearly destroyed the Appaloosa. Stallions were gelded, stock was shot, mares were bred to draft horses, and the breed declined and nearly disappeared. Few members of this remarkable breed existed when ranchers decided to protect and promote it in the 1930s. Today's Appaloosa was rebuilt with Quarter Horse and Arabian blood, and resembles those breeds.

LOOKING AT APPALOOSAS

At 14.2–16.2 hands, the Appaloosa is a fairly large stock horse. An Appaloosa has a small, well-shaped head, long neck, short back, deep chest and powerful haunches. The body may be spotted in a number of patterns (see box), but a registered Appaloosa might not be spotted at all. However, all Appys, as they are known, have mottled skin on the nose, lips, and genitals, and their hooves have light vertical stripes.

FUN FACT: An Appaloosa, Ole Wilson, holds the all-breed world speed record for 4½ furlongs, 0:49½ seconds.

PARADE OF PATTERNS

* **Blanket patch:** Solid-colored body with white or lighter-colored rump; the blanket may or may not be spotted.
* **Frost:** Pale coloring with a paler, but not white, barrel and rump and dark spots
* **Leopard:** Light coat with dark spots all over
* **Marble:** Roan coat with dark spots all over
* **Snowflake:** Dark coat with white spots all over

BEAUTIFUL BRAIDS

When your horse is perfectly clean, it's time to throw in some extras. How about braiding? Your chosen discipline may or may not require braids at shows, but you can practice just for fun.

Find out the rules and fashion standards: for example, dressage horses wear a different number of braids than hunters; Saddlebreds wear one long, thin mane braid with the forelock braided tight; draft horses wear rosettes in their manes, which are braided so tightly they can't lower their heads when they're dolled up in parade colors. Or you could get very fancy and turn your horse's mane into a diamond-plaited curtain . . .

Now get out your tools and become very, very good at producing smooth, tight, even braids. This can save lots of preshow agonies, or even become a part-time job.

Horseshoe REVIEW

Braiding Manes and Tails
by Charni Lewis (2007)

Spiral-bound, with a hole so it can hang on a nail in the barn, this full-color book includes step-by-step instructions for 27 kinds of braids, including draft and Saddlebred styles. When you need to know exactly how to make exactly the right kind of braid, this is the book to turn to.

FRENCH-BRAIDED MANE / RUNNING BRAID

Materials needed: Spray bottle or damp sponge, comb, rubber bands, hair gel

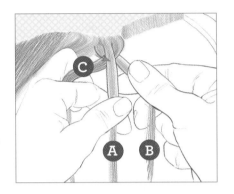

1 **Part off a portion of mane** about 1–1½ inches (3–4 cm) wide. Separate the hair into three sections and start a three-strand braid. With the first turn, cross section **C** over section **B**. Cross section **A** over **C**.

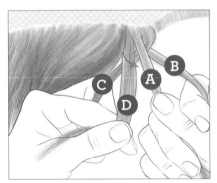

2 **Separate another small portion** of mane (section **D**). Add it to section **A**.

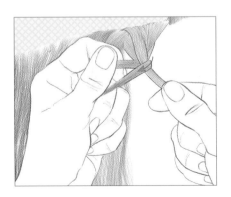

3 **Continue braiding for one turn**: Cross the right section over the middle (as shown), cross the left section over the new middle, and add hair to the middle section. Keep the braid parallel to the crest.

(continued on next page)

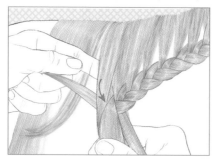

4 **Keep adding hair** to the middle section at every other turn of the braid, and continue braiding until you've reached the withers. Then finish with a three-strand braid.

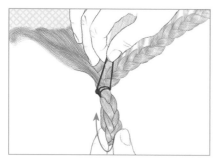

5 **At the end of the braid,** fold the remaining hairs over and wind a rubber band tightly around the end. Then fold the braid up on itself and use a second rubber band to secure the loop.

DIAMOND BRAID

Materials needed: Comb and rubber bands or braiding tape (you can use black electrical tape for a black mane and white athletic tape for a lighter one)

This braid is quite easy, once you get the hang of what to do, and it's so elegant. Just don't leave it in overnight because the tape can become hard to remove.

1 **Use the comb to separate a portion of mane** about 2 inches (5 cm) wide near the poll. Gather the hairs together near the crest with tape or a rubber band, twisting them slightly to make a tighter bundle.

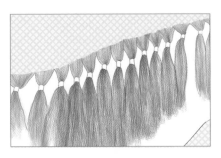

2 **Continue separating out sections of hair** and banding or taping them until you reach the withers.

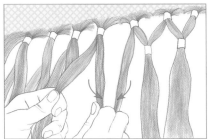

3 **Starting at the top of the mane,** part each lock in half and connect the two nearest sections about 3 inches (8 cm) down with tape or a rubber band.

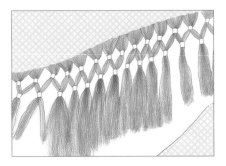

4 **Continue parting the sections** and connecting them all the way to the withers.

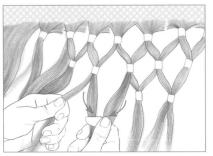

5 **Return to the horse's head** and part each lock of hair in half, and connect each half lock to the nearest half. Make sure you are working in a straight line parallel the crest as you move down the neck.

(continued on next page)

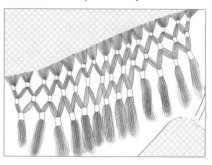

Diamond Braid (continued)

6 **Repeat Step 5 all the way to the withers,** leaving at least 2 inches of mane at the end. You should have 3 to 5 rows, depending on the length of your horse's mane.

PRESERVING A LONG TAIL

Materials needed: Two 2-foot-long (60 cm) shoelaces or thin strips of cloth and a tail bag (you can use a clean old sock instead)

This is a good way help a tail grow to its full potential, or to protect from becoming muddy and tangled during turnout.

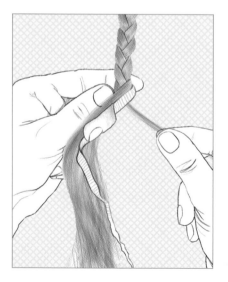

1 **Start a loose, three-strand braid** a few inches below the tailbone. Continue braiding until you are about 6 inches (15 cm) from the end. Fold the shoelace in half and add the halves to the left and right sections of the braid as you continue to the end.

2 **Loop the braid up** and push the end through the top of the braid, below the tailbone. You should have a 6–8-inch (15–20 cm) loop of braid, with the loose end hanging behind.

3 **If the tail is very long,** you may have to make another loop. Use the shoelace to tie the loose end of the hairs around the loop, using a square knot. Be sure to tie below the tailbone.

4 **Slide the tail into a clean sock or tail bag** so that the covering is over the tail but below the tailbone. Use the second shoelace to tie the sock in place. You can also use vet wrap, which sticks to itself but unwraps easily.

FISHTAIL BRAID

Materials needed: Spray bottle or damp sponge, comb, rubber band

This is a fun braid that you won't see at a show but shows off a pretty tail.

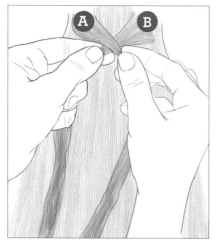

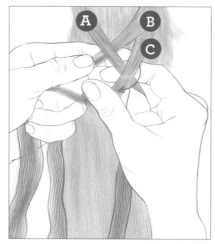

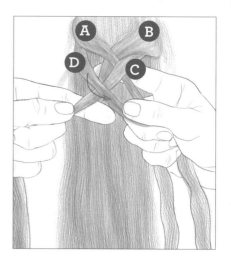

1 At the top of the tail, separate two small sections of hair from the left **A** and right **B** sides, then cross the left piece over the right.

2 Hold these pieces in your left hand. Separate another small section from the right side **C** of the tail, cross it over **A**, and add it to **B**.

3 Hold the two pieces in your right hand. Separate another small section **D** from the left side and add it to **A**. Continue in this way until you are about three-quarters of the way down the tailbone.

4 **Pull a piece of hair** from underneath the right side, pull it over the top of the braid, and add it to the section in your left hand. Continue braiding until you reach the end of the hair. Fasten with a rubber band.

Pony Tales

HEAVENLY HORSES

Did you know that the night skies are full of horses? For example, two of the stars that make up the handle of the Big Dipper are called the Horse and Rider. And several constellations are named after fabulous equine figures or horses of mythology.

Here are few you can look for:

✻ **Centaurus,** thought to represent Chiron, the wise centaur of Greek mythology

✻ **Sagittarius,** the Archer, another centaur and, of course, a member of the zodiac

✻ **Auriga** (oh RYE ga), the Charioteer, represents the driver's helmet rather than his vehicle or horse

✻ **Pegasus,** the wonderful winged horse who helped the hero Bellerophon in his battles

✻ **Equuleus** (ek WOO lee us), the child or brother of Pegasus, depending on which myth you read

✻ **Monoceros,** the Unicorn, found near Orion but hard to see because its stars are dim

Successful Showing Is All in the Attitude

Really successful competitors make showing their lives. At the upper levels you may read about young people who are home-schooled so that classes won't interfere with their show schedules; kids who move in with their coaches; prices for horses that could buy a luxury car or put a down payment on a house.

If you are ambitious, very talented, completely driven, and you have a lot of help, you might make it to that level. But most people want to keep showing horses in a healthy balance with the rest of their lives. So how can you succeed and still have a life?

The most important thing is your attitude. Showing should be fun, for you and your horse. If it's drudgery for either partner, you have a problem. Winning should be a goal, not a need or an obsession. It's only a horse show. The prize is just a ribbon — a little piece of silk that's not even useful. Showing is not real life. It's a game. Enjoy it. It's a pleasure to excel, a pleasure to measure yourself and your horse against others. Anytime it isn't, take a break from it.

How to Strike a Balance

Find a good teacher or coach — someone who explains things so you understand; someone who keeps raising her expectations of you, while making you feel good about what you've already accomplished; someone who puts your health and safety, and your horse's, above ribbons or trophies; and someone you like spending time with.

Practice — but only practice what you learn from a good teacher. Don't get good at riding badly by practicing the wrong thing. It's important to have a knowledgeable outside eye to tell you what you're doing right, and what you need to improve.

Find a suitable horse.
Your beloved backyard companion may be a good show horse, or he may not. If your abilities surpass his, you may need to think about selling him or passing him on to a younger sibling, and then buying a horse that's up to the challenge.

Or you may lease a horse or show a horse for somebody else or ride several different horses from your lesson barn.

Riding one horse all the time can build a deep partnership. Riding a lot of different horses can build an ability to ride almost anything well. Which you prefer depends on your goals.

BE A GOOD CITIZEN IN THE SHOW RING

You can do a lot to make showing more enjoyable for your fellow competitors and the people doing the hard work of put-

#1 Good Citizen Award

Horseshoe REVIEW

Horse Showing for Kids
by Cheryl Kimball (2004)

This is an excellent book about all aspects of showing. It includes checklists for packing for shows, a to-do countdown, information on show officials and what they do, and tips for getting the most out of a show experience.

ting on the event. It comes down to good manners.

Do the paperwork. All the paperwork. Ahead of time. Arrive at the show with your entry form filled out clearly, with all the documents you need and with your entry fee money. Panicky meltdowns at the secretary's tent at the last minute are hard on everybody.

Know the rules. All the rules. Study them ahead of time. After all, you can't practice on your horse 24 hours a day. Spend your nervous energy on reading the rulebook for your particular event.

Make sure you understand what everything means, and that you've mastered the details. If you have patterns to learn, you don't need to practice them on horseback. Walk them. Clop a model horse through them. Trace them with the tip of your tongue on the roof of your mouth.

Be nice to your horse. Winning doesn't matter to him. Because horses are fairly colorblind, he probably doesn't even find the ribbons pretty. What he cares about is knowing what's expected of him, being treated kindly and fairly, and having your approval and friendship. He may enjoy the excitement of the day, too, but he doesn't have a work ethic about it. Don't expect him to pay attention to his standing in the struggle for the championship; that's your job.

Be polite to the officials. They are working hard for little or no pay because they love horses and kids. Don't do anything to spoil that. Shows are exciting and stressful, and stress doesn't always help us be our best selves.

It can be hard to be patient or keep your temper, but look on that as an extra test. Can you handle failure? How

Horse Sense

Even though it's hard to truly feel happy for someone who beats you in a contest, smile. Fake it till you make it!

☀ IF YOU'RE SERIOUS ☀ ABOUT SHOWING

An important organization for the serious show rider is North American Young Riders Championships (NAYRC), which is a member of the International Equestrian Federation (FEI) and holds competitions under its rules. There are junior (14–18) and young rider (16–21) levels. Competition is stiff and academics are emphasized — no giving up school to train your horse. It takes at least a year of working intensively with a good horse to compete successfully at the NAYRC level.

If you do make it, there are a lot of benefits. You'll be competing under the same standards as top world riders, and will be judged by the same people who judge them. You'll learn how to handle tough competition and also to pay attention to the rest of your life. For ambitious riders, NAYRC is a great opportunity.

about success? Horse shows can build character or reveal character flaws. It's up to you.

Be nice to other riders. Congratulate the winners. Encourage people who feel they aren't doing well. If you're disappointed, find a private place to deal with your feelings for a few minutes. Then put that smile back on your face and get out there.

Care for your horse first. He should be watered, fed, rubbed down, and completely comfortable before you take care of yourself.

Don't leave a mess. Grounds or stalls should be in the same condition when you leave as when you arrived — no manure, no trash.

Breed Bits

THE STANDARDBRED
Nothing Standard about This Breed!

Well, there are some standards, the main one being that this breed was developed to race in harness. When the studbook was formed in 1871, horses had to trot or pace a mile in a standard time in order to be registered. That time was 2.30 minutes for the trot and 2.25 minutes for the pace, which was a pretty good clip in those days. Over the years horses and tracks have gotten faster, and the old standard is now considered a training time. These days the best Standardbreds trot a mile in 1.55 minutes; the best pacers come in around 1.47.

The founding sire of the breed, Hambletonian, was born in 1849. The son of an ugly and vicious stallion and a crippled mare, he sired a line of blazingly fast trotters. His offspring were crossed with good Morgans for looks and good temperament, and the Standardbred was born. Morgans could no longer compete, and Standardbreds became America's harness racing breed.

These days, Standardbred racing is popular around the world. In the United States, races are held at county fairs and at large tracks; out in the hot sun and under lights at night. Older people, women, and average-sized people are able to drive in races, making harness racing more accessible to more people. The small breeder can raise and train a foal, take it to the races, and compete.

Standardbreds are also favorite road horses of the Amish, and have a big following as pleasure horses among people who adopt them off the tracks. They can even be trained to jump.

LOOKING AT STANDARDBREDS
Standardbreds are not fancy horses — they are long through the body, with sloping quarters, shorter and straighter necks than the Thoroughbred, large ears, and plain heads. They are sound, sturdy animals; they have to be. Standardbreds put in many more miles of training than Thoroughbreds, including long warm-up laps just before they race. Most Standardbreds are bay, brown, or black; grays, chestnuts, and roans also occur. They average between 15 and 15.3 hands.

A FAMOUS STANDARDBRED
Rosalind demonstrated the strength and heart of Standardbreds conclusively in 1937 when she raced under the greatest handicap ever demanded of a trotter. To give all the horses an even chance, they were started at different points on the track. Rosalind's starting point was 120 feet behind the leaders, 60 feet behind the nearest horse. Race fans feared she'd break her heart trying to win; instead, Rosalind beat the boys and broke the record.

EYE-CATCHING QUARTER MARKS

Once you've braided your horse beautifully, you may want to experiment with quarter marks. These are subtle patterns combed into the hair over a horse's rump — diamonds and checkerboards are common. The pattern is created by dampening the hair and brushing it in different directions; good grooms can do this freehand.

Quarter marks — seen on dressage horses and in some hunter classes — can show off an excellent rump and disguise a skimpy or pointed one. The most common and elegant patterns are variations of the checkerboard, but some riders let their creative juices flow and make hearts, four-leaf clovers, even kiwis! The Canadian Mounties comb a maple leaf pattern onto their horses' rumps.

Experiment before show day to find out what looks good on your horse, and get practice producing it. Some riders use plastic templates; others feel that the patterns are too small and don't show up well enough.

GO FOR THE ☀ GLITZ ☀

Quarter marks are subtle, but they don't have to be — not when you're just out playing with your horse. Use glitter gel (also sold by horse supply catalogs and tack shops) to jazz up your checkerboard.

Polish your horse's hooves — you can buy special glitter for that, too. There are also stencils of flags and flowers commercially available, or, again, you can create your own stencils and turn your horse into a work of art.

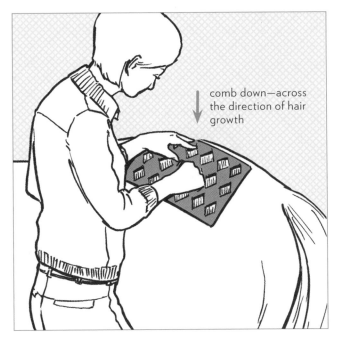

comb down—across the direction of hair growth

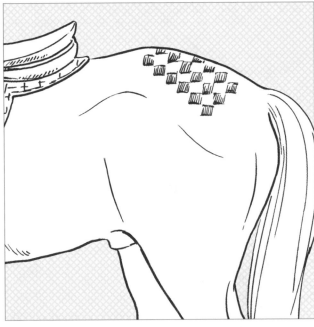

1 **Lightly spray your horse's rump** with water or fly-spray, then brush in the direction of the hair. Using a fine comb — a mane-pulling comb or the fine part of a plastic hair comb — start on the upper left corner of the rump. Line the comb up squarely and comb down toward the ground, across the direction of the hair growth, to create a square.

2 **Move one square down,** and repeat. When you've completed one row of squares, move over one row and comb the alternate squares to create a checkerboard. Repeat on the other side of the rump, being sure to make the same pattern on both sides. Spray with hairspray.

167

EMBOSSING VELVET

Materials Needed

Scraps or lengths of velvet

**Rubber stamp
or other embossing item**

Iron

Ironing board

Clean towel

Velvet that looks like it's been carved by a sculptor is elegant, subtle, and surprisingly easy to make at home. The technique is called embossing, and it's a great way to add an equine emphasis to velvet scarves, blouses, or pillow coverings.

"Emboss" means to carve a design in relief, meaning that it stands out from a flat surface. In this case, the lines of your stamp or other object won't stand *out*; they'll be carved *into* the velvet. Very small details don't come out crisply on velvet. Choose an object or stamp with simple lines. It's easiest to use a stamp that's not mounted on a handle, or one that has a removable handle.

Some velvets work better than others. Experiment with scraps, or buy cheap velvet garments at a thrift store. Fabrics with a high percentage of rayon work best.

⮩ USE YOUR IMAGINATION ⮨

You can create an image on velvet using stamps (see page 66) or you can use metal horse pins or charms. Other possibilities for embossing include metal objects such as currycombs, hoof picks, bridle conchos, curb chains, and (clean) horseshoes. Many objects, such as jewelry, have uneven surfaces; putting a folded towel under them will help your image come out more clearly. Fastening a pin directly to the towel will help it come out well.

If you use a rubber stamp, check with the manufacturer to be sure it's safe for embossing. An online search of "embossing velvet" will help you find the companies' Web sites.

Directions

1. **Set up your ironing board.** Turn the iron on to a medium-high setting such as for wool. Don't use the steam feature.

2. **Lay your piece of velvet, plush side down, over your rubber stamp or embossing object.** You can spray the fabric with water first, spray the reverse side, or not spray at all; experiment to see what works best.

   Note: To avoid flattening the fabric around the image, you may want to place your stamp or other item on a slightly raised surface. I use a metal measuring cup covered with a folded washcloth or sock.

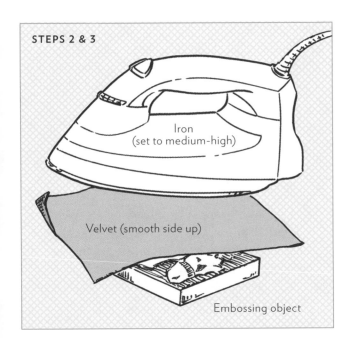

STEPS 2 & 3

Iron (set to medium-high)

Velvet (smooth side up)

Embossing object

3. **Press with the iron, holding for 10 to 20 seconds.** The time, again, depends on your fabric. Experiment on scraps first; practice makes perfect.

   Note: If you are using a steam iron, be aware that the steam holes on the bottom may show through in your design. Gently glide the iron over the stamp after the first ten seconds to smooth the marks out.

4. **Set the iron down on its end, and turn your fabric over.** Your design should be there, subtle but definite. Turn the iron off and unplug it.

EMBOSSING SAFETY TIPS

* **Ask a grownup to help** with the iron settings, and pay attention to safety. Irons can set fires if not managed correctly.

* **Never leave an iron sitting on its face,** even if you think it's turned off. Stand it up on its wide end. When you're finished, unplug it and let it cool standing on a nonflammable surface like a trivet.

* **Don't touch the flat part of the iron** to test the heat. That's a good way to burn your fingers.

* **Work in a well-ventilated room,** and don't work for too long. Half an hour at a time

(continued on next page)

(continued from previous page)

is plenty. This process releases odors and probably chemicals as the surface of the velvet is burned. Work for a little while, then unplug the iron, stand it on a trivet, and take a nice walk in the fresh air. I haven't found any official cautions about embossing health hazards, but it just seems to make sense.

* **When using jewelry,** make sure that it's metal, not plastic. Don't use metal that's been painted; heat may harm the paint and create toxic fumes.

* **When embossing with metal,** remember: that pin or concho is going to be *hot* when you peel off the velvet. Let it cool a few minutes before touching it.

WHAT CAN YOU MAKE WITH EMBOSSED VELVET?

How about a scarf? Or if you're making a horse-themed quilt, you might include some embossed velvet pieces. Velvet and velveteen make elegant party shirts, and very suave gift bags (see page 182). Embossed velvet can also be used to cover decorative pillows.

Be aware that laundering may damage the embossing; most craftspeople advise dry cleaning. Because dry cleaning uses harmful chemicals, it's best to use embossed velvet for projects that won't often need cleaning.

CREATE YOUR OWN GYMKHANA

With a few friends, a riding club, or a class, you can create your own gymkhana. It's a good way to have fun while teaching horses to play well with others. Since it's just for fun, why not emphasize the silly classes, like these?

* **Slow Walking Race:** The last horse across the finish line wins. No stopping allowed!

* **Backing Race:** The fastest horse wins, but you're all going backward. And in a straight line.

* **Apple Bobbing:** Ride to a tub full of water and apples, dismount, seize an apple in your teeth, mount back up, and race across the finish line. (You get points if your horse bobs for apples too!)

* **Sit-a-Buck:** Ride bareback with a dollar clamped between your leg and the horse's back. Last rider holding on to her dollar keeps them all.

* **Egg-and-Spoon:** Use all three gaits, in both directions, as long as it takes for all but one egg to drop off those spoons. Use hard-boiled eggs; otherwise this gets messy.

Competitions for Horseless Horsemen

If you don't have a horse of your own, find a way to compete by joining a horse youth organization that has a hippology quiz bowl (hippology is the study of horses) or a judging program, and start working your way up. You can learn a truly formidable amount about horses, their care, feeding, and physiology just by reading and studying. Here are some ways to get involved:

Pony Club has over 12,000 members, with 600 chapters nationwide. You don't need to own a horse to belong to Pony Club, but you must have access to a horse when required. Pony Club activities and competitions include dressage, eventing, show jumping, mounted games, tetrathlon, quiz, vaulting, foxhunting, and polocrosse.

4-H is about more than horses. Activities range from sewing and cooking to horsemanship and livestock projects. The 4-H focus is on building leadership, citizenship, and life skills. There's a large 4-H after-school program, and 4-H is growing in American cities.

Programs for horse-loving kids include Horse Bowl (or Quiz Bowl), in which you answer questions in a game-show format, and Hippology, a multipart test of horse knowledge. These games let even a horse-deprived person become a true horse geek.

☀ 4-WHAT? ☀
The Hs of 4-H stand for Head, Heart, Hands, and Health.

Horseshoe REVIEW

Flicka
(2006, rated PG)

In this remake, Ken has turned into Katy, and there are major plot additions — a fancy boarding school, a wild horse, a runaway, and a cougar attack. The movie is emotionally gripping, but irritating if you know anything about horses.

Katy, supposedly raised on the ranch, seems to have no idea how people really train horses. Her surprised shrieks become annoying as she's threatened and dumped by horses, over and over and over again. Don't you ever learn, girl?

But the horses are beautiful. So learn from Katy's mistakes while you enjoy this handsome, horse-centered film.

ARABIANS
Beauty, Brains, and Toughness, Too

You know a girl like this — ethereally beautiful, like a fairy, but she's on the Honor Roll, she's a track star, and darn her, she's nice! You're much too mature to hate her. You just want to be on her team.

Arabians were developed from a stew of ancient breeds, in the Arab regions of Iran, Iraq, Syria, and Turkey — not in Saudi Arabia, as many people believe. The Arabs of the Arabian Peninsula began breeding them in around 600 CE; the young man who would become the prophet Mohammed was an early enthusiast, and he encouraged horse breeding. Horses were used in warfare and for racing. They were beloved family members, often living in the tent with the family and sharing all meals. Among many Arab people it was unthinkable to sell a horse; horses were said to know when they were being sold, and to go into mourning.

This lovely and spirited breed attracted fans wherever it went, and can now be found all over the world. The first Arabian in America was Ranger, who arrived in 1760. His half-Arabian son, the Lindsay Arabian, was given to George Washington. Today Arabians are hugely popular in the United States, especially in California and Arizona. They dominate the sport of endurance racing and can be found competing in nearly every equine discipline.

LOOKING AT ARABIANS

Arabians have a straight or slightly dished profile, large eyes, a long arched neck, short back, and high-set tail. The legs are muscular, the hooves are tough, and the coat is fine and silky. They're small horses, standing between 14 and 15.2 hands and weighing 900 to 1,100 pounds. Arabians may be any solid color. The skin is always black. Pinto color patterns are not allowed.

Arabians are spirited, intelligent, and loyal. Among some people they have the reputation of being high-strung; they do need to be handled sensitively, and like to be treated with respect. After all, in the Bedouin tents they were practically royalty, and they remember that!

∾ A HORSE OF ∾
GOOD FORTUNE

According to Islamic lore, every grain one feeds a horse is counted as a good deed. Princess Alia of Saudi Arabia quotes the Prophet as saying "Good fortune is knotted in the horse's forelock until the Day of Judgment, and people are assisted in their care of them, so stroke their forelocks and pray that they be blessed." What a beautiful idea.

All about English Competition

English competitions are rooted in three historic horseback activities. Dressage and three-phase events stem from cavalry training. Hunter classes come from the sport of foxhunting. Saddle seat (park) classes evolved from the use of horses as comfortable and stylish transportation.

Dressage: Elegance in Action

The word dressage comes from the French *dresser*, which means "training." Dressage has a long pedigree: The Greek general Xenophon's book *Per Hippikes* was used as the foundation for Renaissance high school riding. Those arts are preserved today at the Spanish Riding School in Vienna, and the riding schools at Saumur in France, and Jerez de la Frontera in Spain. These schools train young horses from the most basic dressage steps up to the famous "Airs Above the Ground," the athletic leaps such as the courbette and the capriole made famous by the Lipizzans. Modern competition dressage is based on the steps of training used to get a horse to that lofty level.

DRESSAGE COMPETITION
So what is competition dressage? It consists of a series of "figures" — circles, serpentines, changes of gait and tempo — performed in a rectangular arena that's either 20 by 40 meters or 20 by 60. You must have good control over your horse simply to keep him in the arena; the fence is only inches off the ground.

Dressage figures are performed at all three gaits and at different speeds within each gait. Circles must be round, transitions crisp, and the horse must look

Horse PLAY

IN PRAISE OF GRAZING

Taking your favorite horse for a walk and letting him stop to munch is a wonderful way to spend some quiet time together. Especially first thing in the spring, when the grass has just come back. Enjoy the greed and speed with which an enthusiastic horse tears his favorite green treat. Experience the peacefulness of moving one small step at a time. Feel the sun on your shoulders and smell the fresh air. Watch your horse's lips and muzzle work as he crops the grass.

Hand grazing is also a great slow-motion way to introduce your horse to scary things. Horses relax as they lower their heads — and munching something makes it even more relaxing. Graze up to the new bench, the parked hay equipment, the bags of mulch, let your horse sniff them, and likely he won't even give them a glance another time. Here are some tips:

✵ Stay alert for things that might startle your horse.

✵ Don't let a horse eat too much spring grass at once; half an hour is enough.

✵ Use a halter, not a bridle, and a nice long lead rope.

✵ Wear sturdy shoes or boots.

consistently cooperative and supple. Cadence and accuracy are important. At the higher levels, increasing degrees of bend, counter-bend, and collection are required.

Though some of it takes place at a walk, good dressage is far from stodgy. Control must be matched by drive and energy, and many modern dressage champions are extremely large horses. The coiled-spring power of these great warmbloods can be breathtaking.

DRESSAGE TESTS

Dressage tests are taken individually. When the bell rings, you must enter the ring, halt and salute the judge, and perform all the figures of that particular test, in the right place and in the right order. At lower levels you may have someone read the test aloud to you. At higher levels you must memorize it.

Dressage competitors progress through several levels, from Training Level through First, Second, Third, Prix St. George, two levels of Intermediaire, and two levels of Grand Prix. A Freestyle test, also known as a Kür, is designed by the rider and performed to music.

DRESSAGE FUNDAMENTALS

Dressage emphasizes correctness and gradual strengthening and suppling of the horse. Any shortcuts or roughness in the training will show in the test — slow and steady wins this race. The aids should be as invisible as possible. The rider should look at ease and in harmony with the horse.

Warmbloods excel at competition dressage and are very fashionable, but all breeds can compete and win. Large horses have beautiful long strides; it can be harder to teach a pony to lengthen, but the team

Pony Tales

A MARE GODDESS

Epona (Great Mare) was the Celtic mare goddess. She granted easy childbirth, fruitful harvests, and good foal crops. She's often portrayed as a woman sitting sidesaddle on a fine mare, holding an apple or a cornucopia in her hand.

deserves points when that is accomplished. Dressage can help any horse become more balanced and responsive.

At lower levels any English saddle — preferably one with a deep seat — correct English tack, and English riding clothes are acceptable. At the upper levels horses are ridden in a double bridle, riders use deep-seated dressage saddles with long stirrups; a formal long-tailed black coat, black high-crowned hat, white gloves, breeches, and shirt with stock are required. (See Reining, page 184, to learn about Western dressage.)

Jumping: Fun Over Fences

During the heyday of English hunting, lots of riders were jumping lots of big fences, but it all happened off in the countryside where no one could watch. Show jumping (also called stadium jumping) brings the action into an arena where spectators can thrill to the sight of horses and riders leaping intimidating obstacles. Both hunter-over-fences classes and jumping classes involve one horse at a time jumping a course of obstacles. There are some differences, though.

Hunter classes are formal. There's a very precise dress code for horse and rider. Style is important; both rider and horse must look good. Calmness and perfect form are what distinguish the winning hunter. The judging of a hunter class is subjective; the judge's opinion matters. The jumps look like natural obstacles that a horse and rider might confront in a day's foxhunting.

Jumper classes have a less formal dress code. The main criterion is that the rider must stay on. The horse must make it over the jumps without touches or knockdowns, and within the allotted time. Boldness, athleticism, control, and power make a good jumper. The judging of a jumper class is objective and mathematical; whoever completes all the jumps with the fewest penalties wins. Competitors are penalized for touches and knockdowns, refusals, and falls, as well as time.

JUMPING FUNDAMENTALS

Jumps come in a vast array of styles including verticals, spreads, and double and triple combinations. They may be colorful, even alarming. Interestingly, the most difficult jump of all (called a Joker) is the simplest: It's a single natural rail. Without panels or a lower rail, however, it's difficult for horses to judge this jump.

Puissance involves the highest jumps, up to seven feet. Six Bar classes are just what they say; a series of six jumps in a straight line, set at equal distances. Each one is higher than the last, and the jumps are raised if two or more competitors have perfect rounds. Heights can be over six feet. Gambler's Choice classes allow the rider

The Little Horse That Could:
The Connemara Stallion, Erin Go Bragh
(1996, not rated)

This is an engaging inside look at eventing with straight-from-the-horse's-mouth commentary attributed to Go Bragh himself. This could have gotten way too cute, but director Stirlin Harris is a horseman and Go Bragh's voice seems true to character. The little horse makes it all look easy — and fun, too. There's affectionate commentary from his rider, Carol Kozlowski, as well as many behind-the-scenes shots of preparation and horse care. It's beautiful to look at and has nice Irish music.

to choose which jumps to take and in which order. Each jump is assigned a certain number of points, and the competitor with the highest points and fewest penalties wins.

Riders compete at different levels. The most difficult level, with the highest fences, is **Grand Prix,** which means Big Prize — and that's what you get if you win.

Eventing: A True Test of Horsemanship

Three-phase eventing (sometimes called three-day eventing or combined training) is the triathlon of English riding. It comes from the tradition of European cavalry training, when armies needed both skillful riders and bold, well-trained horses for national defense. The modern sport includes dressage, a cross-country phase, and stadium jumping.

The dressage test takes place first. The dressage phase

has traditionally been less popular with riders than the more exciting jumping phases, but that is changing as the cross-country courses become more challenging. Dressage is all about obedience and suppleness, and cross-country courses increasingly demand that kind of discipline.

The cross-country phase is the most popular, but most dangerous, part of eventing. Obstacles on a cross-country course range from 2 feet 3 inches for Beginner Novices to 3 feet 11 inches for Advanced riders. There may be 12 to 20 jumps at the lower levels, 30 to 40 at higher levels.

The obstacles can be natural logs and stone walls, drops, ditches, or combinations. Penalties are assessed for going over or under the time limit, as well as for refusals.

The stadium jumping class takes place last. Horses must show that they've come through the grueling cross-country phase without injury or loss of stamina, obedience, or boldness. The course comprises between 12 and 20 fences, ranging in height from 2 feet 7 inches for Beginner Novices up to 4 feet 1 inch for Advanced riders.

A SHORT HISTORY OF THE CROSS-COUNTRY PHASE

The cross-country competition you see in the Olympics used to be the finale of an event called the endurance phase, the ultimate test of horse and rider ability. The four parts were:

* **Roads and Tracks**, a moderate-paced warm-up on roads and trails

* **Steeplechase**, a very fast run over steeplechase-style fences

* **A slow cool down** and vet check

* **Cross-country course**, a run over solid fences

To accommodate budget and time concerns during the 2004 Athens Olympics, the endurance phase was cut to the cross-country section only. This decision has been controversial. Many horsemen feel that including all four phases is important to the health and safety of the horse; others believe that the shortened version is actually easier on their horses.

The cross-country phase has become increasingly dangerous. The 2007–2008 season alone saw 12 rider deaths in eventing. Courses at the upper levels are becoming more difficult, and course builders seem to feel the lower level courses must also be more difficult, to prepare riders for what's to come. But experienced eventers decry this trend, claiming that at lower levels the cross-country phase should build confidence for horse and rider.

There's also concern that as it becomes more popular, more riders come into the sport unprepared for its difficulty, and perhaps too concerned with speed and glory. In response, the event world is beginning to use more fences with "frangible pins" that allow an obstacle to fall if a horse hits it.

Officials are increasing the penalties for excess speed, and a rider who falls anywhere on the course, whether competing or not, may be eliminated. This sport is changing — stay tuned.

Saddle Seat

Saddle seat riding was developed in the United States to show off high-stepping American breeds like the Saddlebred. Other breeds shown saddle seat include Morgans, Arabians, and Friesians. A saddle seat saddle (sometimes called a park saddle, Lane Fox saddle, or cutback saddle) is an English saddle with a very flat seat and large skirts. The pommel has a semicircle cut out of it, and the saddle sits farther back to allow room for the horse's high withers and high arched neck.

A good saddle seat rider remains in balance even though she is sitting relatively far back on the horse. Her legs are under her body and support her weight; she looks elegant and so does the horse. This method of riding doesn't encourage the horse to round his back up under him; just the opposite. His back hollows down, and his action becomes very high-stepping and flashy, with his knees coming nearly to his chest.

Though he looks like he's bursting with excitement, a good saddle seat horse is well under control and should give a comfortable ride. That's the meaning behind another name for this style of riding, Park Seat. It should give the impression of an elegant ride through a city park, in an era when well-to-do horsemen put on their best clothes and showed off to each other.

Horseshoe REVIEW

The Horsecatcher
by Mari Sandoz (1957)

High on any horse lover's must-read list, *The Horsecatcher* is the story of a Cheyenne boy, Young Elk, who turns his back on killing — a highly controversial decision for a Cheyenne boy in the 1800s — and becomes a catcher of horses. It's a hard and lonely life: The warriors get the prestige and the girls, while Young Elk gets rained on, snowed on, starved, and sometimes captured. But he amasses a large herd of horses, and ultimately makes a great sacrifice for his people. Great details about Plains Indian culture, horses, and survival skills can be gleaned from this story.

Sandoz grew up in Nebraska, the daughter of a frontiersman. She endured poverty and a colossal number of rejections from publishers before her biography of her father, *Old Jules*, was published to great acclaim. She wrote many novels about the West, with great authenticity and sympathy for the Indians.

TYPES OF JUMPS

You'll see dozens of different jumps if you go to even a few different horse shows, but here are a few of the most common. These are the types most riders (and horses!) start with when they are first learning.

You can make all of these from a couple of jump standards, some ground poles, and a few jump cups with pins. Look for patterns in woodworking books or online.

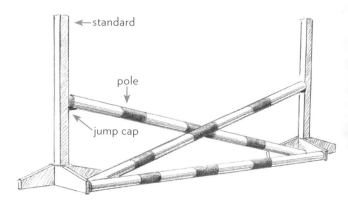

CROSS-RAIL
A cross-rail is usually the first type of jump that you'll take because the horse doesn't have to jump very high. It can be made higher by moving the ends of the poles up a notch or two.

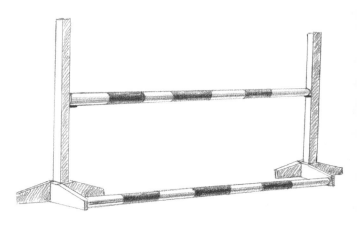

VERTICAL
A vertical jump is made with a single pole going straight between the standards, but as with a cross-rail, putting a pole on the ground helps the horse see where to take off.

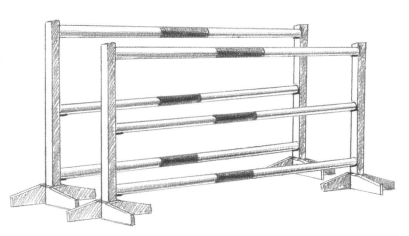

OXER

An oxer is made of two vertical fences placed close enough together so that the horse jumps them both at once. It is meant to be jumped from the lower side.

Jumping for Kids

by Lesley Ward (2007)

This colorful and readable book by the editor of *Young Rider* magazine explains everything you need to know about learning to jump, competing in jumping classes, and teaching your horse to jump. There are even instructions for building your own standards and setting up a course to practice on.

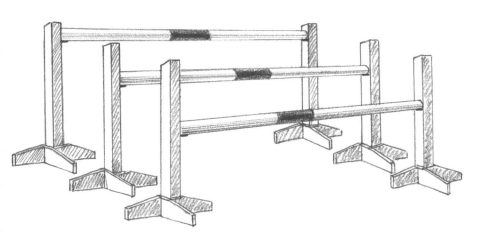

SPREAD

A spread is two or more vertical fences spaced farther apart than an oxer. It is more difficult to jump because of the added width.

FABRIC GIFT BAG

Pinking shears

1 piece of horse-themed fabric, about twice as wide as the bag you want to make

Thread, in a matching or contrasting color

Sewing machine (or you can sew by hand)

Decorative cord for a drawstring (optional)

A fun and fashionable alternative to gift wrap is the reusable fabric gift bag. A handsome bag made of horsey fabric can circulate for years, becoming an old friend at birthday and holiday celebrations, and keeping countless trees out there in the woods where they belong, instead of in the landfill. This is an easy first project for those new to sewing. And if you already sew, this is a good project for using up scraps from a pillowcase or curtain project (see pages 88, 106).

Directions

1. **Use the pinking shears to cut a piece of fabric** that's the same length but twice the width of the bag you'd like to make, plus a half-inch seam allowance all around.

STEP 1

length + ½"

finished size

width × 2 + ½"

pinked edge

2. **With the wrong side of the fabric facing you,** fold down one of the longer sides, about ¼ inch, and crease the fabric with your fingernail, or iron it, to hold the fold in place.

3. **Sew as close as you can** to the bottom edge of the fold. This will be the top hem of your bag — be neat! Run the machine backward and forward for a few stitches at the beginning and end of the seam to make a knot and keep the thread in place.

4. **Fold lengthwise,** putting the right sides together, so that you are

still looking at the reverse (or wrong) side of the fabric. Pin in place along the two open sides.

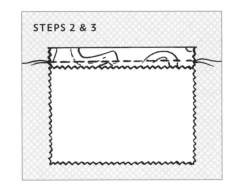

5. **Starting at the bottom corner,** sew along one end of the fabric, using a $^3/_8$-inch seam. Be sure to run the machine backward and forward at the very beginning of your seam.

6. **Turn the corner.** Continue up the long side of your bag. At the top, run the machine backward and forward to knot the thread.

7. **Cut your thread, turn your bag right side out, and voila!** All you need now is a gift to put inside it, and a ribbon to tie around the neck of the bag. What about some baling twine? You can dye twine for a festive yet horse-barny look.

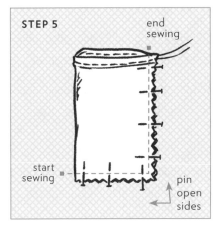

VARIATION: A Drawstring Bag

To make this into a drawstring bag, substitute the following steps after Step 1 above.

Directions

1. **Fold and press the top edge of the fabric over,** wrong sides together, making a $^1/_2$-inch casing (or however large you need the casing to be to accommodate the cord or ribbon you plan to use).

2. **Sew along the edge of the fabric,** going back and forth at the ends.

3. **Continue as from Step 4,** making sure you leave the ends of the channel open, rather than sewing all the way to the ends of your fabric.

4. **To insert the cord or ribbon,** fasten a large safety pin to the end. Work it through the channel. Take off the pin, pop in your gift, and tie it all up with a pretty bow.

All about Western Competition

Western competitions are based on the real work that cowboys and vaqueros have been doing for centuries. They tend to emphasize speed and ease of handling, and often there are cattle involved.

Reining: Circles, Slides, and Spins

Reining is often called "Western dressage," and there is certainly a resemblance. The aids, as in dressage, should be invisible. One horse and rider compete at a time, though they are riding patterns in a much larger arena. All the action takes place at a lope and gallop.

Each pattern includes 8 to 12 movements. Circles should be large, fast, and perfectly round. The transition of speed from large to small circles should be easy to see. Most incorporate a change of direction and fly-ing change of leads. The horse should make the flying change without changing speed. Each reining pattern includes backing up at least 10 feet in a straight line, with a stop and obvious hesitation before the next movement.

Some of the other movements are:

The rundown: a gallop down the long side that leads into the sliding stop. In this spectacular maneuver, the horse plants his hind feet and slides in a cloud of dust, back raised and hind-quarters tucked. The slide must be a straight line. (The slide is such an important feature of reining that many competitions incorporate the word "slide" in their names.)

The rollback: a 180-degree turn immediately after a slid-ing stop. The horse must continue in a lope with no hesitation.

The spin: a 360-degree or greater turn, up to four and a half full turns. As in the dressage pirouette, the inside hind leg is stationary but continues step-ping. Smoothness and correctness are most important; speed increases the difficulty, so a fast, correct turn wins more points. Each pattern includes at least one spin in each direction.

FREESTYLE REINING

There is also a freestyle reining event that is a three-and-a-half-minute musical routine. Props, costumes, and special lighting may be allowed. Some riders compete "no hands" — and sometimes even without a bridle.

Any horse can compete in reining, though of course Western breeds predominate, especially the Quarter Horse. But any horse with powerful haunches and good legs can do well. Many breeds, like the Morgan, have their own breed reining organizations. Reining was first included in the World Equestrian Games at Jerez in 2002.

To dressage-trained eyes, reining might appear a trifle monotonous, with its continual high-speed circles and slides. To reining-trained eyes, dressage may look a little slow and stuffy. But both disciplines involve good training, correctness, kindness, and a sense of artistry.

Into the West
(1993, rated PG)

A beautiful white horse running on a moonlit Irish beach follows the caravan of an old Traveler — a tinker — to a desolate housing project in Dublin, and to two boys, Ossie and Tito Riley. Their mother is dead, their father, once king of the Travelers, has turned to drink to drown his sorrow, and Ossie "breathes funny." But the horse changes everything. Ossie names him Tir na nÓg, after the mystical land beneath the sea, and the boys take him upstairs to their dreary apartment.

Someone calls the police, who take Tir na nÓg and sell him to a rich man for a show jumper. Ossie and Tito take him back, and the manhunt is on as they ride him "to the West," the cowboy West of their favorite movies, and the mythic Land Beneath the Seas of Celtic lore. Their father turns to the Travelers to help find them, and everything leads to a final confrontation on the wild seashore of western Ireland.

This magical movie takes a sympathetic look at the gritty, yet romantic, Traveling life, and the prejudice Travelers endure. It has fine acting, amazing scenery, and that horse! In an elevator. In a bathroom. In a cinema eating popcorn. Best of all, galloping cross-country and along that mythic shore.

CREATE YOUR OWN BRAND

A brand is a design burned onto an animal's hide with hot metal that permanently says "Property of So-and-So." From Ancient Egypt to the American West, brands have been used for this purpose. In the days before fencing, herds of cattle and horses belonging to different owners often mingled while grazing and there had to be a way to sort them out.

Brands for Breeds

In Europe, brands are used as marks of honor, showing that a horse has passed inspection and testing and is worthy for breeding. For example, the Lipizzaner breed uses brands to indicate the lineage of its horses. Each stallion line has its own symbolic brand. Simpler brands, the first letter of the name — such as M for Maestoso — are also used, as is L for Lipizza.

You may not plan on ever branding your horses. But creating your own brand, or a logo for your stable, can be a fun project — something to doodle on the margins of your notebook, to carve into the top rail of the fence, or to paint on the top of your tack trunk.

Some "Brand New" Ideas

Because branding was first used in ancient Egypt, Egyptian hieroglyphs would make good brands. They are simple, which is good, and they're pictorial. You could go for a more European look featuring symbols of royalty, like crowns or oak leaves. Or create a western brand, which is made up of letters, numbers, and simple shapes, used singly or in combination. They may be tilted, they may have wings, they may be reversed or even upside down.

Brands used on cattle have to be simple and readable from a distance. That's a good principle to use in creating your own brand, too. You may want to make a rubber stamp of your brand (see page 66). You'll quickly find that simpler is better for this craft.

Barrel Racing: All about Speed

Though open to everyone, barrel racing is one of the fastest-growing women's sports in the country. It's a simple, high-speed race in which the winning time is usually 13 or 14 seconds. This is a high-stakes sport but it's also one you can enjoy in your own backyard. All you need are three barrels and a horse.

The barrels are set up in a triangle; you ride around them in a cloverleaf pattern. You can choose whether to turn left or right around the first barrel. Your next two turns, however, must be the opposite of your initial turn. Most riders prefer to turn right, left, left. Horses that do better going left, right, right, are called "lefties."

Your approach to the first barrel is critical to your ride. You need to rate your speed to enter the "pocket" — the area around the barrel that will yield the fastest turn.

A barrel race rider needs to sit deep, with her legs held close to the horse's sides to avoid knocking over a barrel (it's a 5-second penalty per barrel, and in a 14-second race, you might as well hang it up if you lose 5 seconds!).

Balance and harmony with your horse are key, though barrel racers ride with one hand on the horn — hanging on for dear life is okay! Horses wear leg bandages. Riders often wear back braces because they can get a lot of torsion on those turns.

YOU CAN TRY THIS AT HOME!

To set up your own barrel race cloverleaf at home, you just need three barrels. Try the local recycling drop-off center. They often have barrels for free. The large plastic food-grade barrels are lighter and easier to handle than oil drums, and are less likely to have had something toxic inside. Or check out a car wash; they may give or sell you their empty plastic soap barrels.

Cutting: Keep Your Eye on the Cow

Cutting is derived from real work that's still done by ranch horses today. Selecting and separating a particular cow from the herd (for individual attention, like branding or shots) is called "cutting." Today cutting, while still important ranch work, is also a high-stakes competitive sport with a nationwide following and a very active youth organization.

The cutting horse sidles into a herd of cattle, disturbing them as little as possible. When the rider has selected a cow and gotten her to the edge of the herd, the rider's job is done. Now it's all up to the horse. The rider indicates the cow. The horse locks onto her, eases her out of the bunch, and prevents her from returning to it.

Each cutting contestant has 2½ minutes to cut at least two cows from a herd. The rider must bring at least one cow from deep within the herd; others may be peeled off the outside edges. As soon as each cow is clear of the herd, the rider must loosen the reins and give the horse its head. As the cow tries to get back to her buddies, the horse acts like a goalie, keeping her from doing so.

IN THE SADDLE

A GOOD HORSE MAKES THE DIFFERENCE

Cutting horses get credit for skill, style, and effort, and they pick up penalties for losing a cow into the herd. Riders may be penalized for quitting on a cow when she's moving toward the horse, or for picking up the reins while the horse is still working the cow.

A good cutting horse reads the cow's intentions and matches her every move, like a cross between a dance and a game of cat and mouse. The distinctive sweeping action of a cutting horse when he "drops on a cow" — settling into a crouching posture, eyeball to eyeball with her — is beautiful to watch.

Each rider has four helpers. Two are herd holders, positioned on each side of the herd to keep it from drifting into the working area. The other two are positioned between the cow being worked and the judges' stand. They turn the cow back to the contestant if it tries to leave the working area.

Any breed can compete at cutting, but Quarter Horses dominate the sport. About 96 percent of horses competing in National Cutting Horse Association events are Quarter Horses.

✳ KIDS IN CUTTING ✳

Riders as young as four have competed in cutting. The youth division includes junior (13 and under) and senior (14–18). Youth cutters can compete in adult cutting classes if they meet the qualifications, regardless of their age. Prize money in many of these classes can be generous, and individual horses and riders can amass quite a lot of cash over a career.

The National Youth Cutting Horse Association (NYCHA) offers a Levels of Excellence Award Program (LEAP). Young cutters accumulate LEAP points throughout their youth career. Activities include cutting competition, of course, but also attending workshops, writing articles, helping at fundraisers, or volunteering at events. Participants in LEAP are eligible for the Youth Hall of Fame. They are also eligible for college scholarships. The Cutters In Action Foundation (CIA) has given scholarships to NYCHA members totaling $800,000. In addition, the Foundation's Crisis Fund helps NYCHA families in need.

NYCHA team cutting is an event in which youth members are responsible for all aspects of the contest; they serve as herd holders, turnback help, show secretary, announcer, and judges. The four-person teams choose themes and dress up in costumes; they are judged on their combined cutting scores and on their creativity.

Team Penning: A Number of Cows

A sport related to cutting is team penning. A team consists of three horses and riders. A herd of 30 cattle is held by riders at the far end of the arena and the cattle have large numbers marked on their backs. There are three of each number, from one to nine. Behind the starting line, a little over halfway down the arena from the cattle, is a small gated pen. When the timer is ready, the team rides toward the herd; as they cross the starting line the judge calls out a number — say, seven.

The team now knows which cattle to focus on. The goal is to separate all three #7 cows from the herd and move them into the pen within 2½ minutes. If extra cows of the wrong number are brought along, the riders need to separate them and drive them back before the bell rings. If more than five cattle with other numbers cross the starting line (which is also the foul line) the team is eliminated.

TEAM PENNING BASICS

Team penning is a low-key, family-oriented, yet high-speed sport. A lot of people do it every weekend. You ride on your friends' teams, they ride on yours; the competition is lively, but ever shifting.

Breeds that do well at team penning are the stock horse breeds — Paints, Quarter Horses, Appaloosas — but any quick, responsive horse should do fine. The horse should not fear cattle, but can't be too aggressive toward them, either. Hurting cows is not allowed.

Pony Tales

A HEALING CHARM

This superstition goes back to a legend of the Norse gods Odin and Baldur the Beautiful. Baldur's horse slipped and broke a leg, and Baldur healed it by tying around the fracture a black thread with seven knots in it, and reciting this poem:

Baldur rade (rode). The foal slade (slipped).
He lighted, and he righted,
Set joint to joint, bone to bone,
Sinew to sinew,
Heal in Odin's name.

For centuries, people believed in the potency of this spell for healing fractured bones; a Christianized version of it existed as recently as a hundred years ago. Who knows? Maybe it really works!

Tack and gear are Western, of course, and in keeping with that, safety helmets aren't usually worn. But team penning has a casual family feel, and if you want to try it and you ride English, you may find tolerance in your area for doing some penning in your dressage saddle with your helmet on.

Working Cow Horse Competition

Dressage is both a stand-alone sport and part of three-phase eventing. Reining is a stand-alone sport and part of Working Cow Horse competitions, which include three events: A 2½–minute cutting event, which involves handling up to three cows; a reining pattern; and fence work, in which the rider handles one cow, controlling and blocking it at the short end of the arena, allowing it to run along the long side and then passing, cutting it off, and turning it repeatedly.

Horseshoe REVIEW

King of the Wind
by Marguerite Henry (1948)

This is the Newbery Award–winning story of the Godolphin Arabian — born in a Moroccan royal stable, shipped to France as a gift to the king, scorned and put to hauling wood in the streets of Paris, then rescued by an English Quaker and taken to England, where he becomes one of the three founding sires of the English Thoroughbred. It's also the story of the mute slave, Agba, who travels with the horse and of the cat, Grimalkin, who shares their fortunes.

Is it true? Like all of Henry's stories, not exactly. The real Godolphin Arabian was a Turkoman horse, probably crossed with an Arabian. Turkoman horses were fast, high-prestige animals frequently given as diplomatic gifts. The export of purebred Arabians was forbidden.

Mr. Coke, the Quaker, a wealthy young horse breeder, knew just what he was acquiring when he traveled to France to buy the five-year-old stallion for the Earl of Godolphin. Godolphin's horse was advertised as an Arabian because the Turkoman breed was not fashionable. Calling him an Arabian commanded higher stud fees and better mares (and Marguerite Henry got a better title!). The decision to fudge the horse's breeding helped establish the most influential founding sire of the Thoroughbred. There's no evidence of a slave boy, but there was a cat named Grimalkin whom the horse loved dearly.

DECOUPAGE TREASURE BOX

Materials Needed

Images (your own drawings, photos, or images cut from magazines)

Wooden or metal box

Mod Podge or other decoupage medium*

Brush

Spoon

Heavy-duty sealer (polyurethane or acrylic)

*** To make your own decoupage medium,** mix one part water with one part white craft glue. The mixture will be opaque in the container but will dry clear.

Everyone needs a treasure box, and making a horse-themed one using decoupage is easy. You can make a box of any size, depending on what you plan to keep in it. I suggest that you buy a tin of Danish butter cookies and eat them. (It's rough, but somebody's got to do it!) For a fun smaller project, embellish a mint tin. For decoration, use your own drawings or photos, or clip a variety of pictures and words from horse magazines and catalogs. You can use decoupage to decorate picture frames, plates, lampshades, Christmas ornaments, and furniture. How about making a unique plaque or nameplate for your door or your horse's stall?

Directions

1. **Cut out your image** or images and figure out how you want to arrange them on the surface of your box.

SCRATCH THAT ITCH!

Finding out where your horse likes to be scratched — and then scratching him just in the right spot — is a great way to bond. Scratching is an important social activity among horses, and joining in makes you one of the herd. You'll enjoy the contortions and lip wiggles a good scratch produces, and you'll add a strong nonfood reward to your training toolbox. Here are some tips:

✻ **Just start scratching and watch his reactions.** If he likes what you're doing, his lip will stretch and wiggle. He may put his head high in the air, or reach around to scratch you back.

✻ **Places horses usually like a scratch:** The sides of the neck, the shoulders, and the chest. More unusual spots to scratch: the center of the back and along the midline of the belly.

✻ **Important:** If you don't know the horse well, avoid possibly sensitive areas like the belly or flanks. If the horse seems annoyed, stop and step away.

✻ **Proceed with caution:** Some horses will want to scratch you back. Some can do so gently and responsibly. Others get carried away and use their teeth — ouch!

If you're feeling teeth or think you're about to, stop scratching for a moment or step away from the pressure. Most horses get the hint to lighten up. Mutual grooming is an important social skill for them; they have a strong interest in doing it right.

2. **If using your own medium,** spread a thin layer on the surface of your box. For a commercial product, follow the directions on the bottle. These products go on cloudy, but dry clear and water-resistant.

3. **Place pictures on glued surface** and press firmly, smoothing the top of the paper with the back of a spoon.

4. **Once the glue is dry,** brush on another layer of glue over the entire surface of your box, including the image. Let dry, and repeat this step until you can't feel the edges of the paper.

5. **When the whole project is dry,** spread on sealer. (If you are using decoupage medium, sealer is usually unnecessary. Follow the directions on the label.)

Everyone Loves a Parade

Your horse is gorgeous, smart, and very well behaved. She loves to be admired and you want to show her off. But you don't have a competitive bone in your body. What can you do? Parade her through the neighborhood for everyone to see?

Well, why not? Parades are an ancient, traditional way of celebrating holidays and special events, and horses have always been a popular part of them. For a lot of us it isn't really a parade without horses. So why not join the fun? Unless you're part of an organization or drill team, you're not apt to ride in a big city parade. More likely it will be a small-town affair. Contact the parade marshal and organizers to find out if you and your horse are welcome. They will assign you a place in the lineup. It's your job to ask what will be in front of you and what will be behind. If it's something that's likely to scare your horse, say so right away. Ask for a different placement, and be prepared to forgo riding in the parade if your horse's needs can't be met.

It Takes a Special Horse

One horse trainer I know says flat out, "Parades are the most dangerous horse-related thing I do." Parades are noisy and full of the unexpected. Parade marshals often don't know much about horses. You and your steed may be expected to prance along near fire engines, bagpipes, full brass bands, or llamas or other unfamiliar animals.

Horseshoe REVIEW

Wild Hearts Can't Be Broken
(1991, rated G)

The real-life story of Sonora Webster, a Depression-era runaway orphan who gets a job mucking stalls for Doc Carver's traveling stunt show. Her ambition is to become a star diving girl, riding a horse as it dives off a 40-foot platform into a pool of water. Sonora is spirited, determined, and charming, and the way she comes back after a disastrous accident is inspiring.

Sonora was a real person and the story is mostly true. She lived to the age of 99 and was able to attend the movie made about her. *Wild Hearts* is suspenseful, romantic, and lovely to look at, with a strong heroine. Both adults and kids will enjoy it.

All of these can be alarming — even terrifying — to the average horse. Which is why a parade horse can't be an average horse. There's simply no room in a parade for a horse who can't quietly cope with the unexpected.

So if you want to ride or drive in parades, spend a lot of time bombproofing your horse. Read *Bombproof Your Horse* by police officer Sgt. Rick Pelicano, which deals with many of the urban hazards a parade horse may encounter. (See Bombproofing Your Horse, page 218.)

BE PREPARED

When your horse is completely reliable with every hazard you can think up — be creative! — then ride her in a smallish parade. It helps to scope out the route ahead of time. If you're driving your horse, find out where the hills are. Starting and stopping on a hill is difficult. If the parade stops

HAIR AND THERE

A fun — and necessary — spring horse activity is to get out there at peak shedding time and just go nuts grooming. Use a shedding blade if you've got one, or a currycomb if that's what you have. Make a blizzard of horsehair. After all, it's gotta be done. You might as well really put your back into it and get totally covered like an Abominable Snowman!

All that loose hair is itchy. Your horse is itching when it's on him. You'll itch when it's all over you. It's a unique way of being at one with your horse. And isn't it fun to get outrageously dirty and disheveled sometimes?

This is a good time to wear old clothes (avoid fleece or wool). No matter what you do, some horse hair will sneak through to tickle you. How does it do that? The science isn't there yet. Maybe you'll be the researcher who makes that breakthrough.

ahead of you, try to plan so you stop at the top or bottom of the hill, not in the middle.

DON'T FORGET THE DETAILS

You've planned. Now polish — your horse, your tack, your own appearance. If you love glitz and glitter, parades are the place for it: ribbons, streamers, silver, and sparkle. Head out, take your place in line. Keep your eyes and ears wide open. Watch your horse's attitude carefully.

If all goes well — and it will if you've prepared — enjoy yourself to the hilt. Thousands of eyes are on your horse. Hundreds of kids are watching hungrily, soaking up your horse's beauty and dreaming of being you. How can a mere ribbon compete with all that glory?

Pony Tales

HORSESHOE LORE

Everyone knows a horseshoe is a good luck symbol. But why?

First, there's the iron, which is said to repel witches, fairies, and even the Devil himself. Where did that idea come from? Perhaps it reflects the vast superiority of iron tools and weapons over Bronze Age weapons. Iron ended many old ways of doing things. It's strong magic.

Perhaps it's the shape that creates the power. The crescent is a symbol of the moon and of the bull, a sacred animal from very early times. In ancient symbology, the horse is a sun animal, the bull a moon animal, and the struggle between them is played out in bullfights. A horse wearing on its feet the symbol of its foe is powerful.

Whatever the origin of the belief, horseshoes are nailed to thresholds to bring good luck and to keep away evil. Traditionally a horseshoe is nailed on with seven nails — a lucky number.

Which way up? Opinions differ. Most legends say the open end should be up, in keeping with the horn/moon symbolism. Others believe the horns should point down, to pin down the luck or pin down the Devil. Blacksmiths hang shoes pointing down so that the luck runs into the forge.

Lord Nelson had a horseshoe nailed to the mast of his ship during the Battle of Trafalgar in 1805. He won the battle, but died of his wounds. Good luck or bad?

The Thrill of the Race

Racing is the oldest horse sport, and the most popular. People race horses around flat tracks under saddle and in harness, and over hilly fields with fences and jumps. Millions enjoy it as a spectator sport — an important option for horseless horsemen. Racing generates billions of dollars in modern economies, and creates thousands of jobs. If you're determined, talented (and in some cases, the right size), you may become a race rider or driver yourself, and experience the ultimate thrill of union with a horse's speed.

Flat Racing: The Sport of Kings

Thoroughbred racing was organized by British royalty in the 1600s. Originally, races were run over distances of up to 4 miles. These days the longest Thoroughbred race is only 1¾ miles.

Racing was popular in the American South before the Civil War. In the Northeast, particularly New England, it was frowned on for religious reasons. The Civil War ruined Southern racing. Bloodstock was killed in battle, rich families were impoverished, and puritanical religious sects sprang up that disapproved of racing and gambling. Racing remained only in Maryland and Louisiana, while new racetracks sprang up in the North. Even today the South has very few racetracks while the North has many.

An exception is Kentucky, which was a border state during the Civil War. Kentuckians fought on both sides of this war, but most of the battles were fought elsewhere, preserving the local breeds, and

My Friend Flicka
by Mary O'Hara (1941)

This is the story of a dreamy boy named Ken who longs for a colt of his own, a horse that will be his friend and companion. But Ken is young and irresponsible, which deeply irritates his ex-military ranchman father.

When he finally gets a chance to choose a colt of his own, Ken chooses badly — a classic plot device for horse stories both true and fictional. Flicka comes from bad blood and seems untamable. It takes an accident and near death to bring about the friendship Ken wishes for.

There are two sequels: *Thunderhead* and *Green Grass of Wyoming*.

the land is exceptionally good for raising horses.

The Kentucky Bluegrass region became the heart of Thoroughbred breeding after the war, and remains central to this day.

The biggest racing event in the United States is the Triple Crown. A horse must win three races — the Kentucky Derby, the Preakness Stakes, and the Belmont Stakes to claim the title (see page 133). The Derby is 1¼ miles, the Preakness 1³⁄₁₆ miles, and the Belmont, which has derailed many a promising Triple Crown candidate, is 1½ miles.

THE HORSES

Bred for speed, stamina, and heart, Thoroughbreds are the core of American flat racing. They begin racing at age two and most of the classic American races are run by three-year-olds. A Thoroughbred who is still racing at age seven is a rarity — though many who finish their flat-race careers go on to foxhunting, steeplechasing, or other sports.

Other breeds also do flat racing: Appaloosas, Arabians, Paints, Quarter Horses, and even mules race at many tracks in the West. Racehorses other than Thoroughbreds are often more affordable, making these races easier to participate in.

THE RIDERS

Jockeys need to be small so they don't overburden their young mounts. They also have to be strong, excellent riders, with a high toleration for hunger, danger, and pain. Most are men, but a few woman jockeys work at a professional level.

Racing employs thousands of people besides jockeys. If you want a job that's related to horses, racing's a good place to look (see Careers in the Horse World, page 341).

The Downside of Racing

Racing provides drama and, of course, controversy. Every few years Americans get swept up in the story of a wonderful horse that is injured in a race. The stories often end sadly — Barbaro is one example.

Are these breakdowns necessary? Are Thoroughbreds raced too young, before their bones are ready? And does the industry care about horses as individuals?

Certainly it generates thousands of Thoroughbreds ready to "retire" at age three or four. Many find useful second careers, but others are used up before they're fully mature, and are left to face a grim future (see The Adoption Option, page 85).

The thrill of racing is simple and profound. It's about speed and courage. More attention to horse safety would only increase its appeal.

 RACING LINGO

Backstretch: the long section of track on the far side of the racecourse, opposite the stands

Breeder's Cup: the annual racing championships — held at a different track each year, with big prize money

Claiming race: a race in which the runners may be purchased at a preset price

Classic: a traditionally important race, like the Kentucky Derby. Also refers to a distance — in America a classic is 1¼ miles, in Europe it's 1½ miles.

Cuppy: describes a track that is dry and crumbling

Furlong: ⅛ mile, 220 yards; comes from the words "furrow long," which was originally the length of a furrow on a square, 10-acre field

Handicap: a race in which horses carry weights based on previous performances. The horse with the best record carries the most.

Homestretch: the final section of track leading to the finish line

In the money: a horse that finishes first, second, or third

Length: about 12 feet. A racing thoroughbred covers that in ⅕ second.

Mudder: a horse who races well on a muddy track

Place: to finish second

Show: to finish third

Silks: the shirts and caps worn by jockeys. Each stable has its own colors and designs.

Sprinter: a horse that's very fast over short distances

Stakes: the fee that an owner must pay to enter a stakes race

Stayer: a horse that can race longer distances and have enough gas left to come on strong at the finish

FELT HORSE

Materials Needed

Carded wool roving* (amount depends on the size of your project; a plastic shopping bag full should be plenty for a 6-inch tall horse)

Thick piece of foam rubber or a 16-inch square of rigid foam insulation for a pad

A size 38 triangle felting needle for most of the project

Tweezers

A size 36 or 40 triangle needle for finer detail work (optional)

** **Roving is wool** that has been washed, perhaps dyed, and carded, ready for spinning. It's fluffy, like batting. Ask for it in yarn shops or look for it online.*

Needle felting lets you create a picture or sculpture out of fluffy wool roving, simply by poking it with a specialized needle. It feels like magic the first time you try it. The roll of fluff stiffens and shrinks as you stab with your needle, becoming denser and taking on shape.

To make a felt horse or pony you'll need carded wool, in natural or dyed colors. You can use white wool to make the basic shape (called an armature) and lay other colors over it. I wanted to make a black horse, so I used black all the way.

WARNING: Felting needles are long and *sharp*! Work with a parent if you're under 10 years old. Work carefully — stabbing the wool is hypnotic and stress releasing, and it's easy to forget you're working with an extremely pointy tool. Try using tweezers to hold the wool as you work.

Directions

1. **Pull a section of wool off** your piece of roving. Roll it into a tube between your hands. This will be your horse's head and upper neck.

2. **Roll the upper end of the tube** (the head section) a little more tightly and bend it at an angle to the neck. Place it on the foam pad and hold steady with tweezers while you start stabbing the head with the 38 triangle felting needle in your other hand.

3. **Use the tweezers to turn the head as you work.** It will quickly begin to stiffen up. Keep stabbing and shaping. You can create indented lines by stabbing deeply and repeatedly in the same place.

4. **Begin to work the neck.** To secure the head-neck angle, stab at your horse's throatlatch area to stiffen the wool. Leave the bottom, shoulder area of the neck loose and open for now.

5. **When the head and neck are stiff,** pull off a larger piece of roving and roll it to make a body. Push one loose end of the larger piece into the loose bottom end of the neck and stab away to graft them together, working along the horse's back and sides. Leave the areas where you'll be attaching the legs loose and open.

(continued on next page)

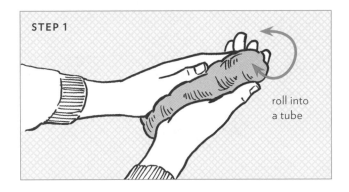

STEP 1

roll into a tube

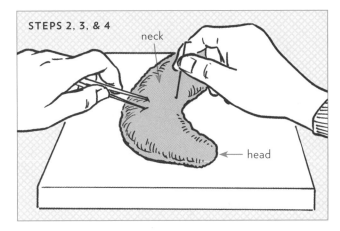

STEPS 2, 3, & 4

neck

head

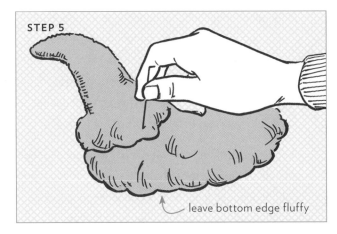

STEP 5

leave bottom edge fluffy

201

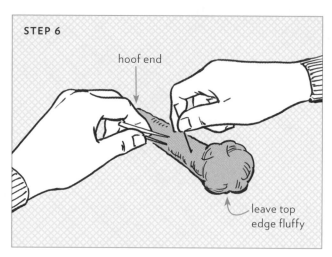

STEP 6

hoof end

leave top
edge fluffy

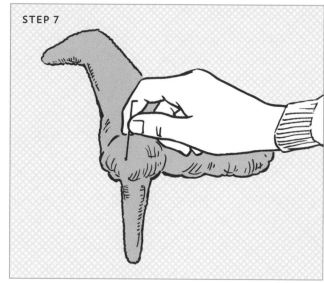

STEP 7

(continued from previous page)

If the body of your horse seems too small, it's easy to add another layer of wool — or several layers, one at a time — until you achieve the shape and size you're looking for.

6. **Now roll some legs.** Pull off four sections of roving that are roughly the same size. Roll them into tubes and start stabbing. The legs need to be quite stiff if you're making a horse that can stand on its own. Legs take a long time. Be patient, and use tweezers to hold the wool. *Note:* Keep the top ends of the legs loose and open, so you can graft them onto the body.

7. **When you have four nice, stiff legs of pretty much the same length,** it's time to attach them. Work with the front end first. Push the loose wool of the body and the loose wool at the top of one

leg together. Stab until the connection between leg and body firms up. Turn your horse over and put on the other front leg. If this leg is a little longer than the first leg, you can shorten it by pushing more of the loose top up into the body; stab until firm. Your horse will be stronger if you stab through both legs at once in the shoulder area. You can also turn the horse on his back and stab the chest and armpit area to make the connection firmer and stronger. Now add the hind legs, using the same method.

8. **When the horse is as firm** and fat as you like, and sturdy enough to stand on his legs, add a mane and tail. For the tail, pull off a small piece of roving. Stab through one end to attach it to your horse's rump. Pull off another small piece

STEP 8

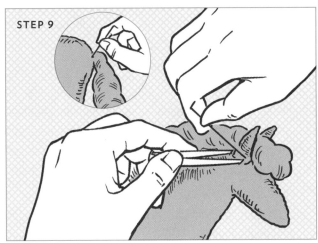

STEP 9

of roving for the mane and attach it by stabbing along the top of the neck. This piece can extend over the top of the horse's head for a forelock.

9. **Make ears by folding tiny pieces of roving** in the right shape and stabbing away. *Be careful with small pieces!* This is where you're most apt to stab yourself, even if you're using tweezers, which you should be. An alternative is to make a stylized horse without ears. That can look great too, especially with a fluffy forelock and mane.

10. **If you are making a more naturalistic horse,** you can add eyes by sewing or glueing on beads or craft eyes, or build a felt eye. On a light-colored horse this is as simple as laying a small dark ball of roving in the right spot and stabbing

it into place. You can even add a white fleck to the center of the eye. For a dark horse it's more difficult. A white rim around the eye makes it stand out, but it may not look exactly horsey. Use the finer needle for these details.

11. **You can overlay colored roving** on your horse to create markings. Just put a piece of roving of the color and shape you want over the body, and stab it to fuse it into place. You may need to keep adding colored wool to keep the underlying color from showing through.

12. **Add thin strips of color** to make a halter and saddle for your horse.

13. **If you want to make an ornament,** use a sewing needle and heavy thread to add a loop near the neck. It may take a couple of tries to find the center of balance so that he'll hang evenly.

Steeplechasing: Speed over Fences

Steeplechasing started in 1752 when two Irish hunting enthusiasts, Blake and O'Callaghan, raced each other "from Buttevant Church to St Mary's Steeple." That and other early steeplechases took place across the British countryside over hedges, fences, ditches, and all kinds of terrain. They began as a way for sportsmen to test their fox-hunters, and evolved into an organized sport that's just as challenging as the original.

The most famous steeple-chase event in the world is probably the Grand National, run in Aintree, England, every April for over 160 years. The race consists of 30 massive jumps in two loops around the course, for a distance of 4 miles, 4 furlongs.

There are several levels of jump racing in the United States. **Point-to-point races** remain closest to the original concept. Amateur riders race over not-very-high fences, sometimes across hunting country. It's considered okay to wear hunting attire rather than racing silks. Point-to-points are a good introduction to jump racing for horses and riders.

Brush races are between 1½ and 2¹³⁄₁₆ miles, over a type of jump called the National Fence. This is a 52-inch-high steel frame stuffed with plastic "brush" to simulate old-fashioned hurdles.

While races over hurdles are held at racetracks, the sport is best known for its beautiful and picturesque **cross-country races**. These races are held over timber fences — natural wood fences made of boards, logs, or post and rail. Their height varies depending on the race.

The Maryland Hunt Cup and Virginia Gold Cup feature fences around 5 feet high. Distances over timber vary, too; the Maryland Hunt Cup and Virginia Gold Cup are the longest at 4 miles.

Steeplechase spectators like to arrive early for picnics and socializing, and then sit on the grass quite close to the fences or the finish line to watch the excitement. Races like the Maryland Hunt Cup are major social and cultural events.

THE HORSES

Steeplechase horses (except in Field Master Chases) are all Thoroughbreds, mostly ex–flat racers. A steeplechaser must be three years old to race over hurdles; for races over timber, the horses must be four.

Steeplechase horses typically have a much longer racing life than a flat racer. Horses competing in a race like the Maryland Hunt Cup are usually 11 to 13 years old. As horses age and slow, they can race in lower level and amateur races, and then retire to eventing, show jumping, or foxhunting.

Some horses have more diverse careers. Bug River, 2004 Maryland Hunt Cup winner, won three stakes races in a disappointing flat-racing career. He was used as a hunter for several seasons before being introduced to steeplechasing. He won his first steeplechase race just

Horseshoe REVIEW

National Velvet
by Enid Bagnold (1935)

Velvet Brown is a British butcher's daughter who is so crazy about horses that she pretends to groom and ride a whole stable full of paper ones cut out of racing magazines. She buys a piebald for a shilling, trains him with the help of an old racetrack hand who works for her father, and rides him in the Grand National.

Some people adore this book. Others don't. I'm one of the latter. Try it and see which kind you are.

a week before his Maryland Hunt Cup win. Some other notable steeplechasers are:

✲ *Billy Barton:* The only horse to win the Maryland Hunt Cup and Virginia Gold Cup in the same year.

✲ *Jay Trump:* Winner of the My Lady's Manor, Grand National Point to Point, and Maryland Hunt Cup in 1957.

✲ *Lonesome Glory:* The only horse to win the annual Eclipse Award five times; he was slated to be a show horse, but was a little too hot — no wonder!

✲ *Mc Dynamo:* The all-time leading steeplechase money winner.

All breeds of horse and pony (including Shetlands) can compete in Field Master Chases; in fact, jumping Shetlands provide many Thelwell moments (see page 298 if you don't know about Thelwell ponies).

Pony Tales

THE BUDDHA'S HORSE

When Gautama Buddha, the founder of Buddhism, left his family to go forth and teach, he rode a white horse named Kanthaka. In Cambodia and China, Kanthaka has long been remembered along with his master. Cambodian pulpits were built in the shape of a horse with a platform on its back where the teacher sat.

THE RIDERS

Kids win steeplechase races. Regularly. That's just one of the cool things about the sport. Steeplechase jockeys can be taller and heavier than flat jockeys; the minimum weight in a steeplechase is around 140 pounds. Amateurs compete on an equal basis with professionals, as do juniors. A junior rider can apply for a license at age 16.

Most meets hold races for junior riders; on reaching age 16, those riders may get a license to compete against adults, both amateur and professional. In 2003, Chris Gracie won the Maryland Hunt Cup at age 16 on Swayo. The next year he won the English Grand National. Women riders like Blair Waterman are also frequent winners.

Races for junior riders are divided between small pony, large pony, and horse. Technically these are called Field Master Chases. Chases are a mile long, over 2½-foot fences. Riders follow a field master, who sets the pace, and are penalized for passing him. The field master leads over the fences, then riders race to the finish.

THE AMERICAN PAINT
A Horse of a Different Color

Is it a color? Is it a breed? Yes. This registered stock horse is descended from Spanish horses brought over by the conquistadores. Plains Indians liked the splashy markings for two seemingly contradictory reasons. First, they blended in with the washed-out colors of the Great Plains landscape and provided camouflage. Closer up, however, they stood out in a crowd.

Legends about different paint markings made these horses even more highly valued. Medicine Hat horses were white, with a dark "bonnet," meaning the ears and poll were colored, and a "shield" of color on the chest. The Comanche considered a warrior on a Medicine Hat horse to be invincible.

✹ A PINTO IS PAINT ✹ EXCEPT WHEN IT AIN'T

The American Paint is a registered breed. In order to be registered, a horse must have at least one registered Paint parent. A pinto horse, on the other hand, can be any breed, as long as it has a colored coat. So all Paints are pintos, but not all pintos are Paints.

Today, Paints are second only to Quarter Horses in reining, cutting, and other Western sports. They also race over $\frac{1}{4}$-mile distances.

LOOKING AT PAINTS

Paints are basically a loud-colored stock horse, similar to a Quarter Horse but lighter in body. In order to be registered, a Paint must have at least one registered Paint parent, and only outcrossings to Quarter Horses and Thoroughbreds are allowed. Paints range between 14.2 and 16.2 hands.

There are two main Paint patterns. The **tobiano** usually has a head marked like a solid-colored horse — dark with white markings. The legs are usually white below the hocks and knees. Spots are regular and distinct, often in round or oval patterns that extend down the neck and chest, forming a shield. Tobianos usually have at least one dark flank. White often extends across the back.

Overo horses rarely have white across the back. All four legs are usually dark. The face is usually white. The white markings are irregular, scattered, or splashy; these are sometimes called calico patterns.

The Fascination of Foxhunting

Steeplechasing arose from the ancient and controversial sport of foxhunting, "the unspeakable in pursuit of the inedible," in the words of Irish playwright Oscar Wilde. In the British countryside it was necessary to control wild foxes, which preyed on farm animals. American foxes are rarely so pestiferous, but American coyotes are, and both are hunted with hounds.

Is this cruelty to animals? Some people feel that foxes enjoy the challenge, others disagree, and the Master of Fox Hounds Association is careful not to attribute human motivations to the fox. That organization, the governing body of foxhunting, stipulates that the prey "must be hunted in their wild and natural state. Any other practice that does not give the animal a sporting chance is contrary to the best tradition of the sport and is strictly forbidden."

It's up to you to decide your stance on hunting. It's been a nearly addictive sport in England for centuries, and is well loved in the United States, as well. The opportunity to gallop cross-country and take all kinds of jumps at speed is some people's ultimate horse experience. And it is possible to participate in cruelty-free hunting in a drag hunt, in which a scent lure is dragged for the hounds to follow.

IF YOU WANT TO PARTICIPATE

Hunting is a formal and highly organized sport. There's a dress code that you need to know and follow. For cubbing — the early season, which introduces young hounds to the pack and gets them in shape — the dress code is less formal. You need a dark jacket, shirt and tie, or turtleneck, a protective helmet, and black leather boots. For the formal hunts, black coats and buff breeches or brilliant red coats and white breeches are required.

THE TENNESSEE WALKING HORSE
Easy to Ride, Easy to Like

What's not to like about Tennessee Walkers? They have easy gaits to ride, great soundness, and exceptionally calm and gentle temperaments; the kind of horse you could put your grandmother on. Walkers are best known for the running walk, a fast, gliding walk that can cover 10 or 12 miles in an hour. As speed increases, the hind feet overstep the tracks left by the front feet by up to 18 inches.

Easy-gaited riding horses were known in central Tennessee from the 1700s on. Frontier horses, like frontier people, had to be able to do it all. A frontier family couldn't afford to keep one team for plowing and another for driving. Starting with the extremely tough stock available to them — Spanish mustangs, Canadian Pacers, and Thoroughbreds — farmers bred horses for good tempers, good attitudes, and versatility.

The frontier Jack-of-all-trades might not be the fastest horse in America, or the strongest, but he was the fastest strong horse and the strongest fast horse. These gentle all-purpose horses survived on whatever forage was available, pulling the plow all week and the buggy on Sunday. If the roads were bad, they could carry five children at once on their backs.

Today Tennessee Walkers are ridden for show and pleasure. It's a surprise to learn that many Walkers of the late 1800s were champion harness racers.

LOOKING AT WALKERS

The Tennessee Walker is an elegant yet solid horse, with a long neck, sloping shoulders, and a short back. The bottom line is longer than the topline. Height can range from 14.3 to 17 hands. All colors are accepted.

The American Walking Pony was developed by crossing Welsh Ponies and Tennessee Walkers. They have the beautiful Welsh head and the smooth Walker gaits, all in a 13.2–14.2 hand package. A special gait of Walking Ponies is the merry walk, fast and smooth with rhythmic head motion — and a lovely name!

THE SADDLESEAT ✸ CONTROVERSY ✸

Don't judge these horses by what you may see in the show ring. The enormous high-stepping strides are the result of heavy shoeing and sometimes cruel methods that don't deserve the name "training."

The best place to get to know a Walker is out in the real world. These are the gentlest horses you'll ever meet, and the ride is almost as easy as sitting in a lounge chair!

209

APPLIQUÉ PROJECTS

Materials Needed

Computer

Digital photo of your horse
(If you have a photo you'd like to
use that's not digital, you can scan
it onto your computer,
or get the negative developed
onto a CD that you can use in
your computer.)

Inkjet or laser printer

**Inkjet or laser-printer fusible
fabric sheets** (like Quick Fuse)

When you're in love, you wear your heart on your sleeve. When you're in love with a horse, you can wear his picture on your shirt or jacket. Yes, you can take a photo to a copy shop and have them make up a T-shirt. But you can create your own projects too, ones that are a lot more individual and personal.

For example, how about making team or barn jackets? Print photos of team members and horses on fusible fabric, cut out each face, and iron them onto a denim jacket as badges, embroidering around the edges to add dimension. Or create a customized dream jacket with photos of your favorite breeds or dream horses — find them on breed or horse sport Web sites. Fuse the photos onto your jacket in collage form, adding beads, stencils, rubber-stamp images — anything that helps you believe in and follow your horse dreams. Here are some more ideas:

* Caps
* T-shirts
* Lampshades
* CD covers
* Backpacks
* Tote bags
* Aprons
* Quilt squares

Directions

1. **Work on the image with a photo-editing program** to center, darken or lighten, add words or a border.

2. **Check that your image is ready** by printing a copy on paper. When it looks good, load one fusible fabric sheet into the printer, fabric side up. Print your image, using the plain paper setting. Allow the ink to dry. Trim around the image, if desired.

3. **Follow the directions on the fabric-sheet package** for fusing the image to the surface. Different products have different directions. (Remember to keep and follow the laundering instructions on the fusible fabric–sheet package.)

4. **You can embellish your project** with embroidery, fabric paints, beads, or glitter — whatever suits your artistic vision. Add stenciled designs or rubber stamped images — your own design or something commercial — for a rich, many-textured project.

VARIATION: Use Fabric

You can cut out individual horses from horse fabric to make appliquéd patches for your jeans or jacket. Buy some fusible webbing (available at fabric stores), cut out a piece to match the size of your patch, and iron both onto your garment; then embroider around the edges, or quilt the whole piece, to make it durable. Add the same kind of embellishment to blankets or curtains.

If sewing is one of your skills, you can save a lot of money and create handsome and personalized riding clothes for yourself, and even clothes for your horse. Patterns are available commercially for everything from grooming aprons to show jackets, saddlebags, horse blankets, and fly masks. This is a great way to combine 4-H horsemanship and sewing projects. Make matching outfits for you and your horse!

When you're ready to move on to something more complex, you might try one of these projects:

❋ Grooming apron and tote

❋ Riding tights and sweats

❋ Sidesaddle apron

❋ Driving apron

❋ Roadster silks

❋ Breeches or jodhpurs

❋ Western and English shirts and vests

❋ Boot, hat, and garment carry bags

❋ Tack protection bags

❋ Saddlebags, cantle bags

❋ Show curtains, valances, name panels

Harness Racing: Keeping Up the Pace

In harness races a single horse pulls a sulky or cutter at a trot or pace. The trot and pace are intermediate gaits, faster than the walk, slower than the gallop. (In the trot, the horse's legs move forward diagonally. In a pace, they move parallel.) If pushed too fast, there's always the danger that a harness horse may break gait — that is, break into a gallop. This isn't allowed. A horse that breaks must be brought back down to the trot or pace; he loses momentum, and, usually, the race.

Harness races generally cover a mile, which a good trotter can do in a little under 2 minutes. Some races are held indoors under lights or at large racetracks where other kinds of races are held. Others take place at country fairs, in a more low-key, relaxed setting.

THE HORSES

The Standardbred is the foremost harness racing breed in North America, but there are others: in Russia, the Orlov Trotter and Russian Trotter, in France the Norman Trotter. Morgans are still raced in harness at some shows. A race called the Vermont Trot takes place on the same stretch of road where Justin Morgan once raced; elimination heats are raced under saddle and in harness. In 2007, the race was won, and a new course record set, by a 22-year-old stallion named River Echo Hamilton.

Harness horses are conditioned very differently than

WHAT'S THE DIFFERENCE?

A **sulky** is a lightweight two-wheeled racing cart made of tubular steel. The driver sits with legs wide apart, very close to the horse's rump. A **cutter** is a lightweight sleigh built for racing on ice or snow.

Thoroughbred racers, with a lot of slow jogging and long warm-ups the day of a race. This type of conditioning has helped the Standardbred breed remain a durable animal with good bone; harness horses do not break down as readily as flat racers, and have longer racing careers.

THE DRIVERS

The small breeder and amateur trainer can participate in harness racing more easily than flat racing. Older horsemen can compete, too; driving is less grueling than riding, and without the difficult weight limits.

Because it's a sport in which average-sized people and amateurs can compete, harness racing emphasizes youth involvement, with a youth organization and summer driving camps.

Horseshoe Review

The Silver Birch Series
by Dorothy Lyons

Dorothy Lyons wrote a number of books that feature a girl named Connie, her friend/boyfriend Peter, and a lot of great horses. They are very "horsey" books, full of details of the 1940s and '50s. But Lyons has no problems with letting Connie be a better rider than Peter, and just a little bit smarter, too. The series includes:

* *Bright Wampum*
* *Copper Khan*
* *Golden Sovereign*
* *Midnight Moon*
* *Silver Birch*

My favorite Lyons books, however, were outside the series. *Dark Sunshine* is the story of a girl crippled by polio who tames a wild mare and takes her on a grueling, high-stakes trail ride. Just when she's winning, she faces the ethical dilemma of a lifetime.

The Blue Stallion is the story of a fatherless ranch girl who inherits a terrific cutting horse — or does she? The old man didn't leave a will, and she's about to lose the horse to the old man's unsavory relatives when — but I won't spoil the ending.

Harlequin Hullabaloo (also published as *Bluegrass Champion*) is about the struggles of a paint Saddle Horse to be recognized as the fine horse that he is. Other Dorothy Lyons titles are:

* *Blue Smoke*
* *Java Jive*
* *Pedigree Unknown*
* *Red Embers*
* *Smoke Rings*

CHARIOT RACING: SOMETHING OLD, SOMETHING NEW

The modern chariot race, a hybrid of harness racing and flat racing, grew out of boredom. Western ranchers and farmers with too much time on their hands in the winter matched their farm teams against one another on the icy streets, pulling light sleighs called cutters.

Today, cutters have been replaced by chariots made of 55-gallon drums sawn in half vertically and mounted on two bicycle tires. The horses are different, too. These days, people use off-track Quarter Horses hitched two abreast. Chariot races are 440 fast yards. Horses race at full gallop.

Chariot racing is organized by regional associations that hold local races and converge once a year for a world championship. Chariot racing tends to be a family affair. It takes a lot of help to get a team and chariot to the starting line. One or two riders usually pony the team and chariot to the starting line. The driver may be the father or grandfather of the family, but girls race, too, and there is a junior division.

There seems to be no central chariot racing organization. An online search leads to regional organizations, and that's a good place to start. Attend a winter festival that includes chariot racing to find out if this high-speed sport is for you.

UNUSUAL EQUINE SPORTS FROM AROUND THE WORLD

The Extreme Cowboy Race is a trail ride/obstacle race, designed to mimic what a horse and rider would encounter in everyday ranch work — only compressed into a very short period of time. A race might start with two circles at a lope and include jumping, riding through a "cowboy curtain" of hanging ropes, swimming a pond, racing around barrels, traversing a rocky ravine, and loading into a trailer — after which the *rider* runs 40 yards uphill.

For all the elements included, this is a short race. The winner might complete the course described above in 4 minutes. You can catch the excitement on RFD-TV.

Ban-ei keiba takes place on the Japanese island of Hokkaido; in it, draft horses (Percheron and Breton crosses) pull iron sleds weighted with iron slabs along a racecourse that includes some fairly steep hills. The single-horse sleds weigh up to a ton when loaded, and the course is 200 meters (about 650 feet). Ban-ei keiba had a large following in the past, but its popularity has declined and enthusiasts struggle to keep the sport alive.

The Tsagaan Sar is a Mongolian race and part of a national celebration dating back to the time of Genghis Khan, and probably earlier. Thousands of Mongolian nomads arrive at the capital, Ulan Bator, for wrestling matches, archery competitions, and a 15-mile race in which all the jockeys are children, girls and boys ages 5 to 12.

The horses travel to Ulan Bator on foot. On the day of the race they travel the 15 miles to the starting point. Then they gallop back to the finish line, which is in the middle of the festival.

Buzkashi is an ancient game, first played on the steppes of Central Asia, that is considered the national sport of Afghanistan. Two or sometimes three teams of mounted horsemen start in a large circle, in the middle of which lies a beheaded calf or goat carcass that is stuffed with sand. All the players make a grab for the carcass, with the successful rider slinging it over his saddle and galloping full tilt toward the goal while his opponents try to take it away from him.

Buzkashi, which means "goat pulling," is not a game for the faint of heart! This is a tough, dangerous sport — players wear little protective gear other than thickly padded coats and they all carry heavy whips to beat off their pursuers. The playing field is huge and sometimes the horses plunge right into the crowd, scattering spectators right and left.

Happy Trails

It lets your horse see new sights, smell new smells, and do some traveling, which is a big part of his nature. It tones your muscles and his. You forget about your troubles. He forgets the fussy details of the other sports disciplines you may be working on, and gets to just carry himself naturally and be a horse. What's not to like?

Noncompetitive trail rides can also be highly organized. Some competitive trail organizations hold annual fun rides, which are great schooling opportunities for horses that will compete later. They offer a chance to ride with a lot of friends, make new friends, and see some different country. Make sure your horse is fit for the distance, and enjoy!

Some charities hold trail rides, where you collect pledges

Most of the approximately seven million horses in the United States are trail or pleasure horses. What is a trail horse? He's a horse you ride out in the real world, preferably the quiet, unspoiled parts of it — back roads, trails, logging roads, and farm roads. He takes you there and back again, mostly just for the fun of it, although many riders also participate in competitive trail events.

Non-competitive Trail Riding

Trail riding is one of the most popular horse sports, and most of it is noncompetitive. You tack up, you ride out, and you enjoy nature in the company of your best friend. It can be as long or as short a ride as you want to make it — no pressure.

Trail riding is relaxing for horse and rider. It lets you daydream and observe nature.

and ride a certain number of miles to raise money for a cause — this gives your ride purpose without competition, and is a good way to give back to the community.

OUT ON THE TRAIL

To go out trail riding for pleasure, you need good riding skills, a reliable horse, and a safe place to go.

Start with your own skills. You may have had a lot of riding lessons, but if they took place in a ring or indoor arena, you haven't faced many of the challenges horses have to offer. Many stables offer lessons in trail riding on horses who know what they're doing.

A good teacher will gradually expose you to greater and greater challenges, and help you learn strategies to overcome them. If you can't get trail riding lessons, go out with another rider, someone who's responsible and experienced, and has a steady horse.

Every horse's reactions are different. When riding your own horse at home, you need to be aware of his personal fears, faults, and strengths. Over the miles, you'll learn to trust each other in challenging situations. Even better, you'll learn how to avoid trouble in the first place.

RIDING ON ROADS

It's great if you can ride right onto trails directly from your property, but most of us can't. You'll likely need to ride on the roads, at least for short distances. You need to know the laws and basic safety rules.

In many states, horses are considered vehicles and ride

 RULES TO RIDE BY

For trail riding to be possible, land must be kept open and available for riders to cross. It's important to obey No Trespassing signs. It's also important to minimize them by behaving so courteously that no one would consider barring you from their land. The rules are simple:

✳ Leave everything as you found it.

✳ Don't pick anything, like berries, without permission.

✳ Close every gate you open.

✳ Leave no trash.

✳ Don't disturb any equipment, like sap lines or water pipes.

✳ Don't be noisy.

✳ Don't be nosy, but if you see something amiss — livestock in trouble, a broken fence — let the owner know.

You want landowners to welcome horsemen on their property. Being courteous is the most important thing you can do to help keep land open for riding.

with traffic on the right — the same side of the road that cars travel. In other states, you're supposed to ride facing oncoming traffic — on the left, as if you were a pedestrian.

Find out what the laws are in your state. Then use your own judgment. It's better to briefly break the rules and ride on the "wrong" side when there's a deep ditch and no shoulder on the "right" side. Here are some more tips for safety on roads and trails:

❊ If there's a scary object on the right that might spook your horse into traffic, take him over on the left until you're past it.

❊ Pavement can be slippery, especially for a shod horse. Walk, don't run, your horse on pavement or blacktop.

❊ Ride at quieter times of day — midmorning might be good in your area.

❊ Wear bright clothing — blaze orange or lime green.

Bombproofing Your Horse

Bombproofing is a way to have fun and make progress with your horse, even in down times. You can work with a young horse who can't be ridden yet, during the winter, or during a time when your horse is lame.

The idea is to introduce scary objects slowly and carefully. Start by putting them outside his fence first and give him time to get used to them before you move them inside the fence and closer to your horse. Repeat with each object, several times a day if possible, until his reaction is, "So what?"

Then try a different object. Balloons, open umbrellas, pieces of cardboard, shiny foil — use your imagination. If you do this thoroughly, your horse won't use his imagination as much out on the trail.

START WITH CARS
Getting your horse used to cars is an important part of

❊ THE YEAR OF THE HORSE ❊

The Chinese Zodiac is symbolized by twelve animals: the rat, the ox, the tiger, the rabbit, the dragon, the snake, the horse, the goat, the monkey, the rooster, the dog, and the pig. Each year has an animal assigned to it. If you were born in the Year of the Horse (most recently, 1966, 1978, 1990, and 2002), you are independent and confident, outgoing and energetic, honest and friendly.

This is the character for "horse" in Chinese, Japanese, and old Korean.

馬

bombproofing. Pasture him beside a busy road if possible. Take the opportunity to first lead him and then ride at a walk around parked cars. Take him to a roadside and just stand there watching traffic.

Get a friend or parent to slowly drive cars past him; when he's bored, graduate to greater speeds, peeling out, slamming the door, honking the horn, and running the lights and windshield wipers.

The key word here is *gradually*. You don't want to be holding him together while a car passes. You want him to be truly unconcerned. When traffic-training, figure out his comfort distance from cars — the place where he barely lifts his head when one passes. Work there first. As famous trainer John Lyons says, "Work where you can, not where you can't."

Very gradually move closer to the traffic — 1 or 2 feet at a time. Your horse will tell you if he's worried. Give him a chance to settle, and if he doesn't, pull back to where he feels safe again. You aren't "losing the fight," you're telling him you'll take care of him.

CLICKER TRAINING HELPS

You can use clicker training to help desensitize your horse to traffic and other scary things. Approach the umbrella? Click and treat. Touch it with your nose? Click and treat. Stand still watching cars? Click and treat. Stand closer, and then closer . . . you get the idea. (See Click, Treat, Train, page 100.)

Make Your Own RUBBER STAMPS

Materials Needed

Block of rubber or a white plastic eraser, at least 2 × 2 inches

Tracing paper

Pencil

A set of tools for carving linoleum, wood, or rubber (you'll need several V-gauges and U-gauges to make different patterns)

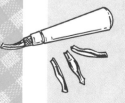

Ink pad, felt tip markers, or fabric pens

Rubber stamps are fun, but they can be expensive. It's easy and fun to make your own, and a lot more personal, too. You can create a stamp of your own horse or a favorite horse hero; you can design your own brand (see page 186) or farm logo; you can even make one with your horse's name, if it's short. How about designing a "chop," as artists call it, of your own name or a symbol to stamp a piece of artwork as your own?

To create a stamp, you select or create an image, transfer it to the stamp material, carve away all parts that are going to be white (meaning the parts that won't get inked), apply ink, and press onto paper. You can purchase stamp-making kits at art stores or you can try making one on your own.

Directions

1. **Choose an image.** Simple is best, especially for your first stamp. Small is good, too, since you won't have a stiff handle and backing on this stamp — though you can make one, once you've created a stamp you know you'll want to use over and over.

   If you're doing a stamp of your own horse, find a small photo that shows him in profile — either his whole body or his head. There are an amazing number of fiddly bits on a horse, so you might want to start with something simpler, like your brand or logo, or a horseshoe, a bit, or a stylized saddle.

2. **Transfer the image to the rubber block.** Using a pencil, simply trace your picture onto the tracing paper. Make sure the image is the same size as the block you are carving! Turn the tracing paper over on top of the block. Press it down, hold securely in place, and rub all over it with the backs of your fingernails or the back of a spoon. The pencil lines will come off on the rubber.

   Newsprint images and freshly printed ink-jet pictures from a printer transfer just like pencil drawings. Laser-printed images can be ironed on, using a barely warm iron.

3. **Carve the image in the block.** Remember: Any part you carve *out* of the image will show as white when you stamp it. Any part you leave on the surface will show up in color. It can take some mental gymnastics to wrap your mind around this.

   Read the directions carefully before you start using these tools, and practice on the edges of your rubber block, or on a spare eraser, before you start carving for real. (I didn't, and made an okay stamp the first time. But by the *third* time, with practice and more careful reading, I made a really good one.)

> CAUTION: The blades on these tools need to be sharp to do their job. They're also rather small. *Be very careful* putting them on and taking them off the handle. Otherwise the first cut you make may be a finger.

IMPORTANT CARVING TIPS:

* **Hold the tool** so the V in the V-shaped blade is upright.
* **Place the point of the V** at the edge of your image.
* **Carve by pushing toward the outer edge** of the block, away from yourself and from your image.
* **You can carve the curves** by rotating the block rather than twisting the tool.

(continued on next page)

(continued from previous page)

* **Use light pressure for carving thin lines,** heavy pressure for thicker lines. It doesn't take a lot of pressure to carve this stuff; don't gouge.

* **To make it easier to carve delicate lines,** or clean up rough edges, try freezing the pad for 15 minutes before carving, or running an ice cube over the area you want to carve. This firms up the rubber so it won't bend away from your carving tool.

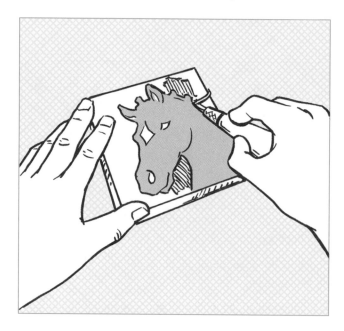

IF THE PINK-ON-PINK *(or white-on-white) effect is making it hard to see as you're carving, try inking the surface of your stamp with a dye-based (not permanent) ink pad — brown or dark blue inks work best. You'll be able to see the contrast between the surface and the carved-away portions.*

INKING TECHNIQUES

Using a rubber stamp is easy, right? Just press onto an inkpad and then onto paper. But did you know that you can get a second, lighter print by "huffing" on the stamp to refresh the ink? Just breathe on the stamp like you would a window or a pair of glasses to fog them up. A lot of times the second, fainter image is better than the first one.

Another way you can ink your stamp is with a good ink marker or a fabric-marking pen. And this is great if, for example, you're trying to produce a three-colored image, say a red-bay mare with a white star and snip. Color the mane black — or blue, if that's what you have; color the face red; stamp, and presto!

You can use your stamp to decorate letters and envelopes, invitations, book covers and school reports, birthday cards, thank-you notes, T-shirts (use permanent ink, like a laundry-marking pen, for that!), anything you can think of that needs a horse stamp or your logo.

MORE TIPS AND TECHNIQUES

* **To make a portrait of your own horse,** work from a good photo. A black and white shot may show the lights and darks more clearly.

* **For a solid-colored horse,** you will be carving away the parts of your horse that catch the light. To see how an artist does it, take a look at an older edition of *The Black Stallion*, one with illustrations by Keith Ward. You'll see how Ward uses white to show the contours of Black's head

and body. The outline remains in black. The eye has a white outline that follows the contour of the skull, and white also reveals the contours of the face.

☀ **Make friends with imperfection.** A picture is a collaboration with the viewer. It *suggests* a horse; the viewer completes the job. If your stamp looks primitive, enjoy that. Primitive is cool.

☀ **Keep at it.** You'll get better at this quite rapidly, so dig in and make some mistakes to learn from. Then reread the instructions. I guarantee they'll make more sense after you've tried this once.

Materials Needed

Heavy paper
(card stock, poster board, oak tag — an old file folder is perfect)

Lighter-weight paper
in a color that contrasts with the first one

Scissors

Glue

Your rubber stamp

Clear adhesive shelf-lining paper or self-laminating plastic (you can find this at an office supply store)

Hole punch

Yarn for tassel

VARIATION: Make a Bookmark

Once you have a stamp, it's easy to create a bookmark.

Directions

1. **Cut the heavy paper into a strip** the size and shape you want your bookmark to be.

2. **Cut contrasting paper** into a slightly smaller strip of the same shape.

3. **Glue the lighter paper onto the cardboard,** leaving a slight margin all around.

4. **Carefully apply your stamp** at the top of the bookmark or make a pattern with it.

5. **To make your bookmark more durable,** seal it inside the shelf-lining paper or self-laminating plastic.

6. **For an optional embellishment,** punch a hole near the top of your bookmark and tie a tassel through it.

Top Trail Riding Breeds

Virtually any breed of horse can participate at some level of trail riding. It's one of the most natural activities we ask of our horses. However, some breeds are more talented than others at certain aspects of trail riding.

Gaited horses are sure-footed and easy on their riders. Morgans are tough and cheerful. Arabs are known for their stamina and ability to travel for miles. Thoroughbreds and Standardbreds are shaped long and lean like radiators, so they vent heat well, and they have great endurance built into their bloodlines.

Some breeds not usually thought of for trail riding have their virtues as well. Draft horses are slow, but strong and patient. Ponies are strong for their size and most have a great will to win. Quarter Horses, Appys, Paints, and Haflingers all have their fans.

 SIGNS OF PROGRESS

The emphasis on vet checks and horse health in trail riding competitions is a sign of how far we've come in our care for animals. The distance-riding champions of old had no compunction about riding horses to death. As recently as the first competitive Ride and Tie event in 1971, there were no vet checks and two horses died.

The founders of the sport resolved that it would never happen again; now Ride and Tie and other trail events feature vet checks, watering stations, and mandatory pulse and respiration recovery. It's not okay anymore for horses to die so people can win a game or get their names in a record book.

TRAIL RIDING ORGANIZATIONS

Many breed organizations have trail programs that award riders based on the number of hours on trails anywhere in the world, as well as in training and showing in cross-country events.

For example, the American Quarter Horse Association's Horseback Riding Program gives awards just for logging the hours you spend on any American Quarter Horse. You keep track of your hours, and at certain points you receive prizes —gift certificates, your picture or profile in *America's Horse*, a silver belt buckle. Non–Quarter Horse owners can also participate, but you get better prizes faster if you're riding a Quarter Horse!

Check your breed association to see if a similar program exists for your horse of choice. For riders who aren't particularly competitive, yet would like to be recognized for the hours they and their horses put in, this can be a fun option.

Competitive Trail Riding

Competitive trail rides are timed rides, judged on your horse's physical conditioning, soundness, and trail manners. Competitive trail rides vary in length from 15-mile rides to classics like the Vermont Hundred Mile. There are three types of ride: Type B is a one-day ride, Type A is two day, and Type AA is three day. You'll ride from 15 to 40 miles per day, depending on the type of ride.

HOW DOES IT WORK?

Riders are sent off at intervals to follow a mapped course marked with signs or letters. Competitors in different divisions may need to follow different sections of the trail — alertness is essential or you could disqualify yourself. You need to finish the course within a set time frame, and you'll be penalized for finishing too fast or too slow.

Along the way you'll stop in at checkpoints where your horse's vital signs will be monitored by judges, one of whom is a veterinarian. These stops ensure that all horses finish the ride in good health. Horses must recover a resting heart rate of under 48 beats per minute within 10 minutes. If not, they are docked one point for each excess beat per minute.

More important, if the horse doesn't recover within 10 minutes he will be held at the checkpoint for 10 more minutes and be checked again. If he doesn't reach the right heart rate after three checks, he'll be disqualified — and that's a good thing. Horses can hide distress, and go until they drop. (A mule won't do that. He always looks out for himself first.)

The hours it takes to get your horse in shape for a competitive trail ride make great bonding time. Seek expert advice on how to condition your horse for a competitive trail ride. He'll need to be in excellent shape, and so will you. Learn how to take his pulse and respiration rate. That way you can judge for yourself how well your horse is doing.

Horseshoe REVIEW

Trail Riding: Train, Prepare, Pack Up & Hit the Trail

by Rhonda Hart Poe (2005)

This book covers everything you need to know about gear, weather, trail hazards, bombproofing horses, and the different kinds of competitive trail riding. It also includes a detailed section on great places to go trail riding all across the United States, and a list of top outfitters and organized trail rides, including some in Canada; a must-own for every trail rider.

ENDURANCE RIDING

Endurance rides are an extremely grueling form of competitive trail riding. Horses race over a predetermined distance — between 50 and 150 miles — within a maximum time. There is no minimum time limit; this is a real race. Beginners may start out on "limited distance rides," which are 25 to 35 miles. Arabs dominate endurance riding, but any horse (within reason) can compete. The ideal endurance horse is built flat, like a radiator, and is muscular but lean.

Veterinary care is good on these rides, because the event veterinarians are part of the judging staff. Horses are checked at designated rest stops; if they are deemed unsound or stressed, they may be disqualified. There are rest stops every 10 to 15 miles, but horses are allowed only 3 hours total rest during a 100-mile ride.

Endurance racing is hard on horses. Dehydration, stress, and food and water changes can lead to colic — another reason for intense veterinary scrutiny. Just completing a ride like the famous 100-mile Tevis Cup in California is a point of pride for a horseman.

RIDE AND TIE

Ride and Tie is a form of competitive trail riding for one horse and two people. One person starts out riding. After a ½ mile or so she dismounts, ties the horse, and takes off running along the trail.

Meanwhile the original runner catches up to the horse, mounts, and rides ½ mile or so past the first rider. Then she dismounts, ties the horse, and keeps on running. Each

⤳ TAILING ON THE TRAIL ⤳

Tailing is a way to climb a hill that's too steep for the horse to manage with a rider or to give him a break while still making progress during a race. The rider dismounts and holds onto the horse's tail while he pulls her up the hill. Endurance bridles are designed with reins that easily unclip from the bit to maintain your contact.

226

☀ FIELD TRIALING ☀
Hound Dogs and Horses and Guns, Oh My!

Field trialing is hunting birds with dogs from horseback; you must control a horse, a dog, and a firearm all at once. There are a lot of skills involved here; field trialing isn't a sport for everyone.

You can also follow the hunt on horseback as an observer. The observers in field trialing are called "the gallery." Riders in the gallery must know field-trial etiquette, and all horses must be absolutely safe around dogs (that means, safe for dogs to be around — hunting dogs are valuable animals).

Field trial horses are ridden hard for 4 hours at a time. They must be fit. Many competitors switch off, using one horse in the morning and one in the afternoon. This is a sport for gaited horses; the rules state that the horse can only advance at a walk. Tennessee Walkers are the traditional breed, but the McCurdy Plantation Horse was developed specifically for field trialing and is gaining popularity.

team must switch off at least six times during a race, but there is no maximum. Ride-and-tie races are between 25 and 40 miles, though novice or fun races may be shorter.

The start of a ride-and-tie race is a mad dash. Riders start first, so runners don't get trampled. After that, strategy is important. Who should ride and who should run along which stretch of the course?

Finding a place to tie your horse can be a challenge. It must be part of the existing landscape, like a tree, telephone pole, or fence post. A good ride-and-tie horse will stand calmly tied only to a clump of grass.

Ride-and-tie races include vet checks, watering stations, and rest stops. A good ride-and-tie horse is fast but calm and will stand tied, alone or when other horses are passing. The kind of horse you ride is up to you, but a shorter horse is easier to mount than a larger one.

COMPETITIVE MOUNTED ORIENTEERING (CMO)

This sport is a bit like a treasure hunt. Competitors ride without trails, using a map and compass to find "stations" hidden out in wild country. Orienteering has been a part of military training since the 19th century. In the American Midwest it became a mounted competitive sport.

In a CMO event you get a map with ¾-mile areas circled. Each station is hidden somewhere within one of these circles — at the edge, dead center, or someplace in between. CMO races begin with a seminar on map and compass reading, and a practice station for beginners to try on. Depending on the rules of the individual race, you may work alone or in teams, and may look for stations in any order.

You don't want to lead competitors to the station. Craft and sneakiness are important. The winner is the rider or team who finds the most stations in the shortest amount of time.

The mileage of a CMO is hard to predict. If you wander around looking for stations you'll log more miles than if you get lucky early. Events are timed and take between 2 and 6 hours. Horses are not vet-checked, as this sport tends to be quite laid-back and family-oriented. But budget for a lot of wandering, and be sure your horse is in excellent condition.

Camping on Horseback

Camping with horses can be a great way to get out into the backcountry — indeed, the only way. It requires excellent planning, sensitivity to the environment, and a safety-first attitude with regard to bad weather, wildlife, and other natural hazards.

A good way to get experience is to join an organized camping trip. Find out about them in *The Trail Rider* magazine. If you're considering this, ask if the organizers follow environmentally responsible principles. Leave No Trace, Low Impact, and Minimum

---

Horse PLAY

YOUR HORSE'S NIGHTLIFE

Go out to the pasture on a moonlit night and find out what your horse is doing. Grazing? Dozing? Listening? You'll enjoy seeing the moon shining on a horse's back, hearing the owls, and feeling the chilly dew. You'll also find out how visible your horse is after dark (unless he's light-colored, not very!). Here are some tips:

✻ Make extra sure all horses in the pasture are aware of your presence before you approach.

✻ Approach with caution.

✻ Carry a flashlight. A wind-up flashlight is good here, because you can be sure it won't run out of juice.

✻ Don't wait to make a nighttime visit until you have a sick horse to nurse and you're too worried to enjoy the experience. Do it when all is well.

Impact are labels for some of these philosophies; find out which your guides follow, and what exactly they mean. At a minimum you should aim to:

✤ Travel and camp on durable surfaces.

✤ Properly dispose of waste.

✤ Leave the land as you found it.

✤ Respect wildlife.

✤ Build and put out fires safely.

Leaving your site as you found it is essential for keeping land open to future campers. Bad citizenship on one camper's part can lose the privilege for all others.

You might also consider going on a backcountry elk hunting trip. You travel with a pack train into the mountains and camp out under the supervision of an experienced guide and horse master. If you're not a hunter, you may be able to ride along without the intention to bag an elk — hunting with a camera can be just as exciting.

Going Back in Time: Historic Reenactments

Historic reenactments are a fantastic way to play with horses in a noncompetitive and unusual way. Reenactments are a popular pastime in the United States. Much of our early history took place on horseback, which means there's a place for horses and riders in this recreation today. Treks, encampments, and mock battles can become a weekend and summer way of life.

Events range from wagon trains to reenactments of historic rides such as the ones by Paul Revere or the Pony Express riders. They can be short events or rather grueling. Every year there's a 10-day reenactment of the Pony Express ride. Five hundred riders and horses cover 1,996 miles between California and Missouri. It's the longest event held annually on a historic trail in the United States, longer than the Iditarod dogsled race. Volunteer riders gather from all over the United States to participate.

If history interests you, find out about local reenactment groups. Most tend to focus on a historical period — Revolutionary War, Civil War, the American West. War reenactors stage battles and marches, while western reenactors often do trail rides that follow the historic trail of a particular group of settlers (see Wagons, Ho!, page 232), and the Society for Creative Anachronism (SCA) reenacts medieval jousting (see page 254).

Modern Safety Concerns

Think about safety as you investigate reenactments. Historical accuracy is important; you may find low tolerance for safety helmets. At the same time, you'll be mixing horses with gunfire and other scary things. Organizers of reenactments may know a lot more about regimental uniforms than they do about horses.

Take charge. Let organizers know what you need. Learn safe methods of picketing horses in camp. Buy a low-

Horse Sense

When retrofitting a helmet for a period look, it's *essential* that any added brim be attached only with Velcro (hook and loop fasteners) so it will detach if you fall or catch it on a branch.

profile safety helmet and put some real work into disguising it as a period hat — consider posing as a heroic wounded soldier with your helmet wrapped in a bloody bandage, for instance. If your horse will be encountering gunfire, spend as much time as it takes — first in a home setting and then on the road — getting him used to gunfire. Be sure to get experienced help with this.

Other considerations are the same as for all camping trips. Provide for insect protection. Accustom your horse to drinking flavored water; then you can flavor the "foreign" water at your campsite, and it will be familiar to him. Listen to the weather reports and take shelter in the event of thunderstorms or other dangerous weather events.

War is hell, on horses and people. Reenactments shouldn't be. Play safe!

FROM THE MIGHTIEST MINI TO THE HUGEST HORSE

✷ **THE SMALLEST HORSE** in the world is Thumbelina, a dwarf Miniature mare who stands just 4.1 hands (17 inches; 43 cm) and weighs 60 pounds (27 kg), full-grown. Thumbelina's parents were full-sized Miniatures; her dwarfism was unintended, and she will not be bred. Thumbelina sleeps in a dog house, has a guard-dog companion, and goes on tour to raise money for children's charities, travelling in her own customized RV. She has no idea how small she is. She bosses the larger horses and has even faced down an elephant.

✷ **THE LARGEST HORSE** in the world as of 2008 is a gray Shire from Australia, named Noddy. Noddy is 20.1 hands — that's over 6 feet (nearly 2 m) at the shoulder and his head is much higher than that, of course. Noddy weighs 2,600 pounds (1180 kg) and he's still growing! He has a ways to go, however, to match the all-time largest horse. Samson, also a Shire, lived in England in the 1800s. He reached 21.2 hands, and weighed 3,360 pounds (1,525 kg).

Wagons, Ho!

A unique way to celebrate American history and have fun with horses is to go on a wagon train trek. Many of these treks retrace the settlers' routes west. The Pendleton Round-Up Wagon Train, for example, follows a section of the Oregon Trail for six days and is open to riders as well as those who'd rather travel in a wagon.

A typical event includes 15 to 20 wagons and 150 or more people, as well as a support crew ferrying in supplies in pickups.

This is a slow-moving, noncompetitive form of trail riding, but it can still be grueling. Blisters and accidents do happen. But with an experienced group of people leading a wagon train, and the right amount of support staff, joining a wagon train can be a great way to enjoy horses with your whole family, even the nonriders. Here are some things you'll want to know:

☀ *How many miles will the train travel per day?*

☀ *What are the arrangements for food preparation and delivery?*

☀ **ALMOST AROUND THE WORLD** ☀

The record for the most miles logged in competitive trail riding by a single horse was set in October, 2008, by a 37-year-old half-Arabian gelding named Elmer Bandit, owned and ridden by Mary Anna Wood. How many miles did this pair cover together? So far, 20,720 and counting! The earth measures about 24,901 miles (40,075 km) around the equator, so they don't have too much farther to go!

- ✤ *Will there be grain, hay, and water for the horses?*

- ✤ *Is the food for people prepared and stored safely?*

- ✤ *Are cold drinks available?*

- ✤ *Will you change camps nightly or stay in one place for several days?*

- ✤ *Will there be portable toilets or showers?*

- ✤ *Will the environment be a concern for this group (such as recycling, trash collection, proper manure and human waste disposal, care for trail conditions)?*

The Rounders
(1964, not rated)

This fun B-Western stars Henry Fonda and Glenn Ford as cowboys who run up against a horse they can't ride. Old Fooler is played by a horse who really seems to be acting. The bucking scenes are impressive, but horse lovers will especially appreciate this horse's face in quieter moments. Ears back, sulky, Old Fooler really seems to be planning something. He earns Ben's and Howdy's hatred, and then something like love, and then . . . well, see it for yourself.

This good-natured, funny movie is the antidote for when you've seen too many movie horses tamed far too easily. Although it's unrated, I'd give it a PG for brief partial nudity.

Spirit Rides

Spirit rides are a Lakota (Sioux) Indian ceremonial ride. People ride to sacred sites, often on the summer solstice, June 21, to pray for peace and unity. The 2003 Big Foot Peace Ride went to Wounded Knee.

Another ride went to the Little Big Horn, known to the Lakota as Greasy Grass, where a reenactment of the battle was held from the Lakota perspective. Originally confined to the Lakota people, Spirit Rides are now taking place worldwide.

✳ FAMOUS TRAIL RIDERS, YOUNG AND OLD ✳

Bud and Temple Abernathy were two ranch kids from Oklahoma who became folk heroes in the early 1900s because of their long rides. Their first, in 1909 — at five and nine years old! — was a mere 1,000 miles from Oklahoma City to Santa Fe and back again. They made this ride alone but with parental permission.

The following year, they struck out for New York City and arrived there in only a month. They met Orville Wright and were offered a ride in his airplane, were greeted by President Taft, and rode in a victory parade with Teddy Roosevelt and the Rough Riders.

They were 7 and 11 in 1911 when they made their most famous ride, 4,500 miles from New York to San Francisco. It took them 62 days, again without adult supervision. This ride has never been equaled, though it has been imitated.

For more about these amazing kids, read *Ride the Wind* by Miles Abernathy and *The Abernathy Boys* by L. J. Hunt. You can also check out the Long Rider's Guild, an association devoted to equestrian travel (see Resources, page 358).

OTHER FAMOUS DISTANCE RIDERS

✳ *Dmitri Peshkov:* 5,500 miles from Siberia to St. Petersburg, 1889

✳ *Roger Pocock:* 3,600 miles from Fort Macleod, Canada, to Mexico City along the Outlaw Trail, 1891

✳ *Aime Tschiffely:* 10,000 miles from Buenos Aires to Washington, DC, starting in 1925

✳ *Louis Brunhke and Vladimir Fissenko:* 19,000 miles from Tierra del Fuego to Prudhoe Bay, Alaska, starting in 1993

✳ *Otto Schwartz:* 30,000 lifetime miles on five continents

✳ *Alberta Claire:* In 1912 Alberta Claire rode her horse Bud 8,000 miles, from Wyoming to Oregon, down through California, and then from Arizona to New York City. Her ride was in support of women's right to vote and to ride astride (she rode astride).

That year Teddy Roosevelt endorsed women's suffrage, and sidesaddles began to lose favor. Next, Alberta rode to Mexico, where she filmed Pancho Villa in battle. You can read a story by Alberta on the Long Rider's Guild Web site.

❧ HORSES AND THEIR FRIENDS ❧

Horses are sociable. They evolved to live in bands and herds. They like company, they like knowing how they fit into their own society, and most are followers. They'll do what the other horses are doing.

This leads to problems when horses have to live less naturally. Some horses get herd-bound; they won't leave their buddies. Others get overexcited around strange horses; they want to mix it up and see who's boss.

Horses can live alone, but most prefer some kind of companionship. It doesn't have to be another horse, though.

 Thumbelina, the world's smallest horse, has a dog companion that she shares her food with.

 Barn cats world wide have discovered the benefits of a horse's warm back on a cold night. The Godolphin Arabian had a cat friend for many years, a tabby named Grimalkin who appears in paintings with the famous stallion.

 Many nervous race horses have goat companions — but not every horse likes goats. Seabiscuit literally threw his goat over the stall door; he preferred the company of a pony.

 A Morgan mare living on a sheep farm spends her days with the rams, and everyone seems to get along.

And horses will bond with people. Sometimes it seems like they've mostly bonded to the grain can, but people who use natural horsemanship techniques, and spend many hours with their horses, become important members of the horse's personal herd. Horses like calm, confident people with an ability to solve horse problems. And yes; "I've run out of food" is a serious horse problem!

Drive Yourself Horse Crazy!

Driving is enjoyed by people of all ages, and has special benefits for people with physical disabilities. Many people find driving a great way to continue horse sports as they age or deal with physical handicaps. Others take to driving when they outgrow a beloved pony and want to keep playing with him.

The driving world includes every breed of equine, from Minis to drafts, donkeys to Arabians. Draft breeds are shown in farm horse contests, pulling contests, hitch classes, pleasure classes, and even compete in some cross-country marathon sports. They also provide the power for wagon train treks (see Wagons, Ho!, page 232). Mules have their own enthusiasts, and Minis are driven far more often than they are ridden.

Pleasure Driving

Pleasure driving in the real world, as opposed to showing, is just that. You hitch your horse up to a sturdy vehicle and do whatever pleases you, whether that's traveling along a country road or across fields.

Driving is a horse sport you can share with a friend. Only a dedicated — and fast — jogger is going to go out running with you on your horse, but anyone can join you on the seat of a carriage. You can take a well-behaved dog along, or a small child who's not yet ready to ride. In many ways driving is physically easier than riding, for people and for horses.

For example, most horses aren't ready to be ridden at two. Their bones are still growing, and they can be damaged. But a two-year-old can be trained to drive, and if not pushed too hard, can happily take you places. This may also be a way to keep using a horse or pony with soundness problems. Horses can pull much heavier weights than they can carry — just like us!

That's why there are all those luggage carts in airports.

NOT AS EASY AS IT LOOKS

Driving has its disadvantages, too. It's not a simple skill, though it might look like it when you watch a good driver. A vehicle can't turn as sharply as a horse can because it's long and has rigid shafts. You have to learn how to turn, how to help your horse brace going down hills, and how hard your horse has to work to go up hills.

So if you want to drive, here's what you should do:

* Find an expert trainer for you and your horse.

* Seek experienced help choosing a cart and harness.

* Go to clinics and learn everything you can.

* Wear a helmet.

Before you go out on the road, give a lot of thought to where you'll drive. Roads are great if they're quiet, but are

Pony Tales

MOON HORSES

In some mythologies, the moon is pulled through the sky in a chariot. For the Romans it was Diana who drove the moon chariot, pulled by a team of milk-white steeds.

The Norse have only one horse for the moon, Alsvider (All-Swift) who crosses the heavens pursued by two wolves, Skoll (Repulsion) and Hati (Hatred). An eclipse was believed to be a time when the wolves caught up and nearly devoured horse and moon together.

you likely to meet a logging truck on that back road? Is the road wide enough for cars to pass you? Where are the barking dogs and darting small children, and what will your horse do when he meets them? Think through as many factors as possible ahead of time; the fewer surprises, the better.

Competitive Carriage Driving

If you become serious about driving or would like to watch more experienced drivers competing, you have

several options. As with riding, there's a wide range of styles, sports, and vehicles to go with them. Here are a few ways to embrace driving.

CARRIAGE PLEASURE DRIVING

Carriage pleasure driving is a show ring competition in which single horses, pairs, and teams pull antique or replica vehicles. There are classes in reinsmanship in which the driver's skills are judged, working classes in which the emphasis is on the horse, classes in which turnout (and even carriage dogs!) are judged, and obstacle courses.

Obstacle courses include fast cones courses, slower courses that may include bridges and ground poles to negotiate, and the popular Gambler's Choice, in which drivers choose which obstacles to take, with the goal of getting through as many as possible in the allotted time.

RIDE AND DRIVE CLASSES

Ride and Drive classes are a part of some shows. The horse is first judged as a driving horse. Then he's unhitched, saddled up, and is judged as a riding horse.

These classes hark back to a time when hunters were driven to the place where the day's hunt would begin. Usually two horses were driven tandem, with the hunter taking the easier position as leader.

ROADSTER-TO-BIKE

Roadster-to-bike is a class that owes a lot to harness racing. Drivers wear silks and goggles like race drivers, and the "bike" is a two-wheeled sulky. Horses show in a clockwise direction at a jog, then reverse as on a racetrack, and are asked to exhibit a road gait, which is a very fast yet stylish trot.

When the call, "Drive on!" comes over the loudspeaker, horses are urged to their top trotting speed. The trot must stay correct and balanced, with no hitching or breaking. (Roadsters are also shown under saddle in silks.)

FINE HARNESS

Fine harness is a class for the breeds of horse that are shown saddle seat or park seat (those are English pleasure competitions that emphasize flashy, high-stepping movement). The park harness horse is shown in a four-wheeled fine harness buggy. A flat-footed walk is not required; the trot is high stepping and animated. Grooming and turnout are important in this event.

COMBINED DRIVING: EVENTING ON WHEELS

Combined driving is similar to three-phase eventing. It includes dressage, a cross-country marathon, and a cones course. As in ridden dressage, a driven dressage test is judged on obedience, freedom and regularity of movement, impulsion, correct position, and training of the horse.

The cross-country phase includes obstacles — bridges, streams, and so on. Drivers are given a map. They must take the obstacles in sequence, keeping red flags on their right, white flags on their left. Beyond that, they're free to take any path through the obstacle. Drivers and grooms may walk the course ahead of time, but no horses are allowed on course before the start of the event. (A groom rides with all drivers to help navigate, and to assist if anything goes wrong — a great opportunity for horseless horsemen.)

This phase is judged on time minus penalties. Penalties include: groom or driver dismounting, driver putting down the whip, course error, knocking down any part of an obstacle, or turning over the vehicle.

Cones courses take the place of stadium jumping. They are timed, fast-paced races involving negotiating a twisty obstacle course made of road cones with tennis balls balanced on top. Knocking off a ball docks seconds from your time.

Divisions within combined driving include singles (one horse), pairs (two horses hitched abreast), tandem (two horses hitched one in front of the other), and teams (four horses hitched two abreast); they are also divided by horse and pony.

 # THE SADDLECHARIOT

The saddlechariot is the invention of avowed coward and non-horseman Simon Mulholland. His daughters were given a Miniature horse, Henry, who grew to 41 inches — too big for his breed, too small to be particularly useful. Mulholland felt sorry for Henry, who was bored on pasture and needed exercise.

Mulholland didn't like traditional driving vehicles. He wanted to be able to bail out if he or Henry got scared. He wanted something made of modern materials and with every safety device he could think of. Around 2006, he started tinkering and had his wife test the early prototypes, most of which crashed. When she'd proven the saddlechariot safe and sturdy, he took over.

The name of this vehicle is derived from the name for the ancient chariot of Mesopotamia (now Iraq): the straddle car. Mulholland didn't like the word "straddle," but he could see the resemblance, and came up with saddlechariot.

The saddlechariot driver stands with the support of a small bicycle-type seat. In emergencies — or moments of timidity — he simply steps off, 8 inches back and 8 inches down, and pulls a ripcord. The chariot detaches from the pony, leaving the driver on the ground, reins in hand and still in control, "if you ever were," notes Mulholland.

The saddlechariot can handle rough terrain, though Mulholland suggests hopping off on steep downhill slopes; and with its fat rubber tires it can even take small jumps. A cart or garden implements can be attached in the rear. Mulholland plans to take Henry and the saddlechariot the length of Hadrian's Wall, a fitting journey back in time to when chariots were a common vehicle in Britain.

Heigh-ho, Heigh-ho, Dashing Through the Snow

A sleigh is a light, horse-drawn vehicle mounted on runners and used on ice or snow. In the old days, when roads were muddy in spring and heavily rutted in other seasons, winter was when northerners traveled and transported goods. Gliding over the snow was smoother and more comfortable than jolting over stones and sinkholes, especially with a heavy buffalo-skin robe to keep you warm. It was also

Pony Tales

HARD TO FIT A HORSE DOWN THE CHIMNEY

St. Nicholas drove a white horse before he became Santa Claus and acquired those eight reindeer. In the Netherlands, Sinterklaas rides a white horse named Schimmel. Kids leave hay, carrots, or turnips in their shoes for Sinterklaas's horse.

fun to get out behind a fast horse and see the world, lifting spirits in a cold, dark season.

Sleighing is still a northern winter recreation, as it is extremely weather-dependent. Sleigh rallies are often canceled or disrupted for lack of snow. But where snow is reliable, sleighing is one way to enjoy and share a horse in winter. Many farms depend on sleigh rides for a share of their income. Often they use draft horses, and the "sleigh" may be the hay-wagon body mounted on heavy runners; on the opposite end of the spectrum, people also race light sleighs called "cutters."

❄ JINGLE BELLS, JINGLE BELLS ❄

The sound of sleigh bells brings thoughts of winter, Christmas, Santa Claus. No wonder they lift the spirits. But why are bells associated with sleighing?

Because they're practical. Snow muffles a horse's hoof beats, and sleighs are more difficult to stop than carts. Bells warned pedestrians and other drivers that a sleigh was coming, and prevented accidents. Laws in many states mandated that sleighs be equipped with bells; those laws are still on the books in parts of Canada.

Sleigh bells come in several forms. The familiar **sleigh bells** or **jingle bells** are a closed bell with a slot in the bottom. They come in many sizes, are usually made of solid brass, and are fastened to the harness in long strings of 20 to 25 bells mounted on leather straps. They may be all the same size or graduated to produce a harmonious sound.

JINGLE ALL THE WAY: TYPES OF BELLS

❄ **Rump bells** are large bells mounted on a broad strap that fastens to the crupper (the strap that runs under the horse's tail). They make the characteristic jingle-bell sound.

❄ **Chimes** are open, bell-shaped bells with a high, clear, carrying tone.

❄ **Pole chimes** are mounted on a steel strap and fastened to the shafts or pole.

❄ **Saddle chimes** are mounted on an ornate framework that attaches to the harness. One bell or several may be hung from the sides and bottom of a draft horse collar. German brewery hitches may wear a sort of heraldic apron that hangs from the horse collar and has bells attached to the corners.

Unusual Ways to Have Fun with a Horse

When most people think about working or playing with a horse, they think of riding or driving. But in addition to these more traditional techniques, there are lots of cool things you can do as an equestrian if you're willing to work hard, learn carefully, and maybe take a few risks.

The Thrill of Vaulting

Time for a quiz: *Which of these best describes the exciting sport of vaulting?*

A. Gymnastics on a moving horse

B. An international equestrian sport recognized by Fédération Equestre Internationale (FEI)

C. One of the six disciplines offered at the World Equestrian Games

D. The safest horse sport

E. The easiest horse sport to learn

F. All of the above

If you answered "All of the above," you scored 100. But how can vaulting be the safest horse sport? Nobody wears a helmet or even shoes. People are somersaulting off cantering horses, standing on their hands, making three-person pyramids — how can this not be dangerous?

The United States Pony Club (USPC) lists three major causes of riding injuries — rider loss of control, poor riding environment or horse suitability, and lack of safety knowledge. According to the USPC, 60 percent of riding injuries are caused by loss of control, and 80 percent are due to falls. (And that doesn't even address the head injury/helmet issue! See Helmets, page 143.)

Vaulting has a solution for all three problems. First, the rider isn't in control. An adult horse handler or longer (pronounced "lunger" but spelled that way because it comes from the French *longeur*) is, so safety isn't dependent on the rider's judgment. Second, the environment is strictly controlled: It's a 20-meter (65½-foot) circle, within an enclosed area, on special deep footing, at the end of a longe line. Third, vaulting is all about the most important safety knowledge a rider can have — how to keep your balance and how to fall right.

JUMPING ON AND OFF A HORSE

As riders, most of us get on the horse and hope to stay on till the end of the ride. A vaulter jumps on and off, on and off, many times during a routine. She has a friendly relationship with the ground — and hitting the ground isn't a big deal when you've mastered the art of landing correctly, and of leaping lightly back onto a cantering horse's back. So why worry?

According to the *USPC Handbook*, with vaulting techniques, "the time required in learning to ride safely can be cut in half. It reduces chances of injury from a fall." Vaulting increases suppleness, balance, rhythm,

Horseshoe REVIEW

The Man from Snowy River
(1982, rated PG)

Tomboy Jessica Harrison, the daughter of a wealthy Australian cattle rancher, wants to help break her father's expensive new colt. He'll hear nothing of it — but when he's off on a trip Jessica joins Jim Craig, a young horse-breaker down from the Snowy River country, to work with the horse.

They're making progress in horse training (and falling in love) when the colt is injured by the same bunch of brumbies that had a role in the death of Jim's father. Jim is banished back to the mountains, and rebellious Jessica goes off to find him. Romance and incredible riding scenes make this movie a winner.

strength, and confidence — if you could do a handstand on a cantering horse, wouldn't you feel pretty confident?

Here are some other great things about vaulting:

* **You can vault at any age,** beginning in preschool.

* **You don't need to know how to ride to get started.**

* **Cost is low** because you share a horse and the expenses of a horse.

* **You can practice without a horse** — in fact, you *must* practice without a horse.

* **You don't have to own a horse.** One horse can provide a dozen vaulters with a half day of practice or competition, so a team needs only one horse to train and compete.

* **You'll make fast progress.** "Virtually instant success is more often the rule than the exception," according to the USPC.

* **You can take part in therapeutic vaulting** as part of the North American Riding for the Handicapped Association.

* **You can compete individually,** in pairs, or in teams.

* **Vaulting events** range from local competitions and clinics to international competition at the World Equestrian Games.

Quick, cheap, great for the horseless horseman, safer than soccer, biking, or playing on the jungle gym — what's not to like?

A horse with a broad back and even gait is ideal, but most important of all is temperament. This horse must put up with almost anything happening on his back, while cantering like clockwork. A large horse may be necessary for team competition, as he may have three riders on his back at once.

⧼ BLUE SHADOWS ⧽ MOUNTED DRILL TEAM

Kids who wanted to use the drill team experience to teach horsemanship, leadership, and responsibility started Blue Shadows in 1957. Routines are based on early cavalry drilling.

Based in Los Angeles County, the group has two posts containing four troops of between 10 and 20 riders. Riders, who are called Remounts when they join, learn the basics of horse care and riding. Then they're promoted to Trooper. Uniforms and helmets are worn in practices as well as competition, and there are monthly tests on horse care. Maybe you could start a drill team of your own!

THE BEAUTY SHOP GAME

This is a great riding school game that builds self-confidence and gives school horses some extra pampering. To play, you'll need to collect a bunch of hair doodads: barrettes, scrunchies, braiding elastics, and so on, along with glitter, beads, and even costume jewelry (nothing too delicate). Include nontoxic tempera paints if you don't mind getting really messy, plus brushes or sponges to apply it (or just use your fingers!). Don't forget hoof polish.

1. **Divide the supplies evenly into buckets** at one end of the ring and set up mounting blocks at the other end (one bucket and one mounting block per team).

2. **The first rider for her team** must mount properly, using the mounting block, then race to the other end of the ring and dismount.

3. **She chooses a hair doodad** or other make-up item from the bucket and applies it to her horse.

4. **Then she leads him as fast as she can** back to the mounting block for the next teammate.

5. **The goal is to make as many trips as you can before the whistle blows.** (Organizers should use their judgment about how much time to allow, based on speed and competence of riders, and the number of doodads available per horse.)

At the end, horses are judged according to categories you'll make up, like: Most Hollywood, Most Punk, and the like.

Of course, Beauty Shop doesn't need to be a race. It can just be a fun way to spend time with a horse on a hot or rainy day. Or hold a horse beauty pageant at the barn with friends.

Polo: Fast and Furious

Often described as "hockey on horseback," polo is one of the oldest and fastest horse sports known. It was played 2,500 years ago in Persia (modern Iran), from where it spread to China, Japan, Tibet, and India. The name comes from the Tibetan *pulu*, which means "ball." British tea planters discovered polo in India and brought it back to England with them. The modern rules were formulated in the 1870s.

Polo is played on a grass field (also called a "ground" or "pitch") measuring 300 by 200 yards. The ground is framed with low boards to keep the ball in. Riders hit a 3-inch willow ball with a bamboo mallet, trying to drive it into the other team's goal. Teams consist of four players.

WHAT'S A CHUKKA?

Matches last just under an hour and are divided into

periods called "chukkas," each lasting 7½ minutes. High-goal matches have five or six chukkas; lower-goal events have four. No pony is allowed to play more than two chukkas per match, or to play two consecutive chukkas. This means each rider needs at least two ponies for low-goal polo, more for high-goal, making polo an expensive sport. Polo ponies are usually 15 to 15.3 hands, and they have strong hocks and hindquarters and very good hooves. They have good

"ball-sense," akin to the cow-sense a cutting horse shows.

SPECIAL EQUIPMENT

Polo players wear helmets, breeches, long boots, and knee protectors. Ponies must wear bandages, a breastplate to keep the saddle from slipping, and a standing martingale, to keep the pony from throwing back his head and hitting the rider in the face. Draw reins and gag bits are often used. In addition to all these reins and a mallet, riders may also carry a whip — it's a lot to handle. Ponies are steered by neck reining and must gallop flat out, turn on a dime, and gallop again from a dead stop.

A lot of polo practice takes place without a horse. Players practice shots while mounted on barrels or wooden "horses."

WHAT IN THE WORLD IS POLOCROSSE?

Polocrosse is a hybrid of polo and lacrosse. It was developed in London in the early twentieth century as a mounted game to teach confidence and riding skills. Originally polocrosse was played indoors by teams of two. It evolved into a four-on-a-side outdoor game, and when players in Australia discovered it in the 1930s, polocrosse took off as a fast-paced organized sport.

Polocrosse players move a soft, four-inch rubber ball down the field using a yard-long racquet with a net. In Pony Club competition, a team consists of three players and a stable manager, who may act as a replacement player if qualified. A polocrosse field is 160 yards long and 60 yards wide, and may be grass or dirt. Chukkas are 6 to 8 minutes, and a game usually consists of four chukkas. Riders must wear helmets; horses must wear bell boots and leg wraps.

Unlike polo, polocrosse players only play one pony per game, for not more than 48 minutes a day. This makes polocrosse much less expensive. Polocrosse horses may be of any breed, size, and age; all they need to be is sound, fast, and steerable. The Australians call polocrosse "the king of one-horse sports."

There is now an active American Polocrosse association, international competition, and, since 2003, a Polocrosse World Cup. Polocrosse is also a Pony Club competition, played at levels from Pee Wee (10 years old or younger, on ponies 14.2 hands or less) through advanced.

Horseshoe REVIEW

A Cat That Plays Polo?

The classic polo story is Rudyard Kipling's "The Maltese Cat." In British India, the Skidars, a lowly regimental team, face the Archangels in the final match of a polo tournament. The Archangels have six ponies each, the Skidars only three, but one of those is The Maltese Cat, master of the game. The ponies talk, though only to each other. The action is thrilling. Find this short story in anthologies or look it up online — it's worth hunting for.

Great Gymkhana Games

Horseback games have doubtless existed since people first mounted up, but modern games trace to the British occupation of India, where gymkhana games were used to train — and amuse — cavalry troops. Many of the games, such as tent-pegging, had been played for centuries in India. British soldiers brought them home, where they became popular with children.

Gymkhanas are competitions consisting of timed horseback games. They can be English or Western — Westerners sometimes call gymkhanas by the Native American term, "Omoksee." Gymkhanas run by 4-H or Pony Club are called mounted games.

Gymkhana races are simple in concept. You ride a pattern, and the fastest time wins; style is unimportant. There's no special equipment needed other than safe boots and a good helmet.

The great thing about a gymkhana is that there is so much variety. The games are enjoyable but are a serious test of your riding skills and ability to handle a horse.

While you're having fun, it's important to remember that gymkhanas and games are grueling activities. Don't overtrain. Keep your horse fresh, physically and mentally.

Here are some of the games you might encounter:

✳ **Single Stake** or **Arena Race (1 pole):** Race to pole; turn around it in either direction; race home.

HORSE WORD

The word gymkhana comes from the English word *gymnasium*, crossed with the Indian word *gend-khana*, which means "ball court." A gymkhana is a day of timed mounted games; this is a popular activity with both English and Western riders.

Horse Sense

Speed can be addictive for horses: If you use your gymkhana or game horse for pleasure and showing, pay close attention to his training and manners. He has to understand that racing out the gate — or any racing — is something that only happens when you ask for it. Monitor his energy level; to keep him obedient and supple, include plenty of steady cross-country miles and schooling on the flat as part of your training.

* **Birangle Race (2 poles):** Race to one pole and turn around it; race to second pole and turn around it in the same direction; race to the finish.

* **Quadrangle Race (4 poles):** Race a birangle around poles 1 and 2; race a second birangle around poles 3 and 4, turning in the opposite direction; race home.

* **Pole Bending (6 poles):** Start in either direction and weave through the poles; turn around the sixth pole; weave back and cross finish line.

* **Cloverleaf Barrel Race (3 barrels set in a triangle):** Circle first barrel from either the right or left; race around the other two barrels in the opposite direction from the first; race home.

* **Barrel and Stake Race (2 open barrels, stakes):** Race to first barrel, circling it and picking up a stake; race to second barrel and deposit stake; repeat pattern until all stakes have been moved to second barrel; race home. One stake for riders under 8 years old, two for 8 to 11, three for others.

* **Flag Race (1 flag in a can of sand, centered on a barrel):** Race around barrel, picking up flag; race home with flag in hand.

* **Speedball (1 cone, 1 golf ball):** Race to cone, ball in hand; turn around cone in either direction, dropping ball in cone; race home.

* **Pony Express Race:** Weave through three bending poles; dismount, pick up a weighted envelope from the ground and put it in your sack; remount and weave back; hand off to the next rider.

* **Rope Race:** Rider 1 weaves through 3 poles carrying a 3-foot rope. She meets Rider 2 at C and they weave back together, holding the ends of the rope. Back at the first pole, Rider 1 drops off and Rider 3 takes hold of the rope. Continue until all have finished.

Pony Club Games

One of the USPC's most popular divisions is Games. Horseback games help riders overcome fears and develop skills. By focusing on a short-term, just-for-fun activity, riders learn without getting too intense about it.

But beyond their usefulness in training young riders, games are a blast. They also let riders keep competing on ponies that might be considered too small for them in other disciplines. A good games pony is fast, agile, and short enough to get on and off easily.

Something for Everyone

There are an enormous number of games, and new ones are invented every year. There are even games for lead-line kids — versions of musical chairs and musical statues.

USPC Games are played in teams, usually of four riders. Team races involve some sort of hand-off. Many include dismounting to pick something up or vaulting skills. Others involve skills like leading a pony and having your pony trot beside you. Games include:

* **Balloon Race:** Riders must pop balloons with a lance.

* **Canadian Race:** Combines pole bending with hitting a ball into a goal with a hockey stick.

* **Egg and Racket:** Managing pole bending while carrying an egg on a tennis racket.

* **Housewife Scurry:** Team members collect and drop into a bucket, in order, a potato, an apple, an orange, a carrot, and an onion.

* **Hurdle Race:** Riders lead their ponies while crawling under 2-foot hurdles and jumping over 1-foot hurdles.

* **Stepping Stone Dash:** Riders lead their ponies while dashing along a row of "stepping stones," which are paint cans filled with cement and set on a board.

Games use unusual objects. By the time you've trained a pony to ignore balloons, hula hoops, road cones, and so on, your mount is a lot less likely to shy at a falling leaf or shiny gum wrapper at the side of the road.

Mounted games are fun, fast, and informal, and become many Pony Clubbers' favorite horse activity. There are competitions all over the country and internationally, and jealous parents have joined the fun by setting up teams and competitions of their own.

When show-jumping gets too serious and your brain is tired of trying to get that exact number of strides between jumps; when dressage is too tame; when you're outgrowing a pony you love with all your heart — get into games. You many never leave!

THE MISSOURI FOX TROTTER:
Smoothest Gaits in the West

This might be the most popular breed you've never heard of. Beloved in the Ozarks and the West, they are rarely seen in other parts of North America. But this is an American frontier breed, like the Morgan; easy-gaited, like the Tennessee Walker; great with cattle, like the Quarter Horse.

The breed dates back to the 1820s, when settlers moved into the Ozark Hills of Missouri. They came from Kentucky, Tennessee, and Virginia and they brought good horses with them, mostly Thoroughbreds, Arabians, and Morgans.

The original Ozark horses were bred to race as well as to be good all-around workers, but after the Civil War, the South experienced a religious revival. Horse racing came to be regarded as sinful. Tracks were shut down and racing enthusiasts shamed into giving up their passion.

The times now demanded a good distance horse with smooth action that was easy on the rider. The Saddlebred and Tennessee Walker blood provided the genes for that, and breeders produced a horse with a unique gait called the fox trot.

Missouri Fox Trotters remained useful in the hilly Ozarks even after mechanical vehicles came on the scene. They were used for working cattle and hunting foxes and other game.

NOT JUST A DANCE STEP

In the fox trot, the horse walks with the front feet and trots with the back. This very smooth gait is faster than a walk — 5 to 8 miles an hour over long distances, 10 miles an hour for short stretches. The hind feet slide over the track of the forefeet. The head and tail bob rhythmically, but the back stays smooth and level. So does the rider! Missouri Fox Trotters also do a regular flat-footed walk and a canter. The canter should be moderate, between the low flat lope of a cow pony and the higher, slower gait of a Saddlebred.

LOOKING AT FOX TROTTERS

The Fox Trotter is a solid horse with a straight profile, long back, and excellent feet and legs. It can range between 14 and 16 hands. All colors are allowed, but many Fox Trotters are chestnut or in the palomino range, including cremello, perlino, and champagne.

Fox Trotters still play an important role in ranch work and forest service work; riders who spend whole days in the saddle wouldn't part with these smooth-stepping horses. They are exceptionally sure-footed, making them great trail horses. This is a gentle, easy-going breed, and they are a great choice for handicapped riding programs.

The Wild West: Cowboy Mounted Shooting

Have you ever wanted to be a movie cowboy? Ride full tilt, blazing away with a pistol? Do you like fast horses, the smell of gunpowder, and Old West clothes? Then Cowboy Mounted Shooting (CMS) may be for you.

This high-speed sport has divisions for kids as young as 6 (though shooting is restricted until you reach age 12) as well as adults. There's a cavalry division and even a therapeutic version for handicapped riders. As one enthusiast says,

"Horses, guns, and costumes — what could be bad about that?"

In CMS, contestants ride a pattern, similar to barrel racing, while shooting at balloons with a pistol. Riders use two single-action revolvers, each loaded with five rounds of blank ammunition. The first five balloons are set in a random pattern and there are over 50 possible patterns.

On the day of the event, you draw the pattern you'll ride out of a hat. You ride that pattern, shooting with your first pistol; then holster your first

gun and race to the far end of the arena, drawing your second; turn around a barrel and you're ready for the last five balloons, laid out in a straight line called a "rundown."

You're scored on your time, plus penalties: 5 seconds for each missed balloon, 5 seconds for dropping a gun, 10 seconds for riding the course incorrectly, 60 seconds for falling off your horse. Times typically

Horse Sense

Gun safety is strongly emphasized in CMS. Live rounds are strictly forbidden at events. An armorer loads each gun as the rider enters the arena. Someone else unloads the gun when the rider is finished. No one may carry a loaded gun — even one loaded with blanks — outside the arena or when not competing.

fall between 15 and 35 seconds. With margins like that, it's the penalties that get you.

You may be wondering: Do the balloons pop if you're only firing blanks? Yer darned tootin' they do! The cartridges are .45 Long Colts, a brass cartridge loaded with black powder, similar to what cowboys used in the 1800s. They'll break a balloon at about 15 feet.

DRESSING THE PART

Tack and clothing are from the 1890s American West. Men wear shirts without collars, and high-waisted pants with buttons, not zippers. You may wear modern jeans as long as you pull a pair of chinks (a type of chaps) over them. Colors are more subdued than in some Western show circles.

Ladies may compete in pants and shirt, or in skirts, dresses, or period riding habits. Some women compete riding sidesaddle. As with many Western sports, and in

keeping with the period dress code, hard hats are not worn (though you could certainly wear Troxel's new felt-over helmet hat). Clothing is available from Western catalogs, but you can save money, and exercise your own creativity, by sewing your own.

Riders use older-style Western saddles, with a deep, flat seat and high cantle. Most use a breastplate and tie-down. Any breed of horse can excel in CMS, as long as he's fast, steerable, and doesn't mind the sound of gunfire. Quarter Horses, Paints, Appaloosas, Spanish Barbs, and wild-caught mustangs have been used, and at least one rider has been successful with a retired rodeo bucker. Ex–barrel racers don't make great mounted shooting horses; they have that barrel race pattern drilled into them and that's the one they want to run.

✷ **THE TALE OF NEVADA JOE** ✷

In 2002, a bay mustang was rounded up with a group in Nevada. He was adopted as a mascot by the Wahl Clipper Corporation, which named him Nevada Joe. Joe has had an amazingly varied career. He has done barrel racing, roping, Extreme Cowboy Racing, and Cowboy Mounted Shooting.

Joe's also an ambassador for the North American Riding for the Handicapped Association (NARHA). He travels the country visiting horse expos, schools, and camps, and has been a mount for therapeutic Mounted Shooting.

Joe impresses his trainers with his kindness, intelligence, and ability to do so many different jobs. He's a great ambassador for wild mustangs, too.

WOW, I WANT TO DO THAT!
How do you get started? Contact the Cowboy Mounted Shooting Association (CMSA) to find out about the regional association nearest you. CMS is done all over the United States, and around the world.

You're best off starting out on an experienced CMS horse, one who's very used to the sound of gunfire. Getting a horse used to guns is not a job for a novice. (Note: Most riders use earplugs for themselves and their horses, but some horses find the earplugs more annoying than the shots.)

Divisions in CMS include Senior (19 and up) and Junior (12 to 18) for men and women, and Wrangler Class for kids, 11 and under. Each division consists of six Classes. You start in Class 1 of your division. When you win once in Class 1, you advance to Class 2. Three wins there moves you on to Class 3, and so on. There's also a prize for best overall score, regardless of age or gender.

Wrangler Class is different from the rest of CMS. Kids under 11 ride the same pattern as adults, and they may shoot Hollywood cap pistols if they wish, aiming at the target as they would in higher divisions. But to actually engage the target with .45 blanks, they return to the arena and shoot from the ground, with a parent beside them.

In therapeutic Mounted Shooting, riders accompanied by a ground crew walk up to the target and pop it with a pointed stick.

Knights in Shining Armor

A joust is a combat between mounted knights — and just how many knights do you run into these days? But believe it or not, jousting isn't a thing of the past. It's an organized modern sport, a professional exhibition sport, and is even the official sport of the state of Maryland. It's also a favorite pastime of members of the Society for Creative Anachronism (SCA).

If you love stories about knights and sorcerers, this might be the horse sport for you, even if you only go as a spectator.

Pony Tales

FORGET ABOUT BLACK CATS!

Certain horse colors are considered lucky, depending on where you live. In Spain and Hungary, black horses bring good luck. In France, however, they bring bad luck.

SPORT JOUSTING FOR MODERN KNIGHTS

Jousting is a regional sport in North America, with clubs mostly in Maryland, Virginia, and southern Pennsylvania. Riders travel along an 80-yard track at any gait above a walk, and attempt to spear three small rings suspended above them. The rings are about a ¼ inch in diameter, so there is a lot of skill involved.

Kids compete on an equal footing with adults, and rings are at the same height for all riders — 6 feet, 9 inches above the ground. In spite of this handicap, young riders on ponies are perfectly capable of defeating adults.

Jousting is a timed event. Horses can be of any size and breed. The best are small or mid-sized, and have a steady temperament. A smooth canter is very important, as most riders adopt a standing position, jockey-style. Competitive divisions include Novice, Amateur, Semi-Professional, and Professional.

There's no particular dress code for jousting. Whatever you normally ride in is fine. Clubs may have colors, or wear either a sleeveless tunic called a gipon (pronounced gee-PON) or a bright sash. Or you may have a title or heraldic emblem embroidered on your shirt.

Helmets are not required in jousting, but are highly recommended. You'll be riding between wooden or iron arches and trying to spear rings suspended on metal rods; you don't want to bang into either with an unprotected head.

Jousters often give themselves titles, like Knight of Cupcakes, Maid Myrtle the Mad, or whatever suits their fancy.

SCA JOUSTING: OUT OF THE ORDINARY

Now for something completely different: jousting with the Society for Creative Anachronism (SCA). SCA is an international, non-profit educational organization that, according to its Web site, is "dedicated to researching and recreating the arts and skills of preseventeenth-century Europe. Our 'Known World'

Horse Sense

Professional exhibition jousting is undoubtedly thrilling to watch, but it's not at all safe for participants. Professionals try for a level of authenticity that gets much too close to the real thing. Injuries and deaths from jousting aren't a relic of the medieval world — they occur today, too.

consists of 19 kingdoms, with over 30,000 members residing in countries around the world. Members, dressed in clothing of the Middle Ages and Renaissance, attend events that feature tournaments, arts exhibits, classes, workshops, dancing, feasts, and more."

SCA has several equestrian guilds that participate in games at SCA events. The equestrian games sanctioned by SCA include:

❧ HOW THE ARROW FLIES ❧

In ancient Japan the art of **Yabusame**, shooting arrows from a galloping horse, was a form of fortune telling. If a Samurai shot well, he knew he would defeat his enemies in his next battle. The hoofprints of his horse were read to predict the harvests.

❋ **Rings:** The rider spears rings suspended from arches.

❋ **Heads:** The rider weaves through a set of poles mounted with fake human heads and tries to knock the heads off with a padded sword called a "boffer."

❋ **Reeds:** The rider takes a straight line between poles with reeds set atop them, and tries to knock the reeds off with a boffer.

❋ **Quintain:** A shield-shaped target is set on a pole; the rider attempts to strike the target with a lance.

- **Pig Sticking:** The rider tries to spear a target (don't worry, it's not a real pig) on the ground.

- **Mounted Crest Combat:** Two riders, wearing steel helmets with crests on top, try to knock each other's crests off with boffers.

- **Jousting:** Two riders try to strike each other's shields with lances. In the SCA, the lances have breakaway foam tips.

SCA event rules show an impressive level of attention to safety for horses, riders, and spectators. Riders must have a knowledgeable helper on the ground at all times. Helmets and safe footgear are required.

SCA Jousting offers riders a chance to build skills and have fun with horses in costume. Some of us horse people can get just a touch too serious — but how serious can you be when you're walloping each other's crests with boffers?

Pony Tales

LEGENDARY SLEEPING HORSEMEN

Many ancient kings and soldiers rest under untold hills and castles with their faithful horses beside them. The most famous is probably **King Arthur**, who sleeps under an unknown hill in Cornwall, waiting to rise again when England needs him.

The Irish **Earl Gerald of Mullaghmast** rides around the Currah of Kildare once every seven years. Legend has it that when his ½-inch-thick silver horseshoes wear thin as a cat's ear, a six-fingered miller's son will blow his trumpet and Gerald will ride forth with his troops.

In Serbia, **King Marko** and his horse Sharatz (which means "piebald") sleep in a cavern in Mount Urvina. The king's sword is slowly rising out of the mountain's summit. When it's fully visible, Marko will mount Sharatz and come to save his country. (Sometimes he nips out early to help Serbs in difficulties.) King Marko was the son of a *veela*, or fairy queen, and a dragon. Sharatz was Marko's closest friend for 160 years, before they went into the mountain.

The Bohemian **King Wenzel** sleeps in a rock-crystal cave under Mount Blanik. Anyone who visits this cave may find that a year, or 10 years, passes in a single night. If you go into any of these kingly caves and blow the King's hunting horn, the soldiers will awake and ask, "Is it time?" In the stories it never is time, but if it were, soldiers and king would waken and ride forth to save their country from any menace.

High-Speed Skijoring

Skijoring is skiing while being towed by a horse; it's also an exciting high-speed winter sport. The word means "ski-driving" and is pronounced "ski-yoring."

Skijoring originated hundreds of years ago in Scandinavia, when travelers on skis got the idea of hitching a ride behind a reindeer. It was a backcountry mode of transportation until 1928, when it was demonstrated at the Winter Olympics in St. Moritz.

The form of the sport that caught on in Europe, and continues there today, is a race on a flat, snowy straight or oval course. The skier drives his horse with one hand. With the other he holds onto a light whiffletree attached to the horse's harness. A long, colorful fabric apron keeps at least some of the flying snow out of the skier's face.

In the late 1940s, skijoring was demonstrated at the Steamboat Springs, Colorado, Winter Carnival. Two horsemen brought the idea back

THE THRILL OF PULLING

You'll find horse pulling at country fairs large and small, all over the United States. In this sport teams of horses pull progressively heavier loads, sometimes on a sled called a "stone boat", other times pulling against a special machine called a "dynamometer". The pull is a measured distance that varies regionally. The work looks hard, but horses are conditioned for it.

Divisions are based on the weight of the team, though all sizes of horse may compete in a free-for-all contest. There's also a pony division.

to Leadville, Colorado. Tom Shroeder was a skier and Mugs Ossman was a horseman. Together they inaugurated the first U.S. skijoring race in 1949.

American skijoring is a two-person, one-horse sport. A rider controls the horse. The skier holds a rope in one hand. He or she may have a spear in the other. The skier is towed over a course of jumps and slalom gates and may have to spear rings. Teams have two go-rounds over a course that's a minimum of 600 feet. This is a timed event with penalties deducted.

Snow-sport-approved helmets are required for skiers. Riders under 18 must wear an ASI-approved riding helmet. The rope, not over 33 feet long, is attached either to the saddle horn or a breastplate.

Of the many and precise rules in this sport, Rule 9 is the most important: "The skier must be in an upright posi-

The Horse in the Gray Flannel Suit
(1968, rated G)

An advertising executive under pressure to create a new ad campaign for the antacid Aspercel and to buy his daughter a horse combines the two goals: a horse named Aspercel who must win championships and fame. But Aspercel doesn't win enough, the daughter hates showing, and the executive is about to lose his job, when the girl's beautiful coach steps in to ride Aspercel in a dramatic jumping championship at the National Horse Show.

Silly, yes, but also fun. The horse is gorgeous, he does not rear and nicker constantly, and the jumping scenes are dramatic and suspenseful. This light and enjoyable movie is vintage Disney.

tion with the rope in one hand and on at least one ski when crossing the finish line. Both ski tips and boots must cross the line." None of this is a given, especially the "upright position" part! In spite of the risks, this fast-paced sport is growing in popularity.

There are several divisions in skijoring competition. Open is for riders and ski-

ers 18 and up; Local involves any age combination; and Junior is for competitors aged 11 to 17. In the Peewee division, for skiers under 10, the rider must be an adult.

Because two people compete with one horse, skijoring is both economical and a good choice for a horseless horseman with a horse-owning friend.

Horseball: Basketball on Horseback

Horseball is an old sport that's new on the scene in the United States. It originated in Argentina, where the game called *pato* has been played since 1610.

Pato means "duck" — the original "ball" in this game was a live duck in a basket. Pato was a violent game, and not only for the duck. Many gauchos (South American cowboys) were killed either during the course of play or in knife fights that broke out during or after the games. Because of this, pato was forbidden at various times in Argentina's history.

Pato was formalized and regulated during the 1930s, and was declared the national game of Argentina in 1953. FEI recognized pato, renaming it "horseball," in 2004.

According to International Horseball Federation rules, the game is played by four-man teams, over six 8-minute periods. Riders score by throwing the ball through a vertically mounted hoop into a net. The ball must pass through the hands of three members of the same team before a goal can be scored. A player can hold the ball for no longer than 10 seconds. Ill treatment of horses is prohibited and penalized.

These days, the ball is the size of a soccer ball, with leather loops sewn to it for handholds. You can pull the ball out of an opponent's hands. If it falls to the ground, you must scoop it up without dismounting. To make this easier, stirrups are tied together under the horse's belly, or to the girth, for stability.

Horse and rider must wear protective equipment: helmets and shoulder and knee pads for riders, leg-bandages and overreach boots for horses. Horses are ridden in a snaffle bit, with a breast collar and martingale for greater control.

≈ HORSEBALL ≈ THE ENGLISH WAY

The British Pony Club adopted horseball and added some interesting twists of its own. Pony Club horseball is played without a saddle. Instead riders sit on a girthed pad with two handholds. You can use the handholds when you bend down to scoop up the ball from the ground. To keep ponies' mouths from being pulled, Pony Club players must drop the reins when catching the ball. These adaptations make this version even more challenging, and it's a great training game for both horse and rider.

Horseball is slower than polo. The ball can only go as far and fast as the best player can throw it. This means there's no special breed requirement for the game.

Horses need to be reasonably quick, well trained, and tolerant of other horses being close by. Any good horse can play horseball at some level. In international league competition, Anglo-Arabs and Andalusians excel.

TRY IT AT HOME!

One appeal of horseball is that the equipment can be made at home, cheaply and easily: sew some leather loops to a soccer ball, put a hoop up sideways and hang a hay net on it, strap on protective gear, and you're ready to play among friends.

Or you can join a league and aim for glory. The sport is making headway in the United States, with leagues in several Western states, in Texas, Florida, and in the Northeast.

Going to Horse Camp

If this is your idea of ultimate summer fun . . .

❋ Ride every day

❋ Show often

❋ Try carriage driving, vaulting, drill team, hunter pace, gymkhana games

❋ Go camping with horses, swimming with horses, on picnic rides with horses

❋ Eat, sleep, and breathe horses

. . . then horse camp is for you!

There are horse camps at all levels of experience, and all disciplines. Check out a local horse periodical for camps near you. (February and March are good months to look for camp listings; camp directors like to think ahead, and so should you.) Or contact the American Camp Association (ACA) for a list of accredited camps. ACA accreditation is a good indicator of a camp's quality, as this organization strongly emphasizes safety and high operating standards.

Many youth organizations also sponsor camps or clinics that offer overnights, intensive lessons, and lots of horse time; to find the right horse camp for you, check out 4-H, Pony Club, a sport organization like the Harness Horse Youth Foundation (HHYF), or search online for "horse youth camps."

 A DAY AT HORSE CAMP

8:00 a.m.	Feed horses
8:30 a.m.	Breakfast
9:00 a.m.	Clean stalls
10:00 a.m.	Riding lesson
Noontime	Lunch & lecture about horses
2:00 p.m.	Trail ride
4:00 p.m.	Swimming or activities
5:00 p.m.	Feed horses
6:00 p.m.	Dinner
7:00 p.m.	Sing horse songs, tell horse stories
9:00 p.m.	Go to bed and dream about horses

How Do You Choose a Camp?

Obviously, you should choose a camp that offers work in your discipline, unless you're looking to branch out and sample a wider range of horse activities. Make sure a parent talks with the camp director and understands the camp's values and philosophy. You don't want to inadvertently end up at some sort of boot camp. Here are some questions to ask:

✻ *Are helmets required for all mounted activities?*

✻ *Is each camper assigned her own horse?*

✻ *How many hours a day will you spend with your horse?*

✻ *How much of that will be riding and lesson time?*

✻ *What other activities are available?* Some camps also offer swimming, hiking, mountain biking, pottery, kayaking, wilderness skills, art, tennis, and archery.

✻ *What's the age range of campers?* You'll probably want to spend time with kids around your own age.

✻ *Is it an overnight camp or day camp?*

✻ *Are the instructors licensed? With which organization? How much experience have they had?*

✻ *What is the ratio of staff to campers?* ACA requires different ratios for different ages. Horseback riding should have a higher ratio, as it is considered a high-risk activity.

✻ *What's the background of the camp director?* He or she should have a college degree and camp administration experience.

✻ *What safety and medical provisions are available?*

Horse PLAY

STABLE SCAVENGER HUNT

Here's a good rainy-day barn activity and a way to keep younger horse campers or siblings amused. It's easy to set up — you simply need to make up a list of items to find, such as a horse with one white sock, a standing martingale, a set of purple polo wraps, or three horses with stars on their foreheads. These must be things that actually exist in your barn — but they don't have to be easy to find!

Photocopy your list, hand it out, and start the clock. The person who finds the most items wins a prize.

Use Scavenger Hunt to teach good barn manners. As excited as kids may be to win the prize, it's important that they keep voices down, not surprise horses in their stalls, and leave all equipment hung up neatly out of the way. Points may be deducted for violations.

* *How many campers and staff return each year?* This gives a clue to how satisfied people are. A good rate for returning staff is 40 to 60 percent — if it's lower, try to find out why.

* *What exactly does tuition cover? Will there be extra charges for certain activities?*

In addition to asking all these questions, try to visit the camp before you sign up. The pictures in that fancy brochure might have been taken a long time ago! It's also okay to ask for the names of previous campers you can contact to get a sense of their experience.

And contact a local vet. Find out if the camp horses are generally healthy, sound, and experienced. Happy and healthy horses are usually safer.

Making the Most of Horse Camp

Don't be too picky about the horse you're assigned to ride. The short ones, the fat ones, the dumpy ones, all have their own great qualities, or they wouldn't be there. Get to know your horse and find out what her virtues are.

Even if your horse is a bit of a disappointment at first, remind yourself that all excellent riders have ridden a lot of not-so-excellent horses along the way. Every horse has something to teach you.

However, don't be afraid to speak up if you are uncomfortable. If your horse is much too easy for you, or much too difficult, talk to your instructor. If things are going on in your cabin or socially that don't seem right, have a private talk with a counselor.

Don't work so hard that you don't have fun. But don't have so much fun that you don't learn, or that you interfere with other people learning.

Be helpful to the adults who are working hard to make this a good experience. It's not easy, and good camp citizenship can make a big difference. Follow the rules and listen to the counselors and teachers.

Be yourself and be nice. If you feel shy, remember that many other campers probably feel the same way. Sometimes shyness can be mistaken for snobbishness. Be friendly and see how people respond.

If you love your camp but are starting to foresee the day when you'll be too old for it, find out what it takes to be a camp counselor or instructor. Maybe you don't have to outgrow camp after all!

Breed Bits

THE MORGAN
America's "Can-Do" Horse

There was a time when Morgans did everything Vermont farmers needed. They took the farmer to market on Saturday and the family to church on Sunday; pulled logs and plows and hay wagons all week. And on Friday night—time to party! Trotting race? Sure. Running race? Bring 'em on! Morgans were the original Jack-of-all-trades equine, and their cheerful willingness to "try anything once" exactly suited the mood of Vermont's early settlers.

AN ORIGINAL AMERICAN

Every Morgan horse is descended from one stallion, a 14-hand bay given to a singing teacher named Justin Morgan in 1792 to settle a debt. The horse turned out to be a great puller, trotter, runner, and sire, tackling every challenge cheerfully and willingly. He was named Figure, but came to be called "Justin Morgan's horse," then just "Justin Morgan."

Morgans were great driving horses, used for both transportation and racing. But over time the Standardbred — faster, but not as pretty — replaced the Morgan on the racetrack. Automobiles replaced them on the roads. The breed was disappearing in the late 1870s when Colonel Joseph Battell and the University of Vermont established the Vermont Morgan Farm at Weybridge.

At first they bred Morgans as cavalry mounts; the Vermont Hundred Mile Trail Ride was established to test cavalry horse stamina, and Morgans dominated it in the early years. Today they are show horses and pleasure horses, saddle horses and driving horses. Some work cattle, and a few still pull logs and do some farm work. A related breed, the Morab, is a cross between Morgans and Arabians. It was developed in California to work cattle, and is now a beautiful pleasure and driving horse.

LOOKING AT MORGANS

The Morgan is a compact, powerful horse, with a beautiful head; high, arched neck; long sloping shoulder; well-sprung ribs; and a deep body. He has sturdy legs and excellent feet, and often shows high-stepping action. Morgans range between 14.1 and 15.2 hands, and weigh between 1,000 and 1,300 pounds. The most common colors are bay, chestnut, and black, but palominos and other more exotic colors have been developed. This is an intelligent, cheerful, friendly, and gentle breed.

FAMOUS MORGANS

- *Black Hawk:* Champion trotting horse and great sire
- *Ethan Allen:* Model for the Morgan weathervanes that top many New England barns
- *Comanche:* The only survivor left on the battlefield after the Battle of Little Big Horn

Help and Hope Through Horses

On a horse, human athletes become larger, faster, and stronger. If we're disabled, horses have even greater power to expand us past our limits. Helping to make that happen is the mission of the North American Riding for the Handicapped Association (NARHA). Each year, NARHA programs help more than 30,000 people with disabilities find joy and healing through riding, driving, or other contact with horses.

Why horses? Many people with disabilities are horse lovers. Beyond that, riding is good for people with physical limitations. A horse gently and rhythmically moves the rider's body in a way that's a lot like walking. If you can't walk, or if you walk with difficulty, that motion is priceless. The brain also benefits from the gentle alternate motions of the legs walking or being lifted and gently dropped by the swaying of a horse's barrel. Contact with horses builds confidence, patience, and self-esteem.

Horseback riding provides many health benefits: improved balance and coordination, increased muscle tone and flexibility, increased range of motion, improved respiration and circulation, improved appetite and digestion, increased body strength and stamina, and faster reflexes.

Those are the clinical reasons, but here is what it means to real families. Terri Handy, program director for Miracles in Motion in southern New Hampshire, says, "Parents come to us in tears saying: 'My child never smiles.' One mom with a little guy said he didn't have a sense of humor until he started to interact with me and the horse." Therapeutic riding is all about love, over-

coming fears, and feeling the magic of horses.

How You Can Help

Want to help bring a smile to a child's face for the first time? It's simple. Handicapped riding programs need lots of volunteers: fundraisers, stall muckers, exercise riders, side walkers, and leaders. Contact local child development services centers or NARHA to find nearby handicapped riding programs.

For horseless horsemen, this is a chance to be close to horses while improving people's lives. You can be part of someone's healing, and you can help the hardworking horses, too. This is a high-stress job. Even good therapy horses can sour on it without pampering and downtime. Taking therapy horses for relaxing rides and keeping them in condition can be one of the rewards for a responsible volunteer.

Another way to help is by donating a suitable horse. A good therapy horse is a jewel. Ideal therapy horses are 8 to 15 years old, calm, athletic, and sensible. Any breed, from pony to draft horse can be used as a therapy horse, which makes a fine second career for a horse or pony you've outgrown. If you want to maintain ownership and control, you may be able to arrange a free lease arrangement with a NARHA program.

CHECKING CREDENTIALS

NARHA's Premier Accredited Center Program lets handicapped riding centers demonstrate excellence through a peer review system judged by trained volunteers.

There are three levels of instructor certification: Registered, Advanced, and Master. There are also specialty discipline certifications for driving and interactive vaulting. Teachers at centers

☼ HORSE ☼ RIDING CAN HELP

Therapeutic riding can assist an exceptionally wide variety of people with many different needs, including those with:

- ☼ muscular dystrophy
- ☼ cerebral palsy
- ☼ visual impairment
- ☼ Down syndrome
- ☼ mental retardation
- ☼ autism
- ☼ multiple sclerosis
- ☼ spina bifida
- ☼ emotional disturbances
- ☼ brain and spinal cord injuries
- ☼ amputation
- ☼ learning disabilities
- ☼ attention-deficit disorder
- ☼ deafness
- ☼ stroke

are required to achieve at least one level, as well as having skills and knowledge in equine management, horsemanship, instruction, teaching methodology, and disabilities. Contact NARHA for more about becoming an instructor.

LEARN ABOUT OTHER NARHA PROGRAMS

If you, a family member, or a friend are dealing with a handicap, NARHA may be able to help. Beyond therapy, NARHA programs offer opportunities to ride and compete at the local, state, national, and international levels.

At the upper levels of sports for disabled equestrians is the Paralympics (see page 270). There's a handicapped division of Cowboy Mounted Shooting (see page 252), and many other sports offer chances to compete as well.

Equine Facilitated Psychotherapy (EFP) is an experiential form of psychotherapy. It can incorporate activities like handling, grooming, longing, riding, driving, and vaulting. An EFP therapist needs to be a licensed credentialed mental health worker as well as a credentialed equine professional.

Driving can be a great activity for those whose handicaps don't allow them to ride, even with help. The client handles the reins on a special halter. The instructor has reins that attach to the bit, and can take control if needed. Driving lets many handicapped horsemen compete on equal footing with the nonhandicapped.

 HORSES FOR HEROES

Four Percherons who usually pull the caissons for military funerals at Fort Myers, Virginia, have a happier job these days. They work at Walter Reed Army Medical Center in Washington, DC, in a therapeutic riding program for veterans who've lost limbs.

Working with the horses brings wounded soldiers out into the fresh air, and gives them a sense of freedom and independence.

There are also big emotional benefits: Soldiers gain a sense of accomplishment, increased self-esteem, and that intangible boost from bonding with an animal. The horses bring back wounded soldiers' smiles — just as they bring smiles to every horse lover.

The program at Walter Reed is part of a movement that's catching on around the country. As of 2007, there were close to 20 NARHA centers working on programs with Veterans Affairs offices, and NARHA is launching a nationwide program called Horses for Heroes.

THE AMERICAN SADDLEBRED
Easy-Gaited Elegance

If you were inventing the ideal horse, what would he be like? Gorgeous, right? And smart, and easy gaited, and good tempered — you're probably thinking, "Dream on!" Well, you can open your eyes. That horse is real. You could own one.

The American Saddlebred was developed by Kentucky pioneers who wanted a useful horse with lots of style. They had good bloodlines to work with — Morgans, Narragansett Pacers, Canadians, and Spanish stock. Out of this mix came a type of horse originally called the Kentucky Saddler. The horses were handsome, with easy gaits and astonishing endurance. They made stylish buggy horses, but their greatest importance was as a saddle horse. On a Saddlebred you could go a long way down a bad road, and reach your destination in style (and without a sore backside!).

During the Civil War countless Saddlebreds served as cavalry horses. When the war was over the surviving horses returned to a more pleasant life, carrying people with great style, and impressing them in the show ring, as they do to this day. Outside of the show ring they do everything every other light horse does — trail riding, pleasure riding, driving, parades, even working cattle. Saddlebreds are plenty tough, too. Until 2008 a Saddlebred held the record for most miles travelled in competitive trail rides.

LOOKING AT SADDLEBREDS

American Saddlebreds are beautiful, with chiseled heads, long arched necks, and strong, deep bodies. They range from 15 to 17 hands, and weigh 1,000 to 1,200 pounds. They are built high, carry their heads and tails high, and step high. All colors are allowed, including palomino and pinto.

The special gaits of the Saddlebred are the slow gait (sometimes called the stepping pace) and the rack. They are actually variations of the walk, though you wouldn't guess that to watch them, as the horse lifts and extends his knees with great exaggeration. Besides speed, the differences lie in the percentage of time that each foot stays on the ground in each stride.

✷ CIVIL WAR ✷ SADDLEBREDS

General Ulysses S. Grant of the United States Army and General Robert E. Lee of the Confederate States Army rode Saddlebreds. Do you suppose their horses, Cincinnati and Traveler, met at Appomattox, when Lee surrendered to Grant? What might they have said to each other?

Riding for Everyone: Para-Equestrian

Para-Equestrian is the eighth FEI discipline and has been part of the Paralympic Games since 1996. Dressage and driving are the two sports currently offered under FEI rules; they are governed by the same principles as other FEI disciplines.

Impairments come in many degrees. To ensure fairness, competitors are leveled through the "profile system" and must be assessed by accredited classifiers — either physical therapists or doctors. There are five grades for dressage competitors and two for drivers.

Dressage competitors, depending on impairment, may ride tests at the walk only, at walk and trot, or at all three gaits, with or without lateral movements. Driving competitors must be accompanied at all times by an able-bodied and competent driver.

Rules are currently being developed for Para-Equestrian show jumping and doubtless will come for other disciplines as well. Paralympics is a growing sport: currently there are 650 riders from 38 countries, and 16 international competitions.

As with all sports at international levels, there's a lot of discipline, training, luck, and money involved — but other people have done it, and maybe you can, too!

Horseshoe REVIEW

Casey Jones Rides Vanity
by Marion Holland (1964)

It's becoming painfully obvious to Casey that she's outgrown her pony, Topnotch. She's not ready to pass him on, though, even in the family. But at a show she plays a mental game: If I could have any horse here, which one would I choose? The game ends when she sees the beautiful mare Vanity.

In conversation with Vanity's owner, it turns out that the mare has possibly been abused and that mistreatment results in a bad jumping accident. With Vanity's owner on her way to the hospital, Casey ends up taking Vanity home, rehabilitating her, and falling in love with a horse that belongs to someone else. But don't worry — there's a happy ending to this warm story.

PART THREE

In the Spotlight

The Arts, the Environment, and Some Equine Extras

When I was a kid, we just played with our horse models, making up stories about them as we clumped them along the floor. Nowadays the model horse world offers so much more.

A Model of Perfection

There are shows around the country sanctioned by the North American Model Horse Shows Association, where you can compete for points and the opportunity to show at the North American Nationals (held in Lexington, Kentucky, in odd years, and in Ontario,

Canada, in even years). Model manufacturers like Breyer and Stone hold annual model horse festivals, and at every horse expo worth its salt you'll find opportunities to paint models and learn more about the model horse hobby.

In addition to buying accurate, detailed models of many different breeds, including some pretty exotic ones, you can customize blank models with paint, change their positions with tools, and even buy kits to sculpt your own models and create your own tack. You can also buy rid-

ers, tack, jumps and cavaletti; barns complete with hay, grain, stable-cleaning equipment, grooming kits, and farrier tools. It's a fascinating, absorbing hobby and, oh yes, you can drop a lot of money on it, just as you can with real horses.

And, also as with real horses, you can show them. There are two kinds of model horse shows: photographed and "live." In a photographed show you position your horse and props in a scene. Then you take a picture and send it, by e-mail or regular mail, to the contest judges.

Live shows usually take place in a large hall. Owners exhibit their models live and in person — the horses, alas, don't come to life. To participate in a live show, contact the North American Model Horse Shows Association to find an event near you. Send for a show packet, which will give class lists and requirements. Showing and cus-

Horse PLAY

HOLD A HORSELESS HORSESHOW

If you and your friends don't have horses — or some do and some don't — you can still enjoy showing. Stage a horseless horse show with jumping classes, a barrel race, whatever seems fun and doable. Real horse show rules must be followed. "Riders" must pass left shoulder to left shoulder in the ring, make proper round circles, and follow all patterns correctly. No tailgating allowed! A Pairs Class or Ribbon Class allows competitors to work together.

tomizing can be done with all sizes of model horse.

What to Expect at a Model Show

Models are shown in halter and performance classes.

Halter classes are usually breed classes. Within halter there are two divisions — Original Finish (OF) and Customized (CM). OF models are judged on how well they meet breed standards, as well as the condition of the model, its color, finish, and rarity or collectibility. CM

models are judged on how well the artist has reworked and improved the original model to look like the breed.

Performance classes have horses set up in the ring with miniature tack and props. Judging is based on the realism of the set-up, and how capable the horse looks of accomplishing the task — be it a dressage test or a cutting class.

Showing model horses takes a lot of organization. Plan to bring only your best models and only a few of them. Don't overwhelm yourself. You'll want time to look at other people's exhibits, swap information and materials, and make notes on how to improve your showing abilities.

At the show you'll be given a home table. That's your "stable." The "rings" are large tables, usually in the center of the hall. When a class is announced, you'll bring your models to the ring, where you'll place them and their props in the best place you can find to catch the judge's eye. You may wait and watch the judging, as long as you stand back out of the way and don't talk to the judge or to your friends. But chances are you'll be competing several models and will have to hurry away to take another entry to another class. Here are some tips for successful positioning and good show etiquette:

* Choose a spot with good lighting.

* Make sure your horse's best side is turned toward the judge.

The Horse Whisperer
(1998, rated PG-13)

Fourteen-year-old Grace is badly injured in a terrifying accident that leaves her and her horse, Pilgrim, physically and emotionally scarred. When Grace's mother hears of a special horseman who may be able to help, the three embark on a long trip west to seek redemption.

The horsemanship techniques, at least in theory, are based on those of master horsemen like Tom Dorrance, who pioneered the natural horsemanship techniques being promoted today by trainers like Monty Roberts, John Lyons, and Pat Parelli.

Because this movie purports to be about a specific training method, it's worth pointing out that some aspects are controversial. A good horse doesn't turn rogue after a single accident, for instance, and a rogue horse is not "cured" by being worn out, tied down, and sat upon.

Enjoy this movie as a story, remembering that real trainers, including Buck Brannaman, who consulted for the movie, are much more subtle, flexible, and safety oriented than the demands of filmmaking will allow.

- Position your horse at least 8 inches from other models, if possible.

- Never pick up or move another competitor's horse.

- Don't place your horse so it blocks the judge's view of someone else's horse.

- Place your horse and props quickly and quietly, and leave the ring as soon as you've finished.

Several classes may be judged at once at larger model shows. Pay attention, and remove your entries once ribbons have been awarded. It's a good idea to keep a checklist of your scores with each horse. You may need to bring a model back into the ring for a championship round. See Resources (page 358) for more ways to learn about model showing.

YOU COULD BE HOOKED!

Model horses are less expensive than real horses, and there's no manure to clean up and no vet bills. But this can still be a costly hobby. People don't usually stop at one, or even a dozen, model horses and then you need a barn, corral, fake grass and snow, tack, and more.

A model show may be lacking something in the sweat, manure, runaways, and whinnying departments. But competing successfully takes attention to detail and to the rules, a lot of organization, and an instinct for showmanship; it's good preparation for competing with a real horse.

If you're a seriously horse-deprived person, or a horse-lover with allergies, model horses can help fill the gap. They're beautiful and quite realistic-looking. Through a model-horse hobby you can learn a lot about the real thing. And if you're a hands-on horseman who knows a lot, your knowledge can help you excel at showing models.

Pony Tales

A REAL GEM

During the Middle Ages, Europeans believed that wearing a turquoise gem would protect a rider from being thrown and his horse from becoming overtired.

THE FUN STUFF — FINDING AND MAKING PROPS

Finding and making props is a big part of the model horse hobby, and an important part of successful model horse showing. It's also one of the most fun and creative parts.

Study *Just About Horses (JAH)*, the model horse magazine. Look at magazine photos of the real thing, too. What do jump courses look like these days? What kind of tack does a Peruvian Paso wear? Authenticity of tack and props is important — get the details right!

You'll find yourself looking at all kinds of small doodads, knickknacks, even trash and wondering, "What can I make with that?" Here are some examples (you can probably think of many more):

* Soup cans make good barrels.

* Restaurant coffee creamers make great flowerpots or buckets.

* A mesh garlic bag filled with dried grass can be a hay net.

* A cardboard soapbox covered with hay and tied around with twine makes a nice hay bale.

* A round shoelace with the plastic tips cut off and knotted becomes a lead rope.

* The orange tops of glue bottles can be road cones.

* Cut a washcloth into smaller pieces to make towels.

* Moss; sticks; dry, crumbled pine needles; and stones from the yard help create a natural scene.

* For snow, try cotton batting, sugar, rice, or flour.

* A mirror with the edges disguised serves as a pond or puddle.

* Go to a store where flours and grains are sold in bulk. Look at what's available. Bulgur for the grain in a bucket? Semolina or steel-cut oats for sand?

* Make board fences out of painted craft sticks, rail fences out of twigs, and electric fence out of slender white dowels and white yarn (or flat shoelaces for electric tape).

You'll need to build up a good supply of craft materials and supplies. Keep on hand wooden dowels of various thicknesses, wooden craft sticks, paint, brushes, glue, and tiny nails. Also cardboard in various thicknesses, scraps of cloth, wire, etc. Especially etc.

Hone your yard-sale skills. Visit shops that specialize in dollhouses and miniatures, model train shops, and slot-car racing shops. These are all good sources for in-scale hinges, bricks, trees, and traffic signs.

SET UP YOUR OWN ☼ SCHOOLING SHOW ☼

You don't have to wait for a scheduled model horse show. Why not put on a schooling show, like dressage riders do to help themselves and their novice horses get ready for prime time?

To make it more authentic, send for the show packet of an upcoming show. Invite some friends to study it and decide together how closely you want to follow the rules. Then schedule your show, get your models ready, and make some snacks to share. If you know an experienced model shower you could ask him or her to judge. Or decide to just critique one another.

Prepare to become quite good at building and painting very small things!

Setting the Scene

When you create a scene, the background is important, as are all the tiny details. Paint a background — sky or trees, or a scene that relates to the theme of the contest — a roundup or a horse show.

In a Christmas scene, did Santa fill the horses' stockings? Make sure there are tiny apples or carrots in there. How about a Christmas tree? It would look great with little lights on it.

Simplicity can be a winner, too. A single dark horse in deep, fluffy snow, set against a background of fir trees with snow on his back and a wreath around his neck, can say Christmas just as well. Depending on the scale of your model, flour might make good snow, or rice might mound more realistically. Take pictures both ways and see which looks best.

Customizing Your Model Horse

Customizing takes the hobby of model horses to a new level, and lets you be the creator of the horse as well as the set. It can also be nerve-wracking and just a little gruesome. Put your horse into near-boiling water? And then take a saw to him? Gross!

Luckily he's not a real horse, but this is still a big deal and there's a lot to learn. Before you put the pot on to boil and get out the hacksaw, do some studying. Read back issues of *Just About Horses*. Go on the Breyer Web site and familiarize yourself with the process. It's very involved. Besides heating, cutting, and bending your model, you will sometimes have to fill in the gaps you create with wallboard filler. This needs to dry for several days before it can be filed and sculpted.

And then you'll be painting. Again, this is quite a specialty. Read up on all your options and do a lot of practicing before you try a new material or technique on your favorite model. Acrylic paints are cheap and challenging: they dry very fast. Oil paints are gooey, smelly, more toxic than acrylics, and dry slowly — giving you more time to make changes; they're also very rich and beautiful. Some artists use pastels, others use airbrushed acrylics; all have advantages and disadvantages.

Pony Tales

LUCKY MARKS

A horse with two white hind feet and a star on the forehead is considered lucky in France.

✳ FAMOUS HORSE MODELS ✳

Many models are based on famous horses, recent or from long ago.

- ✳ *Scamper:* Barrel racing champion
- ✳ *Man O' War:* Racehorse
- ✳ *Smarty Jones:* Racehorse
- ✳ *Theodore O'Connor:* Event horse
- ✳ *Kennebec Count:* Morgan driving horse
- ✳ *Black Hand:* POA foundation stallion

HORSE TALK AROUND THE WORLD

It's a great idea to know another language, but they don't always teach you the important stuff right up front. Here's a chance to brush up on your horse-related language skills.

ENGLISH	SPANISH	FRENCH	GERMAN
Horse	el caballo	le cheval	das Pferd
Pony	el poni, petiso	le poney	das Kleinpferd
Stallion	el semental	l'étalon	der Beschäler
Colt	el potro	le poulain	der Junghengst
Mare	la yegua	la jument	die Stute
Filly	la potra	la pouliche	die junge Stute
Hoof	el casco	le sabot	der Fuss
Mane	las crines	la criniére	die Mähne
The walk	el camino, paseo	le pas	der Schritt
The trot	el trote	le trot	der Trab
Colic	el colico	la colique	die Kolik
To mount	montar	se mettre en selle	aufsitzen
To dismount	desmontar	mettre pied à terre	absitzen
Stall	el establo	la stalle	der Stand
Saddle	la silla	la selle	die Sattel
Stirrup	el estribo	l'étrier	der Steigbügel
Reins	las riendas	les rênes	die Zügel

THE LITTLE GUYS:
Four Popular Pony Breeds

What exactly is a pony? The general definition is "a type of horse that stands 14.2 hands or less when full grown," but it's not that simple. The Caspian, at 10 to 12 hands, is a horse and looks like one. The American Miniature, 38 inches or under, is also called a horse, and some look like horses, while others look very much like ponies.

It's all about proportion. A pony is longer than it is tall. Depth of heart-girth equals length of the leg. The head length equals the shoulder length, and the shoulder length equals the back length. A pony is round, sturdy, cute, with small pointed ears, large eyes, and packs a lot of power in a small package.

CONNEMARA PONY

ORIGIN: West coast of Ireland

THEIR STORY: Wild ponies have lived in Britain since the Ice Age. This breed was developed from wild native ponies crossed with imported Andalusians and Spanish Barbs. The Irish used their ponies for carting, driving, and hunting.

DESCRIPTION: 13–14.2 hands; a straight head and long, well-formed neck; long back, deep, wide chest, and muscular sloped croup; excellent legs and hooves; gray and dun are the most common colors; the dense, plushy coat keeps out rain. They are hardy, agile, and intelligent.

GOOD AT: Jumping, hunting, dressage, eventing, competitive driving, light draft, trail

A FAMOUS CONNEMARA: *Cannon Ball*, the first stallion registered in the Connemara studbook, won the Farmer's race at Oughterard for 16 years in a row, and frequently brought his sleeping master home from market. His death was marked with an all-night Irish wake.

PONY OF THE AMERICAS (POA)

ORIGIN: Iowa

THEIR STORY: In 1954 an Arabian-Appaloosa mare gave birth to a foal sired by a Shetland. The colt was white with large black spots. Because the marks on his flank formed the shape of a hand, he was named Black Hand. His owner decided to form a breed of children's pony around this unique colt. He used small Appaloosas, Arabians, Welsh and Shetland ponies, and spotted ponies from Mexico and South America to create one of the few breeds developed especially for kids.

DESCRIPTION: 11.2–14.2 hands; a small Arab head with a muscular, Quarter Horse–type body; bold Appaloosa coloring must be visible from 40 feet away; easy to work with and train.

FUN FACT: POAs are shown in many disciplines, but POA showing is strictly for kids.

SHETLAND PONY

ORIGIN: Shetland Islands, north of Scotland, possibly from Scandinavian roots

THEIR STORY: Ponies arrived in the Shetlands 10,000 years ago during the Ice Age. One of the oldest breeds, they lived wild for centuries, then carried peat for small farmers — they could carry over half their weight for several miles. They are extremely sure-footed and hardy and need very little to eat, living on scanty grass and seaweed. Later, many Shetlands were exported to work underground in English coal mines. Their numbers dwindled, until they became popular as children's ponies in the 19th century.

DESCRIPTION: There are three Shetland types, all under 11.2 hands. The original British type has short legs and back, thick neck, very small ears; dense coat with a heavy mane and tail. The North American "Classic" Shetland is stocky but well balanced, a bit smoother and longer-legged than the British type. The "Modern American" Shetland has Welsh and Hackney bloodlines to create a high-stepping, driving pony, with a more refined body and a high arched neck.

GOOD AT: Pleasure, showing, jumping, driving

FUN FACT: There's a Shetland Grand National held every December in Britain, and Shetlands take part in point-to-point events in the United States, too.

WELSH PONY

ORIGIN: Wales

THEIR STORY: Ponies lived in Britain before Roman times, but the Romans imported Oriental horses, which gave the Welsh Pony its Arab-like appearance. When King Henry VIII wanted to encourage the breeding of large war horses and ordered all horses under 15 hands destroyed, Welsh farmers simply turned their ponies loose and retrieved them years later when the danger was past. Later, ponies were crossed with draft breeds to create the Welsh Cob, the all-purpose horse of Wales for centuries.

Horseshoe REVIEW

Ponies Plot
by C. Northcote Parkinson (1965)

This is the funny and gripping story of what happens when a riding teacher gets married and sells off her ponies. The ponies make grand plans (they are the kind of ponies that talk when no people are around).

Some of the plans work out; others go wildly astray. One pony ends up in space; one does hard time giving pony rides at a beach. Eventually everyone finds a happy ending.

DESCRIPTION: Welsh Ponies come in four types, ranging from under 12 hands to 13.2 hands and up. Handsome, sturdy, versatile; especially beautiful head with large eyes, small pricked ears, straight or dished profile; natural jumpers.

GOOD AT: Jumping, pleasure driving, combined driving, trail, children's pleasure

FUN FACT: A Welsh Pony, *Cefnoakpark Bouncer*, driven by Suzy Stafford, was the first U.S. entry to win gold in an FEI driving competition (2005). A Breyer model has been made of Bouncer.

How to Write Horse Stories

If you like to read horse stories, maybe you'd like to write them too. Writing is a lot like reading — and like riding. You start on a journey. Maybe you don't quite know where you're going. Certainly you don't know everything that will happen along the way. As when you climb on a horse and set out on a trail some sunny morning, you're in for an adventure.

The best horse stories have plenty of action: catching horses, training them, riding them, or winning ribbons on them. As a writer, your job is to grab the reader's attention and hold it throughout the story. The first thing you need is a strong beginning.

Off to a Good Start

There are as many ways to start a story as there are writers. One way is with a great line. Maybe you don't even know what it means at first, or what's happening in the scene.

Sid Fleischman begins *Mr. Mysterious and Company* that way: "It was a most remarkable sight. Even the hawks and buzzards sleeping in the blue Texas sky awoke in midair to glance down in wonder." When he started writing, Sid didn't have a clue what those birds were glancing at. But by asking himself questions about the characters, setting, and what could possibly happen next, he came up with a story.

This is a fun way to write. If you have an intriguing line teasing at the back of your mind, write it down. Then write the next line, and the next. Stories want to get out, and this is how they coax us to write them.

Other writers prefer knowing where they're going and what will happen before they start. They outline, plan scenes, and choose the scene that will make the best beginning.

So what makes a good beginning?

* Start the character's day in an unusual way.

* Start with the day when everything changes.

* Set something in motion. Don't stop for explanations.

What Makes a Good Story?

First of all, you should be able to state the basics simply, as in the following examples. *The Black Stallion:* Boy and wild stallion marooned on a desert island. *Chase:* Boy framed for murder flees, pursued by two men and a mysterious horse. *Afraid to Ride:* Injured girl and horse cure each other's fears.

Secondly, stories need conflict. A good story is about someone you like, in some kind of trouble. She needs something, desperately, and there are lots of obstacles in the way of her getting it.

WORRY THE READER

Stories are about trouble of one sort or another. Even the gentlest stories must have some tension — something the reader hopes for and fears. The reader needs some *person* to worry about, and some *thing* to worry about. Trust me, readers *want* to worry. They want to

Horseshoe REVIEW

In a Class of Her Own: Marguerite Henry (1902–1997)

Marguerite Henry wrote many books about significant horses, particular breeds, or specific equine events. She was a brilliant stylist who wrote crisply, cleanly, and with memorable cadence. Most of her books were illustrated by the equally brilliant Wesley Dennis. Illustrations and text work together to create some of the most memorable moments in children's literature.

Henry also let readers visit other cultures. *King of the Wind* was the first place I ever heard of Ramadan, and it created a hunger and thirst in me to learn more about Islam, and for one of those juicy oranges Signor Achmet eats.

If you only read a few of Marguerite Henry's books, these are the most important: *Misty of Chincoteague* (see page 83), *King of the Wind* (see page 191), and *Justin Morgan Had a Horse* (see page 58). But why stop there? Each one is a great read:

* *Album of Horses*
* *All About Horses*
* *Black Gold*
* *Born to Trot*
* *Brighty of the Grand Canyon*
* *Five O'Clock Charlie*
* *Gaudenzia, Pride of the Palio*
* *The Little Fellow*
* *The Medicine Hat Stallion*
* *Misty's Twilight*
* *Mustang — Wild Spirit of the West*
* *Our First Pony*
* *Sea Star, Orphan of Chincoteague*
* *Stormy, Misty's Foal*
* *White Stallion of Lipizza*

sit wide-eyed, glued to the page. They want to be so engrossed that if their mom says, "I think the refrigerator just exploded," they answer, "That's nice . . ."

The someone-to-worry-about is the main character. In a horse story there's often a pair of main characters: a horse and the young person who loves, wants, or possibly fears him.

PUT YOUR CHARACTER IN CRISIS

For readers to worry about your main character, they need to like him or her, or at least suspect that they're going to. That means the first introduction is important. Show the character doing something. (Sleeping is *not* doing something. Neither is waking up, unless she's waking up because the smoke alarm just went off.)

And that something should be important to the story; something that shows who she is. Let it be an action or event that'll get her in some kind of trouble — soon. Remember, stories are about trouble. The trouble should start as soon as possible. For example:

It was risky, but Gwen couldn't help it. It was study hall, her work was done, and she had nothing to do but miss Corky. The bag was in her pack — perfectly sealed, she had checked! — and the other kids were working, or pretending to. She should be able to get away with it.

She bent over her pack, silently unzipped it, and pulled out the plastic bag, slid the yellow plastic lock back just half an inch, and gave a little squeeze. Out puffed the aroma of home, of barnyard, of Corky. She could see his round pony shape in her mind's eye, hear his nicker —

"Gwen!" Maya hissed from the seat behind her. "What you got?" Mrs. Maxwell didn't hear, but everyone else did. Heads turned. Bored eyes brightened. Olivia, at the front of the room, scribbled rapidly and held up a note. "Cookies? I'll be yr frnd 4ever!"

Gwen crushed the bag into her lap. She hadn't even noticed the gentle, rustling sound of snacks being munched. Now the treats were being held up enticingly. All the faces looked her way, cheerful and friendly as a pony looking at a can of grain. The bag dropped from Gwen's numb fingers and spilled into the aisle. Maya stared in horror.

"Eee-yu! That looks like horse manure!"

Gwen's in trouble already, at the bottom of the first page. Why is she sniffing a plastic bag of dried horse manure? It's because she's homesick, horsesick, and imprisoned at boarding school, which is just about to become *much* more miserable.

Do we know that yet? No. We don't even know who Gwen is, let alone Corky.

That's another thing about good beginnings. They just start. The names float out there unsupported for a while. The page isn't clogged with the characters' whole biographies. Good fiction trusts itself to hook the reader. She'll be dragged deep into the story, where the background can be filled in gradually and naturally. Like this:

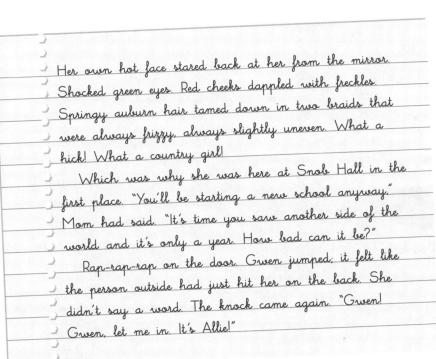

Her own hot face stared back at her from the mirror. Shocked green eyes. Red cheeks dappled with freckles. Springy auburn hair tamed down in two braids that were always frizzy, always slightly uneven. What a hick! What a country girl!

Which was why she was here at Snob Hall in the first place. "You'll be starting a new school anyway," Mom had said. "It's time you saw another side of the world and it's only a year. How bad can it be?"

Rap-rap-rap on the door. Gwen jumped; it felt like the person outside had just hit her on the back. She didn't say a word. The knock came again. "Gwen! Gwen, let me in. It's Allie!"

MAKE IT THROUGH THE MIDDLE

The middle can be the hardest part of a story. You jump in with a good line and good characters — and now what? Remember: worry your reader. Afflict your character. Things need to go from bad to worse. Your character will need to face challenges. She'll have to lose sometimes, get hurt, even fight.

She'll need something, or someone, to fight; something she needs or wants, and a major obstacle in the way of getting it. And a subplot can help. Without the complications it brings, your story might be too simple and lack energy.

Here's our story so far: Gwen, a country girl stuck at a high-class boarding school, misses her pony so much she even brings a bag of pony poop to class. When she gets caught sniffing it, everybody teases her even more than before. Okay, but now what?

There are lots of possibilities. Maybe another girl who's also being teased wants to be friends with Gwen. Gwen doesn't like her and thinks that's a bad basis for a friendship, but this girl is the daughter of the school's stable manager. If Gwen plays her cards right, maybe she can bring Corky next semester.

Or maybe that night, as Gwen cries herself to sleep, she hears a snort outside her window. (Make it a fourth-story window.) What can that be? Gwen goes to look and finds a winged pony nuzzling at the latch. Further adventures are bound to ensue in this scenario, like what will school officials think when the rain gutter atop a four-story building is blocked by pony poop?

ENGAGE YOUR READER

Writing is a collaboration. You put some words down on a page. The reader looks at those little black marks and out of the clues you've given, she creates a movie in her head. If your clues are good enough, you create a virtual reality for your reader.

Stories take place in the world. How do we know where we are? We can *see*. Not only see, we hear, smell, touch, even taste the places around

Pony Tales

FAIRY TALES

If a horse lacks energy and seems tired all the time, it's possible he's being ridden at night by witches or fairies. Dreadlocks in a horse's mane are a sign that the fairies have been visiting. They tangle the mane into stirrups, and ride in great numbers.

us. Good stories appeal to all our senses — not all five in every scene, but enough to keep the reader interested.

To create a full experience you must give sensory clues. What can the character see, hear, smell? The character is the reader's virtual-reality glove. If the character doesn't experience something or the writer doesn't describe it, then the reader can't experience it.

Here's an example:

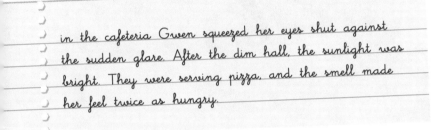

in the cafeteria Gwen squeezed her eyes shut against the sudden glare. After the dim hall, the sunlight was bright. They were serving pizza, and the smell made her feel twice as hungry.

This line uses the reader's own experience. We all know what pizza smells like — no need to describe it. We've all been hungry — no need to go into detail about that, either. Now if this was Mongolia and it was a lovely pot of kumiss Gwen was smelling, the reader would only have half a clue. This is one of the things that makes historical fiction hard to do well.

MAKE YOUR CHARACTERS REAL

One easy way to make your narrator real is to make him or her struggle in a way that the reader will identify with. But you have to remember what you've created. If Gwen sprains her ankle on page three of this story, she's not going to be running on page eight. Hobbling, maybe, but not without saying "Ow!" with every step. (If the narrator is a horse, this rule applies to him or her, too.)

～ SOME GOOD BOOKS ～ ABOUT WRITING

* *The Elements of Style*, by William Strunk, Jr., and E. B. White (4th edition, 1999)
* *The Abracadabra Kid, a Writer's Life*, by Sid Fleischman (1996)
* *Blood on the Forehead: What I Know About Writing*, by M. E. Kerr (1998)
* *If You Want to Write*, by Brenda Ueland (1938)

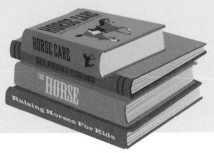

Another important element is to write realistic dialogue. This can be quite a challenge. Try to write as though you are talking to your friends — your characters will sound more natural that way. But don't write exactly the way you talk. Those "ums" and "ya knows" that work fine when you talk don't work on a page.

Describing characters is where many authors walk a fine line. It's a classic cliché, but it works, to have the character look at herself in the mirror and bemoan her mousy hair or small eyes or whatever. But sometimes the main character is barely described at all. That character usually feels like a mask or identity that the reader puts on for the length of the story. You don't need a description of her, because she's you.

To make horses in stories seem real, think about what real horses are like. They do things you don't want them to do, like take fright at the sight of a blowing newspaper just when you're concentrating on a hard jump or a cute boy. They pass gas as you walk behind them. They step on you.

They also catch you unexpectedly with their beauty, just doing simple things like walking beside you, like drinking from a trough. Watch how a horse drinks; lips smiling on the surface of the water, the way you can see the lump of water course down the long throat, the way the ears twitch with every swallow. Don't forget how it sounds; *gnk, gnk, gnk.* Don't forget how they raise their heads, and the drips fall back into the water and make rings. Write it all down exactly. Don't leave out any details. Observation is what good writing is all about.

WINDING EVERYTHING UP

The story arc comes to completion — or you can see how it might end. A satisfying story arouses anxiety in the reader, and then reassures her convincingly. The reader needs to believe that the story would end just that way; that in fact, it's the only ending possible. Here's our story's end:

Gwen and Allie, the stable manager's daughter, struggle to keep the winged pony a secret, but he's too much fun — and there's only one of him. Trying to share one flying pony and survive boarding school at the same time means that one day they make a big mistake.

It turns out carrots don't agree with flying ponies; they're a root crop, after all, and they weigh the pony down. He gets stuck in a dangerous place, and without the help of the girl who's teased them most, Gwen and Allie will be unable to save him.

Horseshoe REVIEW

Black Beauty
by Anna Sewell (1877)

Sewell was an invalid who was dying when she dictated *Black Beauty* to her mother. The book is a plea for the humane treatment of horses, which were the engines of the economy in the 1800s. *Black Beauty* follows the fortune of a well-bred horse who is injured on the job and works his way steadily down the social ladder, ending up hauling a London cab and being hired out as a hack to brutal riders.

The book was intended for adults, but has always been loved by children. It's told in Beauty's voice, but many other horse and human characters speak as well. This classic of horse stories is lively and hard-hitting, and nowhere near as sentimental as you might expect. A good introduction to Victorian writers.

At story's end, the pony is safely down from the tree. He may never fly again, but he's a wonderful earthbound pony, and he and Allie have fallen in love. Meanwhile, Allie's mother and Gwen's have agreed: next week Corky's coming to school and every-thing's going to be a lot better.

Then, a big storm comes up; water begins pouring through the upper-floor ceilings. The rain gutter is apparently blocked, but by what? Gwen isn't admitting anything. Pony poop's gotten her in enough trouble already!

NEAR MISSES
Three Breeds on the Brink

Extinction doesn't just happen to dinosaurs. It happens to modern species and it happens to domestic animal breeds. Here are a few stories of success, failure, and suspense.

IRAN: THE CASPIAN

These tiny horses from northern Iran resemble chariot horses on the royal seal of King Darius the Great (521–486 BCE) and were mentioned in ancient writings as long ago as 600 CE. When chariots went out of favor, these horses were forgotten, but a remnant of the breed ran wild in the mountains near the Caspian Sea. American Louise Firouz rediscovered them in 1965 and gathered as many as she could find. As of 2005, there were 540 Caspians in the United States, with 75 foals registered per year, and small populations in Europe and Australia; they are probably extinct in their homeland. These ancient treasures rate American Livestock Breeds Conservancy's most urgent rating of Critical.

BAHAMAS: THE ABACO BARB

The Spaniards set up horse-breeding farms on many islands in the Bahamas in the 1600s, including the Island of Great Abaco. During the American Revolution, British loyalists moved to Abaco to wait out the war, bringing more Spanish horses with them. The island was later abandoned except for loggers and hunters, and the horses ran free, grazing with cattle where the island was turned into farmland and later living in the citrus orchards that eventually took over the land.

The conditions were not ideal for horses; they suffered from obesity and the effects of chemical fertilizers. In 2002 concerned horse lovers donated a forest preserve in an attempt to save the breed, but the forest is currently at risk as impoverished Haitians cut trees for firewood. No foals have been born for several years; the future of this breed is in doubt. In 2008, only eight Abaco Barbs remained on the island.

IRELAND: THE KERRY BOG PONY

Small, wild ponies have lived on the peat bogs of southwest Ireland for hundreds of years. They survived on heather and sphagnum moss and were able to travel through the treacherous marshes with ease, probably because they are lightweight and don't track up when they walk. That means the hind feet don't step into the footprints left by the front feet, which spreads their weight more evenly.

Local people caught them to carry the peat they burned in their houses and stoves. As donkeys became more popular pack animals in Ireland and peat became less important as a fuel, the ponies were abandoned to run wild again.

John Mulvihill of Kerry could find only 20 ponies in the 1990s. He established a small herd on his farm starting in 1994. Two Americans developed an interest in the breed and imported a small group to the United States, but only about 150 Kerry Bog Ponies exist worldwide. As of 2005, there were just 11 in the United States.

HOW MANY HORSES DOES IT TAKE
✸ TO CHANGE A LIGHTBULB? ✸

Various versions of this list have been going around the Internet for a while, but it's hard to figure out who started it. If you know, please tell me!

✸ **THOROUGHBRED**: Who ME?? Do WHAT? I'm scared of light bulbs! I'm outta here!

✸ **ARABIAN**: I changed it an hour ago. C'mon you guys — catch up!

✸ **QUARTER HORSE**: Put all the bulbs in a pen and tell me which one you want.

✸ **STANDARDBRED**: Oh, for Pete's sake, give me the darn bulb and let's be done with it.

✸ **SHETLAND**: Give it to me. I'll kill it and we won't have to worry about it anymore.

✸ **FRIESIAN**: I would, but I can't see where I'm going from behind all this mane.

✸ **BELGIAN**: Put the Shetland on my back, maybe he can reach it then.

✸ **WARMBLOOD**: I was sold for $75K as a yearling, but only because my hocks are bad, otherwise I would be worth $100K. I am NOT changing light bulbs. Make the TB get back here and do it.

✸ **MORGAN**: Me! Me! Me! Pleeease let me! I wanna do it! I'm gonna do it! I know how, really I do! Just watch! I'll rewire the barn after, too.

✸ **APPALOOSA**: Ya'll are a bunch of losers. We don't need to change the light bulb, I ain't scared of the dark. And someone make that darn Morgan stop jumping up and down before I double barrel him.

✸ **HAFLINGER**: That thing I ate was a light bulb?

✸ **MUSTANG**: Light bulb? Let's go on a trail ride, instead. And camp. Out in the open like REAL horses.

✸ **LIPIZZANER**: Hah, amateurs. I will change the light bulb. Not only that, but I will do it while standing on my hind legs and balancing it on my nose, after which I will perform seven flying lead changes in a row and a capriole.

✸ **MINIATURE**: I bet you think I can't do it just cause I'm small. You know what that is? It's sizeism!

✸ **PAINT**: Put all the light bulbs in a pen, tell me which one you want, and my owner will bet you twenty bucks I can get it before the Quarter Horse.

✸ **POA**: I'm not changing it. I'm the one who kicked the old one and broke it in the first place, remember? Now, excuse me, I have a grain room to break into.

✸ **GRADE HORSE**: Um, guys? I hope you don't mind, but I went ahead and changed it while you were all arguing.

BALING-TWINE SCRUBBIE

12 lengths of baling twine, cut from square bales

1 pair size 13 knitting needles, preferably metal

⚜ MORE BALING-TWINE USES

✷ Tie into a skimpy tail to enhance fly swatting.

✷ Braid a dog leash.

✷ Amuse a cat.

✷ Tie up an electric fence (baling twine doesn't conduct electricity).

✷ Hang a water bucket.

✷ Make an emergency halter.

✷ Bundle up electric fence posts.

If you know the basics of knitting, here is a simple-yet-satisfying item you can make for your horse. The scrubbie gives a lovely scratchy rub and is excellent for loosening the muddy crust on a horse who's been rolling.

When saving baling twine for this project, if you cut your twines off the bale, make sure to cut them at the knot. (Yes, you do need one more thing to think about when you're feeding your horse on a frosty predawn school day! How else are you going to learn to pay attention to details?)

Directions

1. **Cast on** 14 stitches.

2. **Knit every row.** Knit loosely, leaving plenty of slack. The baling twine can really tighten up. So can your hands. If they get sore, take a break and rub on some of your favorite horse liniment.

3. **As you approach the end of a piece of twine,** splice in the next one by tying the ends together. No need to be fussy — the scrubbie doesn't have to be beautiful.

4. **When your scrubbie is long enough** to cover your hand front and back when folded over on itself, bind off.

5. **Sew the two long sides of the scrubbie together.** You won't need a needle — just double your twine and push it through the loops with your fingers.

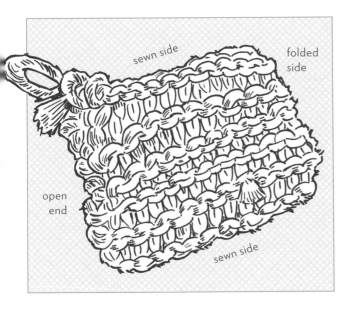

sewn side

folded side

open end

sewn side

6. **Tie the tail** you left when casting on to make a hanger loop.

7. **Find a muddy horse** and scrub, scrub, scrub!

The scrubbie is free, it's recycled, and it's pretty neat looking. If you're really inspired — a lot of baling twine, long winter evenings with nothing to do — you might try knitting other baling-twine articles. A rug? A coaster? A sweater? (Ouch — maybe not!)

Horseshoe REVIEW

A Fun Author to Try

Patsey Gray wrote some very entertaining horse stories set in California. They often, but not always, center around showing, and were illustrated by Sam Savitt, one of the classic horse illustrators. (See page 294.)

* *4-H Filly*
* *Blue Ribbon Summer*
* *Challenger*
* *Diving Horse*
* *Doggone Roan*
* *Flag Is Up*
* *Galloping Gold*
* *Heads Up!*
* *Horse in Her Heart*
* *The Horse Trap*

* *Horsepower*
* *Jumping Jack*
* *Loco the Bronc*
* *Lucky Star*
* *The Mysterious Buckskin*
* *Norah's Ark*
* *Show Ring Rogue*
* *Star Bright*
* *Star Lost*
* *Star, the Sea Horse*

How to Draw Horses

Drawing is a skill that can be learned by anyone with average eyesight and average eye-hand coordination. If you can thread a needle or catch a ball, you can draw. Drawing is not very difficult. Seeing is the problem.

— Sam Savitt (1917–2000; official artist of the USET)

Many illustrators who are terrific at drawing mice, dogs, landscapes, and people have a phobia about drawing horses. They didn't grow up around horses and don't know much about them. There's no question that knowledge helps. The artist Sam Savitt advised artists to visit horses whenever possible, talk with them, "run your hands over their sleek backs and hard legs. Observe them constantly wherever and whenever you can, in real life, in photographs, in movies, and on television." (Rough, huh?)

Savitt went even farther. "As a child I actually wanted to *be* a horse. I copied their actions in every way I could." That love and attention made him a great horse artist. It can help you, too.

The best way to learn is practice. Doodle: while you're taking notes in class; while you're waiting in a doctor's office; while you're waiting for a lesson or for your mom to pick you up at the barn; instead of watching TV!

Trying to draw something beautiful can make you freeze. You create a line — good enough — but then you make a few more and all of a sudden a promising horse drawing looks more like a hot dog with toothpick legs. Here's the good news: Professional artists don't get it right the first time, either. They sketch and doodle and scribble and practice, practice, practice.

MEET TWO HORSE-CRAZY ARTISTS

You've no doubt noticed that this book has two very different styles of artwork.

GALIA BERNSTEIN (NEW YORK CITY)

When people who know me well heard about this book they laughed. It couldn't be more perfect for me. I suppose I was a horse-crazy kid, but it was more about drawing them than anything else. I always liked drawing animals more than people. I think because horses are quite hard to draw, I took it as a personal challenge.

I started my career as a graphic designer and illustrator in the Israeli army (for the weekly magazine) and have worked as an art director, illustrator, and comic strip artist for kids magazines and books. I'm also a textile designer, which means I really love patterns as you can see by the endpapers and part openers in this book. You can see more of my work at *www.dancingkangaroo.com*.

ELARA TANGUY (PORTLAND, OREGON)

I grew up on a small farm where I often drew horses along with all the animals of the barnyard. In high school I became horse crazy when I started riding a half-Arabian mare named Minasha. I spent every day after school grooming her and taking her on trail rides with my other horse-loving friends.

My mom's art studio was part of our living room, so I was always watching her work. Everyone figured I would grow up to be an artist as well, but first came wanting to be an animal therapist, then a horse trainer, then a fashion designer . . .

I often need to research a subject before I can start drawing, so I've gotten to learn about camping and survival techniques, cattle farming, and lots of crafts. For this book I got to learn more about horses, one of my favorite subjects.

What I like most about horses is how peaceful I feel when I'm around them. I know that Minasha helped me get through those often-stressful high school years. She seemed to possess some knowing spirit that made being a teenager okay.

Ready, Set, Draw!

Here are some strategies to get you doodling, and help you progress as a horse artist.

* **Choose a drawing instrument** that feels good. Ballpoint pen can be quite nice. So can mechanical pencils.

* **Copy other people's** drawings and photographs.

* **Draw easy poses,** and then try harder ones.

* **Don't be afraid** to make a bad drawing. That's how you learn to make good drawings.

* **Focus on the different parts** of the horse. Draw hooves (they're hard!), pasterns, lower legs, knees, ears, eyes, nostrils (another hard part).

* **Use only straight lines and boxes** — making it very small will help.

* **Draw a lot of little horses,** doing lots of different things.

* **Try a "life drawing"** of a model horse. Draw the same model from different angles.

* **Studying books can help.** If you're serious, you'll want to learn about perspective and vanishing point and all the other elements of drawing.

* **Study horse anatomy,** especially bones and muscles.

Horse PLAY

DRAWING ON HORSES

Painting your horse doesn't have to mean sitting down with an easel and creating a masterpiece on canvas. Your horse can *be* the canvas and you can paint right on him. Use child-safe water-based tempera paints. They wash off easily and are nonsmelly. Apply with a brush or your fingers, being careful not to drip paint near his eyes.

Have an art show; decorate your horse for Christmas, Halloween, or the Fourth of July. Just be sure it's a warm enough day that you can wash the paint off without giving your horse a chill.

TRY DIFFERENT STYLES

You can aim for realism, or create a stylized horse or cartoon character with impossibly long legs and a short, arched body; or maybe an exaggeratedly fat body with just the suggestion of legs, neck, and head.

Take any shape: oval, rectangle, square, or star. By scribbling, adding lines, and shading, can you make it suggest "horse"?

Try drawing horseshoes and horse tracks and horse equipment as well as actual horses. Saddles and bridles can be a challenge.

A big part of drawing is being willing to slow down. See every strap and how it is connected to the other straps. Concentrate on the details.

You may find you're not that kind of artist, at least not yet. Maybe you prefer to be more gestural and produce a lovely ink scribble or a few sweeping lines that gives the merest impression of a horse.

A TIP FROM A PRO

Has this happened to you? You doodle the best horse you've ever drawn, but you do it on the bottom of some homework or the back of an envelope. On a good piece of paper, you can never draw a horse this good!

Or you draw a horse with a great front end, a great back end, and much too long a middle. Or he's perfect, but he needs to be facing the other way. What can you do? Follow the example of some professional artists, and whip out a piece of tracing paper. Even the pros don't get every drawing right the first time. They trace. (I find it very freeing to know that.)

Lay a sheet of tracing paper or vellum over your drawing and trace the lines that work best. Horse too long? Trace the front end, slide the paper until the back looks right, and trace the back end. Just leave out the bits you don't want!

Tracing paper can help you see mistakes in your drawings, too. Sam Savitt used to start a drawing on tracing paper, then turn the paper over. Seeing his drawing in reverse gave him a fresh perspective. He would correct mistakes on the other side of the paper, then turn the paper over to the original side and erase lines he didn't like. If the paper tore or smudged, he'd put a fresh sheet on top, trace the lines that he liked, and keep drawing.

HEY, HOLD STILL!

Drawing horses from life is hard. They move. Still, trying to draw a horse you love is a great way to learn to truly see him.

When you set out to draw a horse from life, be prepared to sketch quickly, and to abandon a sketch and start a new one whenever your horse moves. It's best to be outside the stall or paddock; horses are curious and yours will want to sample your paper and knock over your jar of pencils.

✤ THE UNMISTAKABLE THELWELL TOUCH ✤

Beginning with *Angels on Horseback* in 1957, British artist Norman Thelwell created several enduring cartoon books for young horse and pony lovers. The Thelwell pony has short, knobby legs, a fat body, an enormous mane and tail, and a boundless supply of mischief. The Thelwell rider is a match for him — passionate, determined, and eloquent. What is this girl saying (do we really want to know?).

No other author or illustrator captures so well the conflict and frustration of the pony/child relationship — but Thelwell also does love, pride, and concern. Find these books. You'll laugh and laugh and laugh.

Other titles by this author include:

✤ *A Leg at Each Corner*

✤ *Riding Academy*

✤ *Thelwell Country*

✤ *Thelwell Goes West*

© 1962 The Estate of Norman Thelwell. Reproduced by permission of Momentum Licensing from Thelwell's Pony Cavalcade (Methuen)

The natural aids to horsemanship are the hands, the legs, the body and the voice –

HORSE WORDS

Hold your horses! Curb your enthusiasm. (Hard to do when horses are involved).
Give free rein: Release from restraint. (Note that it isn't free "reign." That's a mistake a true horse-lover would never make!)

THAT'S DIFFERENT!
Five Unusual Breeds

These horses are all quite rare, but you'll take a second look if you're ever lucky enough to see one.

AKHAL-TEKE

WHAT'S DIFFERENT: The coat has a metallic sheen; unusual structure of the hair shaft refracts a golden glow, whatever the color of the horse.

ORIGIN: Turkmenistan

DESCRIPTION: 15–16 hands. Long, narrow, deep chest, with a high head carriage; gaits are soft and floating; noted for great feats of endurance.

FUN FACT: Akhal-Tekes were fed unusual diets to ready them for races; foods included eggs and cooked chicken.

GYPSY VANNER, GYPSY DRUM HORSES, GYPSY COBS

WHAT'S DIFFERENT: Big hair — very big hair; long, full manes and tails, voluminous feathers on lower legs

ORIGIN: England

DESCRIPTION: 14–15.2 hands. Strong and compact with powerful neck and back and heavy bones; resembles a draft horse; excellent gaits; extremely gentle and intelligent

FUN FACT: Gypsy cobs pulled the caravans of the traveling folk, the Gypsies (or Romani), around the English roads and countryside.

AMERICAN CURLY OR BASHKIR CURLY

WHAT'S DIFFERENT: Born with dense, curly coats, curls in the ears, curly eyebrows; mane may be wavy, too.

ORIGIN: United States northern plains, an American Indian horse

DESCRIPTION: 14.2–15.2 hands. Sturdy, muscular, resembles old-type Morgan; many are gaited.

FUN FACT: Curly horses were highly prized by the Sioux.

MARWARI AND KATHIAWARI

WHAT'S DIFFERENT: Ears curve inward to touch at tips.

ORIGIN: India

DESCRIPTION: 14.2–15.2 hands. Proudly carried neck, strong, deep body, rounded and compact Oriental body, long legs, excellent hearing, and floating gaits

FUN FACT: Marwaris were developed as warhorses for Indian rajas.

MOYLE

WHAT'S DIFFERENT: Small bony knobs above the eyes that are skin-covered and resemble giraffe horns

ORIGIN: Idaho

DESCRIPTION: 14.3–15.2 hands. Long body with foreleg far forward on the ribcage; long walking stride and exceptional endurance; liver and spleen said to be twice the size of other breeds, which may contribute to their powers of endurance.

FUN FACT: Moyle horses resemble the Chinese Datong horse, called "Dragon Horses," owned by Emperor Mu in the first century BCE.

IT'S ALL ABOUT THE SHAPE

If you are just beginning to draw horses, it can be helpful to have a particular technique. Here is one that I've found useful because it breaks down the elements of the horse's structure into simpler shapes. If you can draw a triangle, a square, and a circle, you can draw a horse!

Kite method for drawing a horse's face:

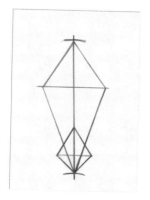 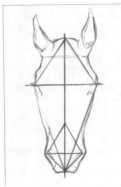 

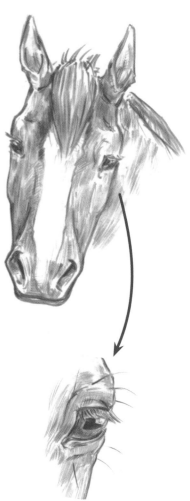

FRONT VIEW DETAILS

1. A horse's face, turned toward you, is shaped like a kite, with a small diamond on the end.

2. The eyes are about one-third down from the top of the skull, just below the ribs of the kite. Place the nostrils below the center line of the small diamond. Draw a faint line cutting off the top point of the kite and add the ears above. They should be the same length as the small diamond below.

3. After you sketch in the outlines and get the lines right, start adding details. Use pencil strokes to shade darker areas and to show the contours and texture of the horse's coat.

SIDE VIEW
DETAILS

A horse's head from the side is
a rectangular box, narrower on
one end.

301

A note about hooves: My mother used to draw all her horses standing in grass, because she couldn't draw hooves. Here's a simple way to draw them:

Basic shapes method for drawing hooves:

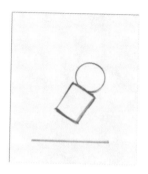   

1. Draw a tiny circle. Add a thin rectangle at an angle to it.

2. Draw a triangle on the end of that.

3. Begin filling out around the basic shapes with light pencil strokes. Remember the bump above the coronet band, and the way the fetlock joint rounds out slightly in the rear.

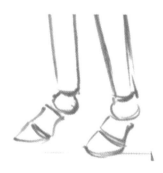  

STEP 1

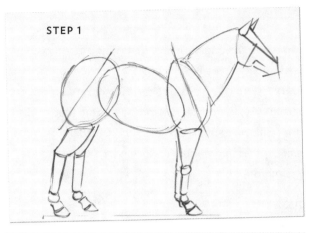

STEP 2

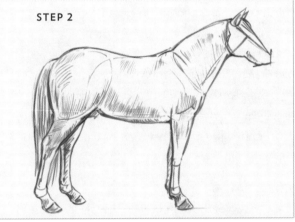

STEP 3

1. Once you've mastered the head and hooves, you can move on to the entire body. Start with a rectangle for the neck. The shoulders are an oval mass, set up on a diagonal. The barrel is a larger oval lying on its side — scoop out the top to give him a nice curvy back. The haunches? Another oval, tilted toward the barrel. Add some legs — triangular shapes on poles for the back legs, poles with ovals in the middle for the front.

2. Now doodle over these simplified shapes. Remember, a horse is solid. He has volume. Fill in, carve out, and add curves, until it looks like a horse. Leave the lines scratchy and scribbly.

3. When you have lines that are right, go over them to make them darker than the wrong lines.

LIVING LIFE LARGE
Looking at Some Draft Breeds

Despite their great size, draft horses are often good movers, and they tend to be somewhat calmer than saddle horses. After nearly disappearing in the 1940s and '50s, they are now enjoying a revival with small farmers, carriage drivers, and other enthusiasts.

AMERICAN CREAM DRAFT

This is the only remaining recognized breed of draft horse that originated in the United States. Like the Morgan, the breed traces back to a single horse, in this case, a draft-type mare of uncertain pedigree called Old Granny, who lived in Iowa in the early 1900s. From her foals, a couple of interested breeders eventually established a distinct breed of medium-weight, light-colored draft horses. Always few in number, the American Cream is still quite rare, with only a few hundred of them registered.

DESCRIPTION: The American Cream stands 15 to 16 hands high. The striking characteristic of the breed is its color. Pink skin is required for registration, though the coat may be light, medium, or dark cream in color. The eyes are amber or hazel (interestingly, foals have nearly white eyes during their first year), and the mane and tail must be white.

BELGIAN

The Belgian originated in Belgium, but has long been popular in North America because of its pleasant temperament and easy keeping qualities. Today there are two types: the original heavy draft type and a more modern carriage-type horse with flashy leg action.

DESCRIPTION: This is a large (16–18 hands), well-rounded, muscular horse. In this country, most are some shade of chestnut with white mane and tail; socks or stockings and a blaze are considered desirable. Roaning and dappling are fairly common.

BRABANT

This massive horse is considered a type of Belgian, though it is much rarer than its cousin described above. Fewer than 100 exist in the United States and Canada.

DESCRIPTION: The Brabant looks as if it were carved out of solid granite. Some Brabants weigh as much as 3,000 pounds! Standing between 15.2 and 17 hands, they are powerfully muscled, with a deep body and strong, heavy legs. Most often red bay or bay roan in color. Black and gray are uncommon.

CLYDESDALE

The best known of the draft breeds, the Clydesdale is the famous hitch horse of the Budweiser brewery. Developed as a packhorse to carry coal in Scotland, its country of origin, the Clydesdale also pulled delivery wagons on the docks and worked in the fields.

DESCRIPTION: A tall horse at 16.1 to 18 hands, the Clydesdale has a short back, deep body, and long, arched neck. It has exceptionally good feet with lots of feather to emphasize its animated action. Most are bay with broad white blazes and high stockings; roaning and/or white spots on the body are common.

NORTH AMERICAN SPOTTED DRAFT

Though this is a relatively new breed in terms of having a registry, heavy horses with spotted coats have been around for centuries. In the mid-1960s, an American breeder began collecting pinto draft horses and in 1995, the North American Spotted Draft Horse Association was formed to promote and develop the breed. With nearly 3,000 horses registered as of 2008, they are increasing in popularity.

DESCRIPTION: Most resemble Percherons and Belgians in build, but have splashy pinto coloring. Blue eyes and white or multicolored hooves are allowed.

PERCHERON

This ancient breed comes from a province in France called Le Perche, where fine horses have been bred for many centuries. Used as a warhorse during the Crusades, the breed became an all-around draft and carriage horse as lighter horses were added to the mix. At one time it was the most popular horse in North America, with three times as many in use as several other breeds combined.

DESCRIPTION: At 16 to 18 hands, the Percheron is a tall horse with a deep chest and broad back. The elegant head and arched neck show Arabian influence; the legs have no feathering. Black and gray are the most common colors.

SHIRE

England is the home of this beautiful breed, whose ancestors carried heavily armored knights into battle. As the age of chivalry gave way to the age of gunpowder, these large horses were used for farm work and as cart horses to pull heavy loads to market. Relatively rare, the

---

❋ HORSEFEATHERS! ❋

Feathering is the word horsemen use to describe long hair on the lower legs of horses. Heavy feathering is essential for horses working in heavy muck. The hair helps drain water off the legs and keeps it away from the skin, where it might promote fungal infections.

Shire is still used for logging, farm work, and in impressive hitches in parades and shows.

DESCRIPTION: The tallest of the draft breeds at an average of 17.1 hands (many reach 19 hands), the Shire has a lean head with a Roman nose set on a long, slightly arched neck. The Shire can be bay, brown, black, gray, or chestnut, but excessive white markings and roaning are considered undesirable.

SUFFOLK PUNCH

This is another English breed, probably the oldest one, in fact. Developed for farm work, it has changed very little over several centuries. The Suffolk's feet are set closer together than other draft horses, allowing it to move carefully between rows of crops. While rare, the breed is well established, with growing numbers in North America.

DESCRIPTION: The Suffolk is a heavily built horse, with an intelligent head and powerful neck. Though standing 16.1 to 17 hands, it has relatively short legs and is known for having excellent feet. The color is always some shade of chestnut and only a very small amount of white is permitted.

How to Photograph Horses

We take photography completely for granted these days. Even our phones can take pictures, and we assume that any fool can snap a photo. But it can be quite tricky to take a good picture, especially of a horse.

The long legs, neck, and nose can look all out of perspective and the ears can prick and look lovely, or droop just as you snap the shot. Not to mention the lighting: Variations in sun, wind, and reflections can make good horse photos hard to achieve.

A few simple rules can improve your chances — and if you want to move beyond those rules, you'll discover a fascinating world of horse photography that can be an art form and even a career.

Learning the Basics

Even a disposable camera can take a perfectly fine horse picture if you follow a few basic rules. Lesli Groves offers some tips in chapter 1 of *Photographing Horses: How to Capture the Perfect Equine Image*. The cheaper and less sophisticated your camera, the more important it is to follow this advice:

1. **Stand the horse so his profile is in direct light.** The sun should shine directly on his side, and his shadow should fall directly behind him.

2. **Stand about 35 feet away and kneel** — unless you're short — so your camera angle is close to the center of the horse.

3. **Use the zoom setting and center his profile.** If your camera doesn't have a telephoto setting, stand farther back. His image should not completely fill the frame.

4. **Wait for a pretty expression.**

5. **Shoot**.

FOCUS ON THE DETAILS

Attention to details can improve your chances of getting a result you like. Follow these tips:

* **Make sure your horse and tack are clean and shiny** — unless you want a fuzzy, scruffy, everyday barnyard shot, and there's nothing wrong with that. Candid shots give us memories of our normal lives, not just our dress-up moments.

- **Use fly spray,** but use it carefully. You don't want to leave wet streaks that will show up in your picture. But you also don't want a fidgety horse kicking at flies and lashing his tail.

- **Make sure tack fits,** and doesn't have distracting loops or tassels. These may look perfectly normal in real life, but in a picture they sometimes seem to be sprouting from a horse's ear or chin.

- **Find a natural background,** or a wall that contrasts with your horse's color. Put a light colored horse against a dark wall, and vice versa.

- **Be aware of how changes in background** — such as a building or tree line — can blur your horse's top line.

- **Think how you'll get those ears up.** Grain or carrots can work. Slightly alarming objects, like squeakers,

Horseshoe REVIEW

Touching Wild Horses
(2002, rated G)

Mark is sent to live on Sable Island with his naturalist aunt after a car accident involving his family. Aunt Fiona is harsh at first, but mellows as the two adjust to each other.

Mark is fascinated by the free, but not particularly wild, Sable Island horses. Canadian law forbids interacting with them or even touching them, and Fiona will lose her home there if she disobeys. But when a foal is orphaned in an accident, Mark feels that he has no choice but to help it, and soon Fiona is involved as well.

An emotional and beautiful film, and the foal, John, is a charmer. The horses may or may not be real Sable Island horses, but they look like they could be, and there's a lot less "movie-horse" whinnying in the soundtrack than in most horse movies. There are some scary scenes, in spite of the G rating.

plastic bags, foil, or mirrors, can work. Best of all is to train your horse to "look pretty" (see page 312).

- **If photographing your horse from the side,** focus your camera at a point just behind the center of his shoulder. Experiment with your own stance. If the camera is too low, the horse may look too leggy. Too high and he'll seem squat.

- **Take lots and lots and lots of shots.** The editor of *LensWork* magazine says, "If you're not shooting 100 negatives for every one you print, you're not being energetic enough."

POSITIONING THE HORSE

When you position your horse for his portrait, follow the rules that George Stubbs and other master horse portrait painters followed, long before the camera was ever dreamed of. These rules apply whether the horse is photographed with a rider or not:

* **All four legs** should be visible.

* **In a profile shot,** the two legs nearest the camera should be farther apart than the other two.

* **Both ears should show** and should be pricked.

* **The tail should hang** straight or drape slightly over the hock nearest the camera.

* **If there's a slight slope,** face your horse uphill.

* **Face him out of the wind,** which may make him put his ears back.

* **If there's something interesting going on,** face him toward that; it'll help get a pretty expression, and keep him from craning his neck to look the other way.

* **Be flexible** — and do what the pros do. Burn a lot of film. Take a lot of pictures, more than you think you need, from different positions and angles.

* **When photographing the head,** you should still follow the rule to "show all parts."

THREE-QUARTER PROFILE

A three-quarter turn should show the eyelash of the hidden eye. Aim the lens at the nearer eye and experiment with angles until you find what's most flattering.

Three-quarter shots should show all four legs, all the way to the top. Look through your viewfinder, count legs, and move until you can see where that diagonal leg joins the horse's body.

Learning the Finer Points

You'll take better photos if you study horse conformation. Standards are different for different breeds. Quarter Horse people like to emphasize the muscular rump. Arabian people are more interested in the head and neck. An Akhal-Teke should look leggy; a Morgan shouldn't. A photographer who knows these differences will be able to take pictures that please horse owners.

Along with conformation, learn about the activities you want to photograph. There's a world of difference between show jumping and saddle-seat equitation. A good photographer finds the important moments and avoids the potentially embarrassing ones.

As you advance, you'll want to learn about photographing people, too. Many of your photos will be of horses with their people. And (surprise!) horses and people are different. It's not just the number of legs, or that horses' ears move; lighting works differently on hair than on skin. The same direct light that flatters horses and shows off their muscles shows people's wrinkles, and washes out their skin tone.

LOOK AT LIGHTING

If you have a choice, take your pictures on a "hazy bright" day — not dark and overcast, and not brilliantly sunny. On sunny days, look for an area of open shade to take your picture. Tree shadows can be uneven and patchy. Be sure you haven't posed your subjects in a spotlight or a dark patch.

WATCH THE ANGLE

Luckily, a zoom function or the "portrait mode" on a camera tends to be flattering to both people and horses. Use that if you have the option.

Focus your camera on the horse, rather than the person. Show a connection between

 THE PERFECT MODEL

One of your problems as a horse photographer is, let's face it, the horse. Horses move, wiggle, make dopey expressions. It's hard to focus on light and camera angles with all that going on.

Photographer and teacher Lesli Groves suggests practicing on model horses first. This lets you find out the effect of different light and camera angles, backgrounds, and so on. Your skills will come in handy if you show model horses, too (see page 272).

Take pictures in different light, at different angles, against different backgrounds. Compare the photos with the images you were expecting. Compare them with each other. What pictures do you like? Why? Do you know what you did? Would you be able to do that again?

the person and the horse — either they should be touching or the lead rope or reins should show in the photograph.

Learn the standard people poses. Don't cut someone off at a joint — wrist, knee, or elbow. Pose people slightly turned. A bent elbow can look more graceful than a straight arm.

TAKING ACTION SHOTS

Action shots are hard to catch, but they are priceless when you get them right. As with everything, there are tricks. It helps to understand what you're watching. If it's a show-ring event you're trying to capture, the hours you spend standing there watching riders approach the jumps will help you feel the rhythm, anticipate when the horse will arrive at a certain point, and know how he'll be looking. Studying horse magazines will give you an idea of typical shots and classic moments in different equine sports.

Horseshoe REVIEW

The Silver Stallion
(1994, rated G)

This visually beautiful movie set in Australia is based on *The Silver Brumby*, by Elyne Mitchell. It's about an author who is writing a story about a wild stallion. The story spills over from fiction to fact and from the past to the present, as "the man" (Russell Crowe) relentlessly hunts the horse down.

Lots of beautiful horse footage here, but will the continual rearing and nickering annoy you? Will it boggle your mind to see a horse gallop for miles and miles and miles without ever apparently breaking a sweat? Will it bug you to hear a golden palomino continually described as "silver"? You'll have to decide for yourself.

For events where an important moment is certain to take place at one particular point — a jump, a barrel, a slide area in a reining event, or a letter in a dressage arena — you can prefocus your camera. The instruction manual will tell you how.

There are standard shots in action photography that work well. The trot, for instance, is best shot when the front foot nearest you reaches forward. It takes practice to see this. Watch that foot as the horse approaches, and count his hoof beats: one-two, one-two, establishing "two" as the beat on which that front foot reaches forward. Click on "two," when the horse is directly in front of you.

Chatting with Horse Folks

Shawn Hamilton, professional equestrian photographer

Describe briefly your work/play with horses.
I cover major international shows such as the last four Olympics, the last five World Equestrian Games, and Rolex every year. I love to shoot eventing.

I shoot the odd local show for stock images but prefer free running horses and wild horses in their natural environment. I am trying to increase awareness through my photos of the perils that wild horses are facing right now. My clients are mostly magazines and advertising agencies.

I have five horses at home. I do dressage with one and go trail riding with another, have two pasture pets who are ridden regularly to keep them in shape, and then there's my daughter's pony.

What's cool about what you do?
Being able to ride and work at the same time! I also love meeting other horse owners and seeing wild horses in their natural habitat. I try to do as many horse-riding vacations as I can. I write a story and take photos about my vacation, and then publish the articles. I've been to South Africa and the American Rockies, and plan to cross the Andes from Chile to Argentina by horseback.

What's hard about what you do?
Sitting at the computer when I would rather be riding and shooting!

What could a kid be doing now to wind up with a career like yours?
Take business courses. You can be great at whatever you do but if you can't market yourself or know how to properly run a business you will not succeed. And shoot your passion — take tons of pictures. Practice, practice, practice!

How did you choose this path in life?
Photography and horses were equal passions in my life. When I had the first of my four children, I did not go back to my full-time position as a computer programmer but followed my love for horses and photography and never looked back.

What surprises you about your work?
How fulfilling it truly is, but also how difficult it can be to make ends meet. The equestrian market is very small compared to other mainstream markets and the pay reflects that.

What's one thing you wish people understood about it?
How much time and effort it takes to capture that great image and how expensive it can be to travel to places to do these things. Even though I'm following my passion, I still need to eat!

CLICK AND CLICK

One of the hard things in photographing horses is catching their ears at the right moment. Photographers resort to waving food treats, crackling plastic bags, making uncouth noises, all in an effort to make the model pay attention. All of this works a few times, but horses become desensitized to scary noises (which is good) and start looking bored or grumpy again (bad).

The solution for the thinking horseman is training. But can you train a horse to put its ears forward? You bet. This is an ideal use of clicker training.

First, both you and the horse need to understand the meaning of the click (see clicker training, page 100). Now you'll do some shaping. Watch those ears. The moment they prick forward, click and treat.

It may take the horse awhile to figure out why he's getting clicked. In *Don't Shoot the Dog*, Karen Pryor describes an Arab mare working this out. "She clearly knew her actions made her trainer click. And she knew it had something to do with her ears. But what? Holding her head erect, she rotated her ears individually: one forward, one back; then the reverse; then she flopped both ears to the sides like a rabbit, something I didn't know a horse could do on purpose. Finally, both ears went forward at once. *Click!* Aha! She had it straight from then on. It was charming, but it was also sad: We don't usually ask horses to think or to be inventive, and they seem to like to do it."

✳ A TRAINING REVOLUTION ✳

For many years, rodeos were the epitome of traditional rough and tough American methods of horse training — symbolized by the term "to break a horse." In the past couple of decades, however, a revolution, led by trainers such as Monty Roberts, Pat Parelli, Julie Goodnight, and Stacey Westfall is taking horse training back to its original roots of working in harmony with the horse's instincts and natural behavior.

Today contests like "Road to the Horse" and "Extreme Mustang Makeover" showcase the new methods. In the latter example, trainers have three months to train a wild mustang. "Road to the Horse" trainers have just three hours, before a live audience, to start a young horse.

Of course, even with such a good start, a lot of work remains to be done before these horses can be considered fully trained!

FIVE EXOTIC BREEDS
You've Probably Never Heard Of

This big old world is full of horses that are unknown to most Americans. There's a whole list of them on page 351, but here are a few in more detail:

CIRIT

ORIGIN: Turkey

THEIR STORY: Bred for the high-speed sport of *cirit* (pronounced je-REET), these horses descend from horses brought from central Asia by Attila the Hun. In cirit, individual players challenge each other and throw sticks at each other; it was the Ottoman equivalent of jousting, and just as dangerous.

HEIGHT: 13.1–14.1 hands

DESCRIPTION: Many have an Arab-type head on a strong, thick neck; strong shoulders, short back

GUOXIA

ORIGIN: Southwest China

THEIR STORY: A very old breed whose name means "under fruit tree horse," which refers to their use in the orchards, where they stood under trees while workers filled the baskets on their backs. They were also court pets during the Han and Song dynasties. They were thought extinct until about a thousand were found in an isolated mountain area. Today they're used in children's parks.

HEIGHT: 9–10 hands

DESCRIPTION: Short, pretty head; short, thick neck; level from neck to croup, rounded belly, good straight legs

KARABAIR

ORIGIN: Uzbekistan

THEIR STORY: An ancient breed from an area known for fine horses for 2,500 years. The Chinese sent diplomatic and military missions to bring back horses from this region. It is related to the Turkmen and Akhal-Teke breeds.

HEIGHT: 14.2–15 hands

DESCRIPTION: There are three types — basic, heavy, and saddle. The most common is the basic, used for both riding and work in harness; lean and well balanced with a deep trunk, it has a lively disposition.

PONY MOUSSEY

ORIGIN: Cameroon

THEIR STORY: Their ancestry is unknown; they may derive from Barbs. They are resistant to sleeping sickness, a dangerous disease spread in central Africa by the tsetse fly.

HEIGHT: 12 hands

DESCRIPTION: Heavy head; short, thick neck; short legs; gentle and extremely hardy

SUMBA

ORIGIN: Indonesia

THEIR STORY: Descended from Mongolian horses, these Indonesian ponies are traditionally ridden without bits. They are used in dance competitions, where they are ridden bareback with bells attached to their knees.

HEIGHT: 12 hands

DESCRIPTION: Small, primitive type of pony, usually dun-colored with a dorsal stripe; heavy head, short neck, long back, straight shoulder, slender legs; tough, gentle, and smart

RHYTHM BEADS

Materials Needed

Cord (strong, and with a bit of stretch) or leather string*

Beads (avoid glass beads, for safety)

Bells (any kind is okay. Hawk bells —called jingle or sleigh bells — are traditional for horses and make a merry, muted sound.)

Alligator clips

___

* *Whatever string you use should be strong, yet breakable should your horse become tangled in something. Don't use elastic!*

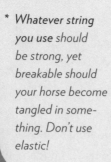

Jewelry for your horse? Why not! Rhythm beads are considered a training tool in natural horsemanship circles. The bells make it easier for you to hear if your horse is moving evenly and in good cadence. Horses are said to listen to the bells, too, and some seem to enjoy influencing the sound by changing the way they move. Many horsemen claim their horses relax and improve their way of going when rhythm beads are added to their tack. The steady jingling provides white noise, calms horse and rider, and on the trail, alerts wildlife and other riders that you and your horse are approaching. Fewer surprises equals fewer spooks.

Horses are very aware of rhythm, and tend to move in sync with it. This is one reason some riding teachers, particularly those working with drill teams, like to incorporate music into the lesson. Adding rhythm beads to a musical lesson can help riders hear if they are working with the beat.

Directions

Rhythm beads commonly come in two forms, mane clips and necklaces.

FOR A MANE CLIP:

1. **Knot one end of a mane-length string** so the beads won't slip through. Slide on beads and bells in whatever pattern and color combination pleases you. You can include feathers and even healing crystals if you want.

2. **Tie a knot in the top,** and fasten to your horse's mane with an alligator clip.

FOR A RHYTHM NECKLACE:

1. **Measure** your horse's neck at the base.

2. **Cut off enough string** to go comfortably around his neck, with enough extra to tie a knot.

3. **Start stringing** bells and beads. You can include a larger bell, array of bells, or pendant that hangs down. It can be on the same string, or you can secure the ornament to the string separately, with a knot or a lanyard clip.

4. **When your necklace is finished,** knot the ends. Secure it using a ring and clasp — something moderately sturdy, like a lanyard clip — or simply tie with a quick-release knot. An alligator clip attached to the mane will keep the necklace from sliding off if your horse puts his head down.

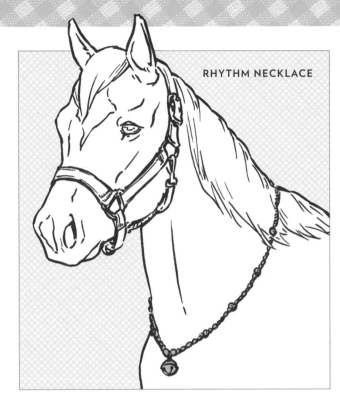

RHYTHM NECKLACE

Horse Sense

Introduce rhythm beads with sensitivity. Show them to your horse. Wear them yourself as you work around him. Drape them over his neck and lead him around. If he seems unworried, tie or clip the beads and let him loose in the ring or round pen to explore the sound himself. Only when you're sure he accepts this new accessory should you head out on the trail wearing them.

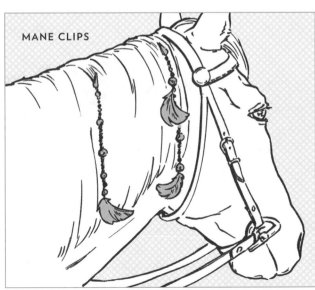

MANE CLIPS

Singing About Horses

Horses and singing go together. The rhythm of hoof beats suggests a tune, and whether we're feeling high spirited or melancholy, soon we're singing. There are walking songs, trotting songs, cantering songs, and songs no doubt to go with all the traveling gaits.

Experiment with counting the beat. You don't need to be on horseback to do this. Mark the beats with your fingers — one-two-three-four for walk; one-two, one-two for trot; one-two-three, one-two-three for canter.

Horses Like Music, Too

Some people who use sleigh bells or rhythm beads notice that their horses enjoy influencing the sound — moving more rhythmically, for example, or stepping out with a livelier gait. Teams of driving horses learn to move in step with each other, probably due to the sound of hoof beats. What's music to our ears is music to theirs, too.

Pony Tales

EQUINE ACOUSTICS

In Britain, horse skulls were believed to amplify sound. A horse skull in the wall would let you hear what was going on out in the yard. Horse skulls were put between choir stalls and in bell towers to enhance the sound. Sometimes they were placed beneath the floorboards of a house, to clarify sound and also prevent dry rot.

☼ PLAY IT ☼ AGAIN, SAM

A fun trick to teach your curious horse is one that clicker trainer Alexandra Kurland calls "Band Practice."

Teach your horse to target on something potentially noisy — a large plastic soda bottle, a dog's squeaky toy, a bicycle horn. After the horse is touching it reliably, withhold the click. Most horses will shove or bite the target, making a sound. As soon as your horse makes a noise, click and treat, even if he seems startled by what he's produced.

Horses soon learn to enjoy making noise and you can have fun introducing him to different items. See what he does with a toy piano. What tune is that horse trying to play?

SOME GOOD OLD HORSE SONGS

Jingle Bells

This familiar favorite was written by James Lord Pierpont after a visit to Medford, Massachusetts, America's capital city of sleigh bells. Sung softly, it sounds a little like sleigh bells.

Dashing thro' the snow
In a one-horse open sleigh,
O'er the fields we go,
Laughing all the way;
Bells on bobtail ring,
Making spirits bright,
What fun it is to ride and sing
A sleighing song tonight.

CHORUS
Jingle bells, jingle bells,
Jingle all the way!
Oh, what fun it is to ride
In a one-horse open sleigh!

Camptown Races

This southern racing ditty was written by Stephen Foster and published in 1830. Foster also wrote "My Old Kentucky Home," which is played every year at the Kentucky Derby.

Camptown Races sing this song
Doo-Dah! Doo-Dah!
Camptown Racetrack five miles long
Oh Doo-Dah-Day.

Going to run all night
Going to run all day,
Bet my money on the bobtailed nag
Somebody bet on the bay.

All the Pretty Little Horses

This traditional American folk song is known to have been sung in North Carolina before the Civil War.

Hush-a-bye,
Don't you cry,
Go to sleep my little baby.
When you wake
You shall have
All the pretty little horses.

CHORUS
Blacks and bays,
Dapples and grays,
All the pretty little horses.

Erie Canal

Canal boating was pretty much a thing of the past when this song was written by Thomas Allen in 1905.

I have an old mule and her name is Sal;
Fifteen miles on the Erie Canal.
She's a good old worker and a good old pal;
Fifteen miles on the Erie Canal.
We've hauled some barges in our day
Filled with lumber, coal, and hay
And we know every inch of the way,
From Albany to Buffalo.
CHORUS
Low bridge, everybody down,
Low bridge for we're going through the town.
Oh you'll always know your neighbor, you'll always
   know your pal,
If you've ever navigated on the Erie Canal.

317

✳ IGIL, CHANZY, KENGIRGE — WHAT? ✳

Did you ever look at the neck and peg head of a violin and imagine you saw a horse there? There's a reason for that. Western stringed instruments descend from instruments invented by horse people on the Asian steppes. They were introduced to Europe and China by Mongol invaders. The original instruments are still played in Mongolia and Tuva, a small, semi-autonomous country in central Asia. In ages past, Tuva voluntarily joined Genghis Khan's empire, and Tuvans revere their ancestor, Genghis's general Subudai.

TOURING TUVANS

Tuvan bands frequently tour the United States, showing off their remarkable singing style called *khoomei*, or throat singing. The sound, produced below the vocal cords, is amazing: deep growls, high whistles, the silvery chink of a wooden-handled whip striking a metal stirrup. Tuvan singers can produce two notes at the same time; a trio of Tuvans can sing in six-part harmony.

Tuvans are horse people, and the rhythm of hoof beats is in the songs. Listen and you'll hear small horses moving swiftly and steadily across endless miles. The music is unique, yet familiar. There's a lonely, wide-open country feeling about it, like many cowboy songs.

THE INSTRUMENTS

Tuvan instruments are similar to instruments played throughout the Mongolian region. The horsehead fiddle, called the *igil* in Tuvan, dates back at least a thousand years. It has a teardrop-shaped body and the peg head is carved in the shape of a horse head — a nice, cresty pony with pricked ears. The body is made of soft wood.

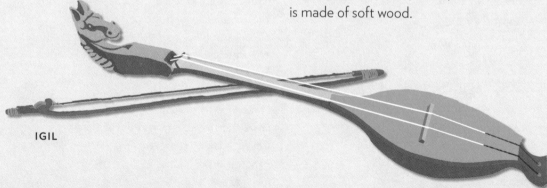

IGIL

The two unfretted strings, tuned a fifth apart, are traditionally made of many strands of horsehair. One string is called "The Mare," the other, "The Stallion." The bow is also made of horsehair.

The igil is held between the knees when played. It is an instrument of great subtlety that can be sweet and melancholy, or establish the strong hoof-beat rhythms on which much Tuvan music is based. Some of the basic rhythms are called "galloping horse," "walking horse," and "walking camel."

Other horse-related Tuvan instruments include the *chanzy*, a three-string plucked instrument similar to a banjo. It has a horse-shaped peg head, like the igil, and decorative horse designs on the sound board.

On top of the Tuvan drum, the *kengirge*, you'll see an instrument called the *shyngyrash*, a string of small bells sewn to a goatskin. Tuvan horses wear bells, and to Tuvans, the shyngyrash evokes horses traveling.

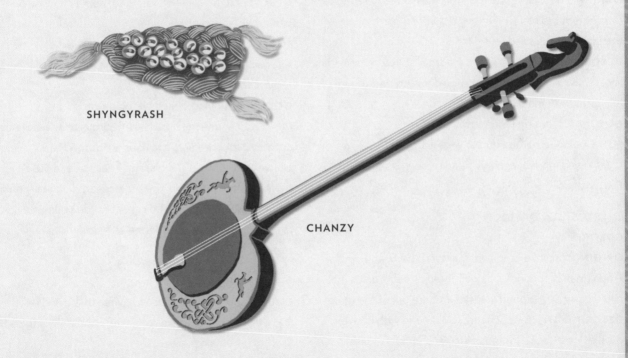

SHYNGYRASH

CHANZY

A HORSE OF THE EXACT SAME COLOR:
Five Single-Color Breeds

Most breeds include horses of many colors, but a few breeds, mostly very old ones, produce horses that are all the same color.

CAMARGUE

COLOR: White (technically gray; foals are born black or brown, and turn white as they mature)

ORIGIN: The Camargue Marsh in the Rhone River delta of southern France, where they run in wild herds along with the black cattle raised for bullfights.

DESCRIPTION: 13.1–14.1 hands; a small sturdy horse with short muscular neck, straight shoulders and back, tough legs, and thick mane and tail

GOOD AT: Herding cattle, endurance

FUN FACT: Camargue horses were admired by Julius Caesar and influenced early Spanish breeds, including the Lipizzan.

CLEVELAND BAY

COLOR: Bay

ORIGIN: Yorkshire, England; Galloway, Barb, and Andalusian bloodlines; originally bred as packhorses that could carry 600-pound loads of iron ore out of the mines

DESCRIPTION: 16–16.2 hands; bold head with convex profile; long neck, sloping muscular shoulders, deep body and moderately long back; level quarters, muscular, strong legs

GOOD AT: Foxhunting, showing in hunter division, dressage, combined driving

FUN FACT: Cleveland Bays performed in Buffalo Bill's Wild West show.

FRIESIAN

COLOR: Black

ORIGIN: The North Sea coast of Europe, in the area once called Friesland, now the Netherlands and Denmark; descended from an ancient wild European type

DESCRIPTION: 15–17 hands; long, noble head; neck carried high, sloping shoulders, moderately long neck, strong legs with abundant feathering; long, full mane and tail; gaits are fluid and high-stepping; gentle and friendly temperament.

GOOD AT: Driving, dressage, pleasure

FUN FACT: Friesians must pass rigorous tests before being accepted for breeding. Stallions are judged as weanlings, yearlings, 3- or 4-year-olds, and finally after a 50-day training program. Then, they're inspected annually until age 12. Failure of any test disqualifies the young stallion for breeding. Mares are judged at 3, and may receive extra status at later judgings.

HAFLINGER

COLOR: Golden chestnut with white mane and tail

ORIGIN: Tyrol Mountains of Austria and Italy; originally used as mountain pack horses

DESCRIPTION: 13–15 hands; beautiful head, powerful shoulders, medium-length back, and strong, sloping croup;

there is a lighter and longer legged pleasure-type and a draft-type used for farm work.

GOOD AT: Pleasure, driving, farm work, lower-level dressage, eventing, and jumping

FUN FACT: Haflingers make excellent all-around farm horses and are popular with the Amish for that reason.

NORWEGIAN FJORD

COLOR: Dun, with a dorsal stripe and zebra stripes, sometimes very faint, on the lower legs

ORIGIN: Norway. Fjord horses (also called Norwegian Duns) were domesticated around 2000 BCE, and were used by the Vikings for warhorses and farm work.

DESCRIPTION: 13.2–14.2 hands; a small, heavy, powerful horse, with a handsome well-proportioned head, short muscular neck, sloping shoulders, and deep body; short, powerful legs

GOOD AT: Riding, driving, packing, farm work, dressage, jumping, lower-level eventing

FUN FACT: The mane is typically roached to stand straight up, showing off its striking color — light on the outside with a dark central stripe.

See page 33 for more about colors.

Pony Tales

COLORFUL CHARACTERS

✹ *Black horses* are lucky in some cultures and unlucky in others. White horses are also lucky in some places, unlucky in others.

✹ *Chestnuts* are supposedly temperamental (like all redheads!). A pale chestnut or bay is said to be sicklier than one of a deep, strong hue.

✹ *Dun horses* have a reputation for extreme toughness.

✹ *Piebalds* are the luckiest horses to meet. If you see a piebald horse, spit, cross your fingers, and make a wish. Keep your fingers crossed until you see a dog and the wish will come true. Also, the hair of a piebald horse cures illness if carried in a pocket.

The main thing to remember is that "a good horse is never a bad color." (Some people say, "A good horse has no color," which isn't quite the same thing.)

321

CROCHET IN A BIG WAY

Materials Needed

SADDLE PAD
**14 3oz. balls
(about 1200 yards total)
of bulky weight acrylic yarn
(suggested: Patons Melody
Quick & Cozy)**

**Crochet hook:
US size H/8
(5 mm), or size you need
to obtain gauge**

Gauge: 3 rows and 6 hdc = 2"

Finished size: 33" × 37"

HALTER PADS
**1 skein (about 125 yards)
of super-bulky weight acrylic
yarn (suggested: Red Heart
Light & Lofty)**

One 9" velcro strip

Two 4" velcro strips

One 11" Velcro strip

Needle and thread

**Crochet hook:
US size J/10 (6 mm), or size
you need to obtain gauge**

Gauge: 5 dc and 2 rows = 2"

If you enjoy crochet, and like making things for your horse in colors of your own choosing, you can make a simple fly fringe, polo wraps, or choose from patterns for fly bonnets that go over the ears. Yes, you can buy these items for a few dollars, but that's not the point. If you make your own you can customize the colors, and have the satisfaction of doing it yourself, while you learn a new skill.

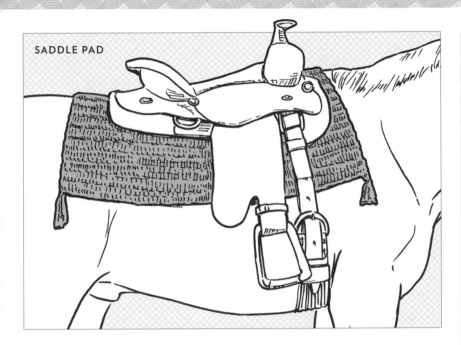

SADDLE PAD

Crochet a Saddle Pad

Yes, it's big, but it's straightforward and there's no shaping or finishing work.

START   Chain 102.

ROW 1   Work 1 half double crochet in second chain from hook and in each chain across. Chain 2, turn.

ROW 2   Work 1 half double crochet in each stitch across. Chain 2, turn. Repeat this row until piece measures 37 inches. Fasten off.

FINISH   If desired, make four tassels and attach one to each corner.

Patterns courtesy of *Crochet Do Dads* (see Resources, page 358).

❋ ADD A ❋ TASSEL

Tassels are easy to make, yet they really help a project look snazzy. Here are the basics:

1. Gather a handful of yarn; each piece should be a little more than twice as long as you want your tassel to be. You can use the same yarn as you used for the saddle pad, or try a different color or texture. It should be the same thickness as you used for the saddle pad, though.

2. Fold the bundle in half, keeping the ends even.

3. Insert the folded end of the bundle through a loop at the corner of the blanket.

4. Reach through with your fingers or a large crochet hook. Pull the loose ends of the bundle through the loop, and pull up snug.

5. If the ends are uneven, trim them with scissors.

Crochet Halter Pads

Halter pads are only marginally harder than the saddle pad. There's no shaping, but you do have to sew some Velcro on when you're done.

HALTER PADS

NOSE BAND

START   Chain 23.

ROW 1   Half double crochet in third chain from hook and in each stitch across. Chain 2, turn.

ROW 2   Half double crochet in each stitch across. Chain 2, turn.

ROWS 3–14   Repeat Row 2. Fasten off.

CHEEK (MAKE 2)

START   Chain 15.

ROW 1   Half double crochet in third chain from hook and in each stitch across. Chain 2, turn.

ROW 2   Half double crochet in each stitch across. Chain 2, turn.

ROWS 3–14   Repeat Row 2. Fasten off.

CROWN

START   Chain 28.

ROW 1   Half double crochet in third chain from hook and in each stitch across. Chain 2, turn.

ROW 2   Half double crochet in each stitch across. Chain 2, turn.

ROWS 3–14   Repeat Row 2. Fasten off.

TO FINISH

Cut Velcro pieces to length. (Use adhesive-backed Velcro, then sew the pieces in place.) Sew one side of strip to the right side of the halter cover. Taking care to line the second piece up in the matching area, sew the second strip to the wrong side of the halter cover on the opposite edge. Roll halter cover around appropriate halter piece.

✲ WHAT THE BEST HORSES ARE WEARING ✲

In the wild, horses are nudists. A horse would rather wear nothing at all, all day long. But we like to dress them up, and sometimes it's necessary, given the way horses live. Here are some common horse duds.

Sheets and blankets (called "rugs" in England) are coverings to keep your horse clean, prevent sun-bleach, keep him cooler, keep him warmer — there's a type out there for every sort of weather and for a variety of living and working conditions.

Turnout blankets are heavy clothing for winter protection, while **stable sheets** are light indoor-outdoor blankets. **Rain sheets** keep off the rain and **fly sheets** keep off flies (that's pretty obvious!). **Exercise rugs** or **quarter sheets** are half blankets that extend back from the saddle; they cover a clipped horse while warming up or cooling down in chilly weather.

Some horse garments sound like people clothes: **Bathrobes** are plushy sheets of fleece, wool, or cotton terry that wick away moisture after exercise or bath. **Pajamas** and **underwear** are stretchy hoods, shoulder guards, or sheets that keep your horse and his blanket clean and protect his coat from being rubbed or chafed by his blanket.

Fly masks protect his eyes and ears from biting bugs while he's in the pasture. **Ear nets** keep flies out of ears while you ride; many have fringe that hangs down the forehead as well.

Leg wraps and **polo wraps** protect and support the legs of horses being shipped or being worked. They're usually made of stretchy fabric. **Tail wraps and bags** protect tails during shipping or keep a show horse's long tail clean and beautiful. **Neck wraps** do the same for the mane and sometimes are used to sweat out fat as well.

Bell boots, galloping boots, splint boots, ankle boots, fetlock boots, and **brushing boots** are usually made of leather or neoprene. They support tendons and ligaments, and protect the legs and feet from being nicked by the horse's own hooves when he is moving or jumping. **Shipping boots** protect against injury when a horse is being trailered.

A **grazing muzzle** keeps a turned-out horse from grazing too freely and gaining too much weight. A horse in a muzzle can nibble a little grass with each bite, but not a lot: surely it's been voted by horses worldwide as "Most Hated Garment!"

A **feedbag**, on the other hand, is a portable grain pail, usually made of fabric, that hangs on the head of a working horse so he can eat on the job. This bag lunch for the working horse would probably win the worldwide horse vote for "Most Loved Garment."

A Horse of a Different Color — How About Green?

You love horses. You love nature: the swing of the seasons, wild animals, blue skies, cool winds, sun, and snow. This wonderful planet has given you everything you've got, including your favorite animal. What have you done for Mother Earth lately?

Unfortunately, methods of modern horsemanship tend to do things *to* Mother Earth, not *for* her. We use fossil fuels to fertilize and harvest hay and grain, and then to transport it. We trailer our horses thousands of miles, behind big pickup trucks that get, if we're lucky, 8 miles per gallon. We house our animals indoors, where we need to turn on a light anytime we're doing something with them.

We dispose of tons of manure and use up tons of shavings and other bedding materials. Some of us drive twice a day to where our horses live to feed them, ride them, and muck them out.

We can do better. A few simple choices can get us started, and make our beloved sport/hobby/life's passion cleaner, greener, and better for the Mother of our horses and ourselves.

Starting with the Basics

Food, shelter, and transportation are the main factors involved with keeping a horse. One of the best ways to reduce your equine environmental impact is to live near your horse. Stable at home if possible. The next best solution is to stable within walking or biking distance.

If you *can* walk or bike, do it! Your horse will thank you for being slimmer and more in shape.

If your horse can't live close to you, look at how you get to him. Is public transportation available? Use it. If the schedule doesn't work for you, let the transportation company know. They may add buses if there's demand.

Can you carpool with friends? Do it. If you must go solo, what are you being driven in? Ask how many miles per gallon the vehicle gets. If there's a choice, ask to use the compact car, not the pickup.

FEEDING YOUR HORSE

The so-called locavore movement encourages people to eat food grown near their homes. Your horse can be a locavore, too. Don't buy hay from a distant location if a local farmer is selling it. You'll be helping to keep him in business, and he'll be helping you by keeping the countryside open and undeveloped. (Hayfields are great places to ride when the hay's been cut; you're doing yourself a big favor keeping them around.)

When buying grain at the local feed store, ask where it comes from. If there's a choice of brands with equivalent

 MANURE HAPPENS

The average horse produces about 50 pounds of manure a day — that's 10 tons a year! About half the nutrients you feed your horse pass out in his pee and poop. About half, if properly handled, can be used by pasture or crop plants in a growing season. Manure is a resource that returns the organic matter and nitrogen to the soil, so less fertilizer is needed.

But storm water washing over your manure pile can leach out nutrients and pollute streams. If possible, store manure and bedding in a lined and covered area, where water can't pour over it and leach into the ground. Use a Dumpster or build a concrete storage area. If that isn't an option, look into composting, or removal services that compost the manure and return it to the earth somewhere.

products, choose the one that comes the shortest distance. Let store managers know this is important to you. It may affect their buying decisions.

BUYING BEDDING

Sawdust and shavings are former trees; so is recycled paper bedding. Trees take many years to grow. Straw grows new every year, as do rice hulls.

Why does all of this matter? Because of the carbon cycle. Plants absorb and bind CO_2 (carbon dioxide) as they grow. That keeps it out of the atmosphere, where it can cause global warming. Plants — and beddings made from them — release carbon as they decompose.

But if you use wheat straw from this year's harvest, the carbon release is balanced by carbon uptake next season, when the wheat field is replanted. If you use sawdust instead, you release carbon that took a tree 20 or 30 years to absorb and bind. Even if trees are replanted, there's a long lag time before the little tree grows large enough to absorb the amount of carbon the big one released.

So what should you use for bedding?

* **Straw** is probably the greenest choice, and is preferred by many horsemen. It is soft, warm, and absorbent. Locally grown straw is the greenest of all.

* **Rice hulls,** if available in your area, are another annually grown bedding that may work well. They are usually used mixed with shavings.

* **Shredded paper** is the greenest choice of the tree-grown products. It's recycled, so it's already been used at least once. Check the source to be sure the bedding is made of newsprint, phone books, and other materials printed with nontoxic vegetable inks.

* **Pellets,** though a non-recycled, tree-based bedding, may be somewhat less wasteful because less volume is needed for bedding overall. The pellets expand in the presence of water, and may clump, making it easier to remove urine.

* **Sawdust or shavings** may be all that's available in your price range. Look for a local source. Use softwood shavings only; hardwoods can cause health problems for your horse.

Whatever bedding you use, put down stall mats first. Mats provide cushioning, so you don't need to bed as deeply. They also prevent horses from digging — or peeing — holes in a dirt floor. They're expensive, but last for years, and can really help you reduce your horse's impact on the environment.

✶ SWEATING THE SMALL STUFF ✶

Small actions have big consequences when multiplied by several million people. Take bottled water. Nobody used to carry water around all the time. But today, 22 billion water bottles are thrown away every year, 60 million each day. Each bottle takes 1,000 years to degrade. Bottled water is no safer than tap water — in fact it may be less safe, as harmful compounds from the plastic may leach into it — and it costs 10,000 times more.

Horse lovers, why not use a canteen instead? It's way cooler — for the planet, for your image, and even for the water, if you get an insulated canteen. A canteen says you're too smart to pay for something you can get free. It says you care about your world.

SOUTH OF THE BORDER
Three South American Breeds

A lot of North American breeds were influenced by ancient Spanish bloodlines; here are some South American horses that share that ancestry. The three described here all happen to be gaited, meaning that in addition to the walk, trot, and canter, they have a special way of moving. Gaited horses are prized for their special gaits, which are usually beautifully smooth and easy to ride. See pages 336–37 to learn about gaited horses from North America.

MANGALARGA MARCHADOR

Developed in Brazil from Portuguese bloodlines, the Mangalarga Marchador is an outstanding cow horse that is also at home on the trail and is known for its great endurance and stamina. A handsome horse, the Mangalarga Marchador has a triangular-shaped head with broad, flat forehead and fine muzzle; an arched, muscular neck; and medium-length body. It stands between 14.2 and 16 hands, and has powerful legs with short cannons and sloping pasterns. It is a gentle, sensitive, and versatile animal.

SPECIAL GAIT: The **marcha**, which is a fast smooth gait in which three feet are sometimes on the ground; an extremely comfortable ride.

PASO FINO

The Paso Fino comes from Puerto Rico, where it was developed from Spanish horses crossed with Canadian horses that were imported to work in the sugar mills.

Other countries, including the Dominican Republic, Cuba, Colombia, and Venezuela, also developed Paso Fino–type horses. This is a lovely horse, compactly built at 14 to 15 hands, with a handsome head, arched neck, sloping shoulders, delicate legs, full mane and tail. It is gentle in hand and spirited under saddle; known to be affectionate and full of personality.

SPECIAL GAITS: The **paso fino** is a highly collected gait that is slower than the walk. The horse takes many rapid, short steps, and each footfall is distinct. In competition, the fino is performed on a sounding board and judged by the quickness, evenness, and precision of the gait. Though the legs move so quickly, a horse can keep up the fino for hours, and it is extremely smooth for the rider.

The **paso corto** is a jogging-speed version of the fino, also very smooth. The **paso largo** extends the gait to a canter or hand-gallop speed.

PERUVIAN PASO

The National Horse of Peru, the Peruvian Paso has been bred over centuries to be a smooth-stepping horse with great endurance. It stands 14 to 15 hands high, with a rather heavy neck, wide chest and sloping shoulders; great depth of body, rounded croup and low-set tail. The hocks are more angled than other breeds. This robust but sensitive horse is known for **brio**, a quality of brilliance and spirit apparent in its performance and its personality.

SPECIAL GAIT: A smooth, soft amble with brilliant high-stepping action; the front legs roll outward as the horse steps forward, a quality called **termino**, that looks almost as if the horse is swimming.

✸ CALCULATING YOUR CARBON HOOFPRINT ✸

The term "carbon footprint" refers to the amount of carbon a person's day-to-day activities release into the atmosphere. All animals and people release some CO_2 just by breathing, pooping, dying, and decaying. But we humans have vastly multiplied the impact we, and our animals, have.

Horses create a large carbon hoofprint when we transport them for competition or clinics. The next largest impact would be production and transportation of feed and bedding. Other impacts include barn lighting and water heating.

Here's how to calculate your show-season carbon hoofprint:

1. Find out how many gallons of fuel are used to transport your horse to and from an event.
   How many miles per gallon does the vehicle get? _____
   How many miles to the event? _____ × 2 (for the round-trip) =_____
   Now divide the miles by the miles per gallon. (For example: 80 miles / 12 mpg = 6.6 gallons)

2. If your truck uses diesel, multiply that number by 22.38.
   That's how many pounds of CO_2 each gallon of diesel puts into the atmosphere.
   (For example: 6.6 gal × 22.38 lbs CO_2/gal = 147.7 lbs of CO_2)
   For gasoline, multiply by 20.
   (For example: 6.6 gal × 20 lbs CO_2/gal = 132 lbs of CO_2)

3. Calculate for all the events you transport your horse to in a season.

Some broad examples:

If you show locally every two weeks all summer, your calculation might look like this:

25 gal of gasoline per event × 8 events = 200 gal × 20 = 4,000 lbs of CO_2

Add to this your everyday horse-related carbon hoofprint. You can get a rough idea of that number by asking yourself these questions:

Do you live with your horse, or do you have to be driven to where you ride? _____

How often? _____

How many miles? _____

And how many miles per gallon does the vehicle get? _____

If you're driven 5 miles each way, 5 days a week, in a car that gets 20 miles per gallon, your calculation looks like this:

5 miles × 10 trips = 50 miles per week

50 miles ÷ 20 mpg = 2.5 gal

2.5 gallons × 20 lbs CO_2/gal = 50 lbs CO_2 per week

Multiply this by the number of weeks a year you keep this schedule. You may be shocked by the number you come up with.

Help Offset Your Carbon Hoofprint

When going to a show, consider buying credits to offset that carbon. Carbon credits are sold by companies (see Resources, page 358) that pool the money and fund projects like tree planting or energy projects like solar, wind, and farm-based methane that produce no greenhouse gases. The price is amazingly reasonable — currently $12 per ton. You become an investor, helping these great projects get off the ground.

Dealing with Pesky Pests

In our natural desire to make our horses lives more comfortable, we sometimes make choices that aren't great for the environment. One example is the propane mosquito trap. These work by giving off CO2, just like our bodies do. The greater concentration attracts mosquitoes to their doom. Great idea, right? Except that CO2 is one of the major greenhouse gases, and these traps release it straight into the atmosphere.

Electronic bug zappers are another less-than-friendly choice. Sure, they make that satisfying sizzling sound as they fry the predators that feed on us, but sadly, they fry the predators that feed on mosquitoes, too. Studies show that only 31 percent of those zaps represent the death of a biting insect — and for every mosquito zapped, a larger number of mosquito predators

(ground beetles and parasitic wasps) are killed, making your basic problem even worse.

What about those ultrasonic sound-wave bug repellers? Mosquitoes are actually attracted to them! And many sprays we use to control and kill mosquitoes are toxic to humans and other animals.

ZAPPING MOSQUITOES

Luckily, mosquitoes are easy to control in an environmentally sound way. Here's how:

✳ **Empty all standing water,** every other day, from pails, birdbaths, plant saucers, and wading pools. This keeps mosquito larvae from maturing.

332

- **Get rid of trash** that can hold small amounts of water, such as old tires, leaf-filled roof gutters, tin cans, etc. Drill holes in the bottom of your tire swing to let the water out. Cover or screen rain barrels.

- **Use *Bacillus thuringiensis israelensis* (BTi)** mosquito products. These come in disks or granules that can be put in ponds, water tubs, and other permanent bodies of water. BTi is a natural bacteria that kills mosquito larvae. It doesn't harm other organisms. You can find BTi at hardware stores, gardening stores, or in natural gardening and pest control catalogs.

- **Put up bat houses.** One bat can eat 700 mosquitoes a night.

- **Use natural insect repellents** on your horse. Many different ones are available in tack shops and feed stores.

- **Feed vinegar to your horses.** Some folks swear that it helps keep flies away.

- **Dried garlic** has the reputation for being a great deterrent to all insects. This can be mixed in the feed or, if you have horses getting fat on pasture alone and you aren't feeding grain, you can mix it with loose salt and let them have it free choice.

SHOOING FLIES

Fly control is a big issue around stables. The body heat and CO_2 that horses give off attract bloodsucking insects like horseflies and deerflies. Manure attracts stable flies.

Stable flies are annoying to people and horses. The solution here is cleanliness. And be sure to do the following:

- **Close windows and doors** during the hours when they are in direct sunlight. Keep window screens in good repair.

- **Sweep the barn aisles.** Put manure in its own pile and locate it as far as possible from the barn. Compost your manure in covered piles.

- **Put up flypaper,** high enough that no one — not even a high-headed horse — will walk into it.

* **Use jar traps inside the barn.** These traps use odor — okay, stink — to lure flies. Once in, they can't get out; they die in there, adding more stink, which lures more flies, in what is called a "virtuous cycle." These jar traps can get pretty ripe; you'll want to locate them as far as possible from where you'll be working or hanging out with your horse.

You can also use beneficial nematodes, tiny insects that kill fly larvae, ticks, fleas, and termites. You can usually find these at your local garden nursery.

Some Solar Solutions

You use electricity in your barn and to run your electric fence. Why not harness the sun and produce your own power? The sun shines everywhere — some places more than others — and your barn roof may be a good location for some solar panels. Solar power can be a lifeline in areas where storms frequently knock out power.

If a full-blown solar power system is out of the question, an easy option for making some of your own power is a solar fence charger (available at most farm supply stores). In sunny parts of the country it can be a great choice to keep that wire hot using free energy from the sun.

Solar-powered flashlights can be a lifesaver on a farm. You just leave your flashlight in a sunny window, or on the dashboard of the truck, and it's always charged. There's nothing worse than a horse emergency on a dark night, with dead flashlight batteries. Choose a flashlight with LED bulbs, and the batteries will last many times as long.

Horseshoe REVIEW

The Flambards series and others by K. M. Peyton

K. M. Peyton's most famous books are in her Flambards series, but you'll find more horses in some of her other books, such as *Fly-by-Night*, *Free Rein*, and *Dark Horse*. These are definitely young adult books; younger readers might want to wait a few years to tackle them.

She also wrote the extremely funny *"Who, Sir? Me, Sir?"* about a reluctant school tetrathlon team that triumphs even though it is under-endowed with horses, experience, and talent.

FLY FRINGE

Materials Needed

A rectangular strip of lightweight leather or denim, 1 inch narrower than your brow band, and long enough to reach from the bridle brow band to your horse's nostrils (6–8 inches should do it)

Scissors

Latigo or Velcro strips

Leather punch (if using leather)

Needle and thread (if using fabric)

Looking through horse books with pictures from Spain and India, you'll see horses wearing bridles with long leather fringes hanging from the brow band to keep flies away. They reach most of the way down the face and look quite elegant. You can make one of leather (elegant and durable) or fabric (funky and functional).

Directions

1. **Fold your leather or cloth** over at one short end, fitting it around the brow band to make a tube.

2. **If using leather:** Punch 2 holes about ½ inch apart, in either end of the folded part, below the brow band; thread a piece of latigo through both holes on each end and tie knots in the two ends, leaving enough tail so you can untie the knots when you need to remove the fringe.

   If using fabric, mark where the edges come together. Hand-sew Velcro patches on each end and attach to your brow band.

3. **With the scissors,** cut the leather or fabric into long strips, starting at the bottom edge and stopping before you reach the brow band.

STEP 3

SMOOTH STRIDING RIDES
Seven Gaited Breeds from North America

All horses can do three basic gaits: the walk, the trot, and the canter (the gallop is a really fast canter). "Gaited" horses have additional gaits — special ways of moving that are often more efficient than the trot and much more comfortable for the rider. These gaits are an inherited trait; they can't be taught to a horse that doesn't have the right breeding. Gaited horses come in many sizes, shapes, and backgrounds. Here's a selection from the northern hemispheres. (For South American gaited horses, see page 329.)

ICELANDIC HORSE

ORIGIN: Iceland, of Norse stock

HEIGHT: 12.2–14.3 hands

DESCRIPTION: Handsome head, long neck, sloping, well-muscled shoulders, moderately long back, muscular croup; friendly, energetic, not always a good choice for small children because of their fiery nature

SPECIAL GAITS: The *tölt*, which is a smooth four-beat amble without suspension and always with one or two feet on the ground; it can be as fast as an extended trot or canter. Also the *skeid* or flying pace, which is a two-beat gait that can be as fast as a gallop. Both gaits are extremely smooth for a rider.

GOOD AT: Trail and endurance

KENTUCKY MOUNTAIN SADDLE HORSE/ MOUNTAIN PLEASURE HORSE

ORIGIN: Eastern Kentucky

HEIGHT: 11–15.2 hands

DESCRIPTION: Handsome head, large eyes and a straight profile; medium-length arched neck; well-sloped shoulders; wide, deep chest; clean legs; a comfortable ride and a gentle nature

SPECIAL GAIT: A fast amble or single-foot, which is comfortable for horse and rider; very sure-footed over rough ground

GOOD AT: Trail, pleasure, light farm work

MCCURDY PLANTATION HORSE

ORIGIN: Alabama

HEIGHT: 14.2–16 hands

DESCRIPTION: Rounded, sturdy, refined horse with broad chest and good bone; gentle temperament

SPECIAL GAITS: The McCurdy Lick, which is a smooth, lateral, four-beat single-foot; also the running walk, the rack, and the stepping pace. Some individuals also perform a gait called the fox trot in which the horse walks with the front feet and trots with the rear, giving a smooth ride that is easy on horse and rider alike.

GOOD AT: Trail, pleasure, field trials

RACKING HORSE

ORIGIN: Southern United States

HEIGHT: 15.2 hands

DESCRIPTION: Handsome head, long arched neck, long sloping shoulders, rounded flanks, moderately sloping croup; good bone, fine coat; temperament is calm, intelligent, ready to please

SPECIAL GAIT: The rack, which is a smooth, lateral, four-beat ambling gait with only one foot striking the ground at a time; emphasis is on speed rather than high-stepping style; they can keep up the rack for a long time without tiring.

GOOD AT: Pleasure riding, trail riding, field trials, showing

ROCKY MOUNTAIN HORSE

ORIGIN: Eastern Kentucky

HEIGHT: 14.2–16 hands

DESCRIPTION: Type varies, with some appearing more Spanish than others; handsome, broad-chested; many are chocolate-colored with a white mane and tail.

SPECIAL GAIT: Single-foot, which is a fast, comfortable, four-beat gait

GOOD AT: Pleasure riding, trail riding

SINGLE-FOOTING HORSE

ORIGIN: American South

HEIGHT: 14.3–15.2 hands

DESCRIPTION: Conformation similar to an old-type Morgan, with breed organizers emphasizing working qualities over show qualities; this very rare breed is described as a horse that's ready to "git 'er done."

SPECIAL GAIT: The single-foot, in which at least one foot is on the ground at all times. This four-beat gait can be performed at trail speeds (7–9 mph), a road gait (12–15 mph), or a racing speed (over 20 mph). With a range like this, Single-Footing horses can work cattle in gait, and compete in Western sports against other breeds. In fact, this is the only gait these horses perform!

GOOD AT: Trail, endurance, ranch work

TIGER HORSE

ORIGIN: Northwest United States; bred as an attempt to recreate the Altai Horse — a spotted horse of the Russian steppes — and also the old-type Nez Percé Appaloosa; still quite rare

HEIGHT: 14–15.2 hands

DESCRIPTION: Lean, with straight or convex profile, high-set neck, great depth of heart girth, well-muscled, clean legs; mane and tail may be scanty; resembles the original Appaloosa, both in conformation and coloring.

SPECIAL GAIT: The Indian shuffle, which is an intermediate four-beat gait, smooth and comfortable for horse and rider

GOOD AT: Trail, ranch work, pleasure

Working on Having a Horse of Your Own

Because that's what you want if you're horse crazy: A horse to groom, care for, muck out, and fuss over; a horse to ride or drive, to take pictures of, to dream about. But what if you don't have room or money for a horse of your own?

First, don't despair. Life is long, and circumstances change. If you want a horse, you'll make choices that will eventually lead you there.

And if eventually isn't soon enough? You still have options, depending on your age, where you live, your skills, and your financial situation.

Look into Leasing

One of the simplest is leasing. This means you rent a horse. Time frames range from extremely short — a few hours on a trail ride — to long-term, possibly several years.

Horses available for lease are usually loved and valued by their owners; that's why they aren't for sale. The owner may be too busy to ride the horse, or she may have health or other issues. The owner wants to keep control of the horse, but is happy to have him exercised and enjoyed by another rider.

Share a Sport

Another option is to get involved in a sport that requires more than one person per horse. Vaulting has the highest human-to-horse ratio.

Other choices include combined driving. If you're someone's steady groom or 'gator (navigator) you'll gain lots of competitive experience and horse time on somebody else's dime. Or try Ride and Tie.

Sign Up to Help Out

If leasing opportunities don't show up, make yourself useful. Mucking stalls at a barn, turning horses out and bringing them back in, and doing the feeding routine give you the contact you crave, teach you horse skills, and puts you in front of people who may notice how responsible you are and think of a spare horse they know about.

Or volunteer in a handicapped riding program. You'll be helping people, and there are often opportunities to ride the therapy horses — they need recreational time, too.

Most important, learn all you can. Take every chance you can to handle horses. If being around horses is your firm intention, you'll find that horses come into your life in unexpected ways.

So if somebody asks if you have a horse, don't say "No." Say, "Not yet."

338

Sharing Your Horse

Horse lovers are a community, even a family. If you are lucky enough to have a horse of your very own, find a way to share with people who don't.

❋ **Bring a gentle horse to a local elementary school.** You can talk to kids about handling and riding horses, and stoke their enthusiasm.

❋ **Bring your horse to a nursing home.** There are old people in nursing homes hungry for the sight, touch, and smell of a horse. If you have a gentle one, and the nursing home authorities will allow it, think about bringing her to meet people. If you have a Mini, she may even be able to come indoors and gladden horse-hungry hearts.

❋ **Give a little kid a pony ride.** Even a slow circle under the trees at a church fair can be the thrilling first ride of the rest of her life. Let people pat your horse, if safe and appropriate.

❋ **Investigate sports that allow people to share a horse.** Maybe you and a friend could compete in Ride and Tie, or she could navigate for you in Combined Driving.

❋ **Finally, just let a horseless friend ride your horse.** Teach her how to be safe and effective. Give her some alone time with your horse. After all, that's what you'd want, isn't it?

THE TAIL END

Wait, there's more great stuff! On the following pages, you'll find information on different ways to work with horses, a checklist with dozens of breeds to start looking out for, lists of all the books, movies, and crafts included in this book (in case you want to start checking those off as well), a glossary of equine words and terms, and a bunch of organizations, associations, and other resources to help you keep learning about and loving the wonderful, amazing, beautiful horse!

APPENDIX A:
Careers in the Horse World

Yes, you love horses, but how are you going to make a living with them? The question, which you may have heard from your mom or dad, implies a not-so-hidden message: Horses are impractical. Get your head out of the clouds and find something real to do!

But there are many jobs and career paths, and thousands of people working with, for, and near their favorite animal. Some jobs are very hands-on, like grooming, riding, and veterinary medicine; some are totally hands-off, like advertising, law, and real estate. Some pay well, some don't, but many offer opportunities to move up in the field.

Horses are big business, small business, and in-between business. There are 9.2 million horses in the United States and the horse industry has a direct economic benefit of $39 billion annually in the U.S. economy. It creates 460,000 full-time jobs. Tell that to your loving parent — and then investigate your options.

Veterinary Assistant

Job description: A vet's assistant goes on rounds to clean and set up instruments, assists with physical exams, and helps the vet with daily duties, plus schedules appointments and does anything that keeps the office running.

You'll need: Good horse knowledge, organizational skills, and the ability to take directions quickly.

Schooling: Most training is on the job, but you may need to complete a certificate program. Some schools that accredit veterinary technicians also offer an assistant program.

Downside: Depending upon where you work, you may end up as a drudge who only gets to do the dirty work. Or you might just do office work. You'll also make approximately five times less than your boss.

Upside: It's hands-on, outdoor horse work, if you're lucky, plus there's no need to get (and pay for) eight years of vet training.

Veterinary Technician

Job description: Vet techs help veterinarians in a professional capacity, doing lab tests, acting as surgical nurses and anesthesiologists, doing exams, and managing the office.

You'll need: A strong knowledge of science, the ability to focus on details, organizational skills, physical strength, and mind-reading skills so you can give your boss what she wants before she knows she wants it.

Schooling: Either a two-year or bachelor's degree in an accredited vet tech program. There are around 80 such programs in the United States.

Downside: Depending on the practice, you may be on call some nights and weekends. It's difficult, physically demanding work at less than half the pay your boss gets.

Upside: You need only about half the schooling a vet needs but are doing professional, hands-on work helping horses. You can do veterinary work without being married to the job, and you're not the one who has to make the terrible decision to put a horse down.

Veterinarian

Job description: An animal doctor is just as qualified as a human doctor. Most equine vets are in private practice, traveling to farms for routine and emergency care. Usually you'll have several nights a week on-call and some weekends. Vets also work for the government and at universities and corporations, developing new products, teaching, or helping understand and control disease.

You'll need: Great marks, especially in science, some outstanding special projects on your resume, organizational skills, and physical strength and stamina;

must understand horses and know how to handle them.

Schooling: Four years pre-vet study, four years vet school, passing a state licensing exam.

Downside: It's difficult, physically demanding work, with long hours and many heartbreaks. Vet schools are more competitive to get into than med schools.

Upside: You're doing essential, lifesaving work, with a direct impact on horses' quality of life. The pay is good and you have lots of contact with horses.

Equine Acupuncturist

Job description: An acupuncturist uses fine needles to treat horses for pain and other problems. This is a growing field as more people in the West learn about the effectiveness of acupuncture.

You'll need: A degree in veterinary medicine (DVM), so you'll need the usual great grades to get into vet school; not to mention, excellent horse-handling skills.

Schooling: In addition to your DVM, mentioned above, you'll also need the tenacity and funds to go back to school to learn acupuncture and become an expert in Chinese medicine.

Downside: Extra schooling beyond your DVM is expensive. Not all human clients will be receptive to your methods and not all horses will be comfortable with the needles.

Upside: You'll be able to do a lot for horses with less invasive techniques and fewer side effects. You'll work in a fascinating, cross-cultural field.

Equine Dentist

Job description: A veterinarian who specializes in dentistry. There is a growing need for equine dentists as we learn more about the problems bad teeth can cause horses.

You'll need: Excellent horse-handling skills, strength, and an ability and willingness to educate your human clients on the need for good dental care.

Schooling: A degree in veterinary medicine (DVM) with further training or certification in equine dentistry, plus an apprenticeship with a practicing equine dentist. Depending on the state, it may be legal to practice equine dentistry without a DVM degree, provided you have certification through an equine dental school. The supervision of a vet is still usually necessary.

Downside: Horses don't like dentists in their mouths any more than you do; this can be hard physical work.

Upside: Your work has an immediate impact; you don't have to wait long to see positive results for the horse. Skilled work for excellent pay, plus an equine dentist doesn't usually need to be on-call; tooth problems can usually wait until morning.

Veterinary Chiropractor

Job description: Chiropractors manipulate the patient's spinal column to correct misalignments and relieve pain. This is a growing field.

You'll need: Strong horse skills, a thorough knowledge of horse anatomy, strong marketing and business skills, and physical strength.

(Jobs in Equine Healthcare, continued)

Schooling: A degree as a vet with training in chiropractic, or as a Doctor of Chiropractic with special training in animal chiropractic, state licensing, and certification through the American Veterinary Chiropractic Association.

Downside: Adjusting a horse's spine can be hard physical work. This specialty is not as formally recognized as other medical fields, so clients may be skeptical.

Upside: Outdoor work with horses; making horses' lives better. No needles, so your patients are glad to see you the second time you visit!

Farrier

Job description: Farriers shoe and trim horses' feet, and correct problems with a horse's way of going (movement). "No hoof, no horse" is the saying — and that makes the farrier an essential part of the horse economy.

You'll need: A thorough knowledge of equine feet and legs, an ability to work with a vet and learn on the job, a strong back, good horse- and people-handling skills.

Schooling: You can either learn by doing an apprenticeship with a good farrier or by attending farrier school and then being an apprentice. Length of study at farrier schools varies. Some farriers specialize in so-called natural shoeing, or in maintaining barefoot horses; there are fashions and theories in this as in all things. Others specialize in racehorses, draft horses, hunter-jumpers, or another specialty.

Downside: This is very demanding physical work, with long hours, being outdoors in all weather, and a lot of driving to service your territory. Not all horses have good shoeing manners; you may find yourself doing a lot of ad hoc training.

Upside: You're your own boss, working outdoors every day with horses, and developing relationships with horse people in your area. You are needed, and you'll be able to get plenty of work.

Pony Tales

BLACKSMITHS

The smithy was a place of heat, fire, and steam, and it's no surprise that many cultures had smith gods. Interestingly many of them were lame, in spite of their strong arms. Hephaestus, the Greek smith god, was born crippled. His father, Zeus, cast him out of heaven in disgust, but he worked his way back with his smith skills and married Aphrodite.

Another lame smith-god is the Anglo-Saxon Wayland, the son of a mermaid and a water giant. His fame at blacksmithing led to his kidnapping by the Swedish king, who ham-strung him to prevent his escape. According to legend, Wayland's spirit will shoe any horse if a coin is left on a stone near his smithy.

Professional Equestrian

Job description: A professional equestrian is paid to ride, drive, show, train, and school other people's horses. She may also conduct clinics or seminars and give lessons in equitation or horse training.

You'll need: Great horse skills, good self-promotional skills, flexibility, and the ability to work well with different kinds of people and horses.

Schooling: Requirements range from coming up through Pony Club or Master Field Trials to graduating from an equestrian college. You may be able to start by simply posting a lot of wins as an amateur.

Downside: It can be a hard scramble to make enough money to live on. It's a demanding, physical life that may involve a lot of travel (sometimes that's a plus!).

Upside: Your whole job is about horses — you don't have to squeeze your passion into a busy life doing something else. You keep improving skills you may have begun learning as a little kid on a pony.

Trainer

Job description: Trainers start, finish, fine-tune, and retune horses. There are as many kinds of trainers as there are horsemanship disciplines.

You'll need: Great riding and horse-handling skills, thorough knowledge of horse behavior and psychology, business skills, self-promotion skills, patience, and flexibility.

Schooling: You might find an apprenticeship or you could learn from clinics and through graded programs offered by Pony Club and AQHA. You could also earn a college degree in equine studies. Countless new theories about riding, training, and the mind of the horse spin off new training protocols each year, so you'll always be learning.

Downside: Training can be demanding physical work for not much pay, especially when you are just starting out.

Upside: You work with horses, day-in, day-out, helping them learn and making their lives better. It's rewarding when your clients, equine and human, do well. Popular trainers can earn a lot of money as clinicians by teaching at clinics and horse expos.

Riding Instructor

Job description: Instructors work with students at all levels, either as an employee at a barn, traveling from barn to barn, or holding classes at their own facility. You can work in a specialized field like reining, jumping, or dressage. The greater your skills, the more in-demand you will be among riders working at the higher levels. Or you can specialize in introducing young children and novice adults to the wonderful world of horses — equally important and very rewarding, though not as well paid. Another choice is to be an instructor to the handicapped. This, too, can be tremendously rewarding, as you see horses help people surmount health troubles that have held them back for years.

You'll need: Teaching and communication skills, riding skills, in-depth knowledge of horse safety and handling, ability to project authority and speak clearly (all day!), patience, and organizational skills.

Schooling: You can apprentice, be a working student, come up through programs offered by Pony Club or AQHA, or earn a college degree in equine studies. Certification is not required, but is recommended as a way to help you increase your skills and as a marketing tool. It can also reduce the cost of your insurance.

Downside: People (not to mention horses!) can be difficult to work with, and it can be hard to make a living, even if you work full-time.

Upside: You work with horses and people every day, helping both achieve their potential. There is a lot of variety and it is rewarding to play a part in other people's progress.

Groom

Job description: Grooms take care of horses in boarding barns, training and riding stables, tracks, breeding farms, polo and hunt clubs, at shows and rodeos. The job usually includes feeding, watering, mucking stalls, cleaning tack, and managing supplies, as well as actually grooming, trimming, and perhaps braiding.

You'll need: Flexibility, reliability, physical energy, good attitude, lots of horse experience.

Schooling: Mostly acquired on the job, though a four-year equine studies degree is helpful in moving to upper-level positions.

Downside: You are not working with your own horses. It's hard, exacting work for little pay or status.

Upside: You're doing hands-on, day-to-day work with horses. Pay may include housing, insurance, or perks such as lessons, board for your horse, or use of a vehicle.

Jockey

Job description: Riding racehorses on the flat or over fences. Lots of people say they want to be a jockey, but only a few actually do it.

You'll need: Courage, self-promotion skills, exceptional riding skills, a small yet strong physique.

Schooling: You'll gain experience in the field or you can attend jockey school. You may work your way up by starting as a groom, stable hand, or exercise rider.

Downside: It's dangerous, demanding work, with no glory when you lose and not much money; plus most jockeys have to diet continually.

Upside: If you're a thrill seeker, there's speed, excitement, fame and glory, and 6 to 10 percent of the winning purse, which can be quite large.

Exercise Rider

Job description: Exercise riders arrive at the track very early in the morning and ride racehorses according to the trainer's instructions, to keep them fit and bring them along to peak condition at race time.

You'll need: A high school diploma, lots of horse experience, great riding skills, and a reliable alarm clock.

Schooling: On-the-job training.

Downside: The hours are early and the pay is moderate.

Upside: You get to ride great horses every day, without the dangers of actual racing.

Hot Walker

Job description: Cool horses out after races.

You'll need: Horse-leading skills.

Schooling: None required.

Downside: The job is a bit lowly and monotonous, with low pay.

Upside: This is one of the easier entry-level race jobs to get and can be a way into the race world.

Outrider

Job description: Outriders lead and follow the post parade on horseback, and they catch loose horses. Some people combine outrider work with exercise riding.

You'll need: Great horse and riding skills, plus a thorough knowledge of racing. You may need to provide your own horse; experience at the track is recommended.

Schooling: On-the-job training.

Downside: It's hard work in all weather with early hours. Outriders work while horses are being exercised as well as during actual races.

Upside: You're on horseback all day while doing essential work in an exciting environment.

∾ A DREAM ∾ NO LONGER DENIED

Have you ever dreamed of riding those magnificent Lipizzans at the Spanish Riding School? That career used to be out of reach for girls, but no longer. In 2008 two young women, Sojourner Morrel and Hannah Zeithofer, passed the rigorous exam and trial period to become *élèves* (cadets).

Cadets get to the stable at six in the morning to feed horses, take a riding lesson at seven, and spend the rest of their day grooming and cleaning stalls. After 3 or 4 years they progress to being Assistant Riders; it can take 15 years to make Chief Rider.

The girls' hardest problem so far? Mounting without stirrups. They don't have the upper arm strength of the male cadets.

JOBS IN UNUSUAL EQUINE AREAS

Rodeo Cowboy

Job description: Rodeo cowboys and cowgirls compete on the rodeo circuit in various events.

You'll need: Courage, cowboy skills, and an ability to tolerate lots of instability and life on the road.

Schooling: You'll be attending the school of hard knocks!

Downside: This job involves constant travel, a high risk of injury, and a lot of wear and tear on the body.

Upside: There's plenty of excitement, a close-knit rodeo community, and the chance to earn a great deal of money if you become one of the top riders.

Packer/Guide

Job description: Guides take hunters, fishers, photographers, and campers on long trips into backcountry.

You'll need: Wilderness skills, hunting and fishing skills, horse experience, reliability, people skills, and maybe cooking skills.

Schooling: You'll need a high school diploma plus experience or attendance at a guide training school.

Downside: There's an element of danger from sudden changes in the weather, wildlife, and unexpected events such as rock slides.

Upside: You're doing outdoor work with horses (or mules), usually in gorgeous surroundings. You'll learn things most people don't know.

Dude Ranch Worker

Job description: Working on a dude or guest ranch offers a number of job possibilities, including wrangler, riding instructor, ranch hand, and guide; ranches also need cooks, wait staff, bartenders, and cleaners.

You'll need: A good attitude, people skills, willingness to pitch in and help wherever needed, and a good appearance.

Schooling: No formal education required; can be a good summer job for college students.

Downside: Hard work and long hours, with six-day work weeks standard and evening activities with guests often required. Compensation usually includes salary plus room and board.

Upside: You'll gain good experience with horses and people and be able to work outdoors, usually in gorgeous scenery.

Carriage Driver

Job description: As a carriage driver, you can own your own horse and vehicle or work for a company that provides rides — city tours, weddings, parades, proposals.

In addition to handling the lines (reins), the driver cares for, grooms, and harnesses the horse.

You'll need: Strong driving and horse-handling experience, a tidy appearance, communication and people skills.

Schooling: You'll need at least a high school diploma. Attending a driving school is recommended.

Downside: It's outdoor work in all weather; the schedule may be grueling.

Upside: This is an unusual job working with horses and people. You spend lots of time outdoors, and you are bringing a bit of magic into people's lives.

Stunt Rider

Job description: Stunt riders, who often have a professional background in another horse sport, work in movies, TV, and for live-action entertainment spectacles.

You'll need: Outstanding riding skills, stunt skills, physical strength, and courage.

Schooling: A high school diploma. An apprenticeship with a good stuntman is recommended for film work.

Downside: Show biz people are often difficult to work with, and you will be seeing the less-than-glamorous underbelly of the business. The work can be hazardous — that's why the stars don't do it. Pay is variable. If you're really good, no one will know it's you!

Upside: Stunt work can be challenging and intriguing. Show biz is glamorous and high profile. You may work with big stars and get to know them. You could be seen in movies and on TV by millions of people.

Commercial Horse Hauler

Job description: People pay to have their horses hauled around the country to events and new homes. Employment opportunities include drivers, attendants, and office workers, or you can build your own business and be the boss!

You'll need: Experience driving a heavy truck and large horse rig, horse handling skills, knowledge of horse health problems, and an understanding of the rules of the road and legal issues.

Schooling: A bachelor's degree is helpful, as is previous experience in animal transportation. Attending truck-driving classes is a good idea.

Downside: You need to serve other people's schedules, and you can be out there on your own with a valuable horse in trouble. Starting a business like this takes a big upfront investment, a lot of time away from family, and long hours. Business can be cyclical.

Upside: A successful business can be financially rewarding. You'll work independently, see the country, and work with horses on a regular basis.

APPENDIX B:
Keeping a Life List of Breeds

Bird watchers keep a "life list," a checklist of the birds they've seen. Why shouldn't horse lovers keep a life list of breeds? A horse lover's life list can be more detailed than a bird watcher's life list. Birders can usually only hope to glimpse their quarry from a distance. Horse lovers can get much closer.

Some of the breeds on this list are quite common. Others are rare or regional.

Most breeds in the Exotic category are only apt to be encountered on a trip abroad, but don't let that discourage you. Many European warmblood breeds are popular in American sports like jumping and dressage. Others may be imported, or may make an appearance as part of a traveling exhibit. It may seem unlikely that fate will take you to Kazakhstan or Cameroon, but if it does, you'll be ready to add to your life list.

 SEEN *Keep track of every horse you've ever seen (you can include pictures if you want — after all, it's your list!).*

 TOUCHED *Tick off every hands-on experience you have with horses of different breeds.*

 RIDDEN *If you're lucky enough to ride different kinds of horses, mark it down here.*

 OWNED *This list will probably be the shortest, but why not count horses your friends and family own or even horses you wish you owned (now that would be a long list!).*

DRAFT BREEDS	👁	✋	🐎	🏠
American Cream	○	○	○	○
Belgian	○	○	○	○
Brabant	○	○	○	○
Clydesdale	○	○	○	○
North American Spotted Draft	○	○	○	○
Percheron	○	○	○	○
Shire	○	○	○	○
Suffolk Punch	○	○	○	○

PONIES	👁	✋	🐎	🏠
American Quarter Pony	○	○	○	○
American Shetland Pony	○	○	○	○
American Walking Pony	○	○	○	○
Chincoteague Pony	○	○	○	○
Connemara Pony	○	○	○	○
Dales Pony	○	○	○	○
Dartmoor Pony	○	○	○	○
Exmoor Pony	○	○	○	○
Fell Pony	○	○	○	○
Gotland Pony	○	○	○	○
Hackney Pony	○	○	○	○
Highland Pony (Scotland)	○	○	○	○
Kerry Bog Pony	○	○	○	○

PONIES, continued	👁	✋	🐎	🏠
Lac La Croix Indian Pony	○	○	○	○
New Forest Pony (England)	○	○	○	○
Newfoundland Pony	○	○	○	○
Pony of the Americas	○	○	○	○
Shackleford Banker Pony	○	○	○	○
Shetland Pony	○	○	○	○
Welara Pony	○	○	○	○
Welsh Pony	○	○	○	○

LIGHT HORSES	👁	✋	🐎	🏠
Abaco Barb	○	○	○	○
Akhal-Teke	○	○	○	○
American Curly Horse	○	○	○	○
American Indian Horse	○	○	○	○
American Paint	○	○	○	○
American Quarter Horse	○	○	○	○
American Saddlebred	○	○	○	○
Andalusian	○	○	○	○
Appaloosa	○	○	○	○
AraAppaloosa	○	○	○	○
Arabian	○	○	○	○
Argentine Polo Pony	○	○	○	○
Australian Stock Horse	○	○	○	○

LIGHT HORSES, *continued*	👁	✋	🐴	🏚
Azteca	◯	◯	◯	◯
Ban-ei Race Horse	◯	◯	◯	◯
Bavarian Warmblood	◯	◯	◯	◯
Belgian Ardennais	◯	◯	◯	◯
Brumby	◯	◯	◯	◯
Camargue	◯	◯	◯	◯
Canadian Cutting Horse	◯	◯	◯	◯
Canadian Horse	◯	◯	◯	◯
Canadian Sport Horse	◯	◯	◯	◯
Cape Horse	◯	◯	◯	◯
Caspian	◯	◯	◯	◯
Cerbat	◯	◯	◯	◯
Chickasaw	◯	◯	◯	◯
Cleveland Bay	◯	◯	◯	◯
Colorado Rangerbred	◯	◯	◯	◯
Costa Rican Saddle Horse	◯	◯	◯	◯
Czech Warmblood	◯	◯	◯	◯
Danish Oldenburg	◯	◯	◯	◯
Danish Warmblood	◯	◯	◯	◯
Datong	◯	◯	◯	◯
Dutch Warmblood	◯	◯	◯	◯
Falabella	◯	◯	◯	◯

LIGHT HORSES, *continued*	👁	✋	🐴	🏚
Florida Cracker	◯	◯	◯	◯
Frederiksborg	◯	◯	◯	◯
French Ardennais	◯	◯	◯	◯
Friesian	◯	◯	◯	◯
Galiceno	◯	◯	◯	◯
Gypsy Vanner	◯	◯	◯	◯
Hackney Horse	◯	◯	◯	◯
Haflinger	◯	◯	◯	◯
Hanoverian	◯	◯	◯	◯
Holsteiner	◯	◯	◯	◯
Hungarian Horse	◯	◯	◯	◯
Icelandic Horse	◯	◯	◯	◯
Irish Draught	◯	◯	◯	◯
Irish Hunter	◯	◯	◯	◯
Kentucky Mountain Saddle Horse	◯	◯	◯	◯
Kiger Mustang	◯	◯	◯	◯
Lipizzan	◯	◯	◯	◯
Lusitano	◯	◯	◯	◯
Mangalarga Marchador	◯	◯	◯	◯
Marwari	◯	◯	◯	◯
McCurdy Plantation Horse	◯	◯	◯	◯
Miniature Horse	◯	◯	◯	◯

LIGHT HORSES, *continued*	👁	✋	🐎	🏚
Missouri Fox Trotter	○	○	○	○
Morab	○	○	○	○
Morgan	○	○	○	○
Moroccan Barb	○	○	○	○
Moyle	○	○	○	○
Mustang	○	○	○	○
National Show Horse	○	○	○	○
Nokota	○	○	○	○
Norwegian Fjord	○	○	○	○
Oldenburg	○	○	○	○
Palomino	○	○	○	○
Paso Fino	○	○	○	○
Peruvian Paso	○	○	○	○
Pryor Mountain Mustang	○	○	○	○
Przewalkski's Horse (a.k.a. Taki)	○	○	○	○
Racking Horse	○	○	○	○
Rocky Mountain Horse	○	○	○	○
Sable Island Horse	○	○	○	○
Selle Francais	○	○	○	○
Shagya Arabian	○	○	○	○
Single-Footing Horse	○	○	○	○
Skyros	○	○	○	○
Sorraia	○	○	○	○

LIGHT HORSES, *continued*	👁	✋	🐎	🏚
Spanish Barb	○	○	○	○
Spanish Colonial/Mustang	○	○	○	○
Spanish Jennet	○	○	○	○
Standardbred	○	○	○	○
Sulphur Horse	○	○	○	○
Swedish Warmblood	○	○	○	○
Tennessee Walking Horse	○	○	○	○
Thoroughbred	○	○	○	○
Tiger Horse	○	○	○	○
Trakehner	○	○	○	○
Westphalian	○	○	○	○
Wilber-Cruce Mission Horse	○	○	○	○

DONKEYS & MULES	👁	✋	🐎	🏚
Hinny	○	○	○	○
Large Standard Donkey	○	○	○	○
Mammoth Donkey	○	○	○	○
Miniature Donkey	○	○	○	○
Mule	○	○	○	○
Poitou Donkey	○	○	○	○
Spotted Ass	○	○	○	○
Standard Donkey	○	○	○	○

APPENDIX C:
Lots of Good Books

AND A FEW GOOD AUTHORS

APPENDIX D:
Lots of Great Movies

APPENDIX E:
Lots of Cool Crafts

GLOSSARY

Action. Degree of flexion of the joints during movement; ranges from high and snappy to low and sweeping.

Aid. A signal from the rider. The natural aids are voice, hands, seat, weight, legs, and upper body. Artificial aids are whips and spurs.

ASTM/SEI. American Standard for Testing Materials and Safety Equipment Institute. Rates riding helmets.

Bars. The gap between the horse's front and back teeth, where the bit rests.

Beat. A single step within a gait; may involve one leg or two. The walk is a 4-beat gait, one leg at a time, 1-2-3-4. The trot is a 2-beat gait; two diagonal legs at a time. The canter is a 3-beat gait.

Breeches. English riding pants, that are tight on the calf to fit into tall boots.

Chaps. Leather leggings worn over pants to protect a rider's legs. Originally Western, they are now used by English riders too. Half-chaps cover only the lower leg.

Cold-blooded. A horse with draft breeding, with heavy bone and thicker skin and hide.

Collection. A compression of movement. A collected horse is light on his feet, well balanced, and very responsive to the rider.

Complete feed. Usually pelletized, this product is meant to meet all of a horse's nutritional needs without feeding supplemental hay or grass.

Contact. Pressure on the horse's mouth through the reins.

Cooling out. Walking a horse after strenuous exercise. Moving air cools a sweaty horse, and gentle motion squeezes metabolic wastes out of the muscles so they don't become sore.

Cross-tie. A method of tying a horse. The horse is held in the center of the aisle by lines fastened to either side of the halter.

Diagonal. A pair of legs moving together at the trot; for example, right front and left hind move forward at the same time.

FEI. Federation Equestrian International, the board that oversees international equestrian competition.

Flying lead change. When a horse changes from one lead to another in the canter without breaking stride.

Forehand. The horse's front end, including the head, neck, shoulders, and front legs.

Gait. A specific pattern of foot movements, such as walk, trot, or canter. The horse has 55 possible gaits.

Gaited. A horse who has an extra gait beyond the most common walk, trot, and canter. Gaited breeds include Saddlebreds, Pasos, Icelandics, and many Spanish-type breeds.

Green. An untrained or novice horse (or rider).

Ground-driving. A training technique that involves driving the horse with long lines while walking behind or to the side.

Ground tying. When a horse reliably stands still, as if tied, when the reins are dropped on the ground.

Ground work. Training from the ground that leads up to and reinforces riding, it includes leading, lunging, and ground driving.

Hackamore. One of many forms of bitless bridle.

Hand. The unit used to measure equine height, from the highest point of the withers to the ground. A hand is 4 inches. 14.2 hands means 14 hands, 2 inches or 58 inches.

Hand grazing. Allowing a horse to eat while on a halter.

Homeopathy. A system of medical treatment using minute amounts of substances that, in large doses, would cause symptoms like the ones being treated. For instance, nux vomica treats colic; in large doses it causes stomach pain.

Hot blooded. A horse of Oriental breeding, such as the Thoroughbred and Arabian. Hot bloods have fine bone and thin coats.

Lead. In the canter, the legs on one side reach farther forward than on the other with each stride. The horse leads with the leg that is to the inside of the circle.

Liniment. A medicinal fluid rubbed onto the skin to reduce swelling and pain.

Longe. To work the horse in a circle around you, on a long (30 feet or so) line.

Lunging (pronounced LUN-jing). Having a horse circle around a handler at the end of a long rope, called a lunge line, at various gaits, for training or exercise.

Roadster. A fast and stylish driving horse.

Tack. Anything that a horse wears, such as halter, saddle, blanket, bit, and so on.

Tack up. To saddle and bridle (or harness) a horse so he's ready for work.

Transition. The change from one gait to another. A downward transition is from faster to slower; an upward transition is from slower to faster.

USEF. United States Equestrian Federation, the national board that oversees equine competition within the United States.

USET. The United States Equestrian Team, which oversees selection and training of national teams in Combined Driving, Dressage, Endurance Riding, Eventing, Reining, and Show Jumping.

Vaulting surcingle. A girth with handles, used for vaulting.

Vital signs. Temperature, pulse, and respiration.

Warmblood. A horse, usually of European origin, developed by crossing saddle horses on draft or carriage horse stock.

✺ VITAL SIGNS ✺

✷ Normal resting temperature is 99–100.5 Above 102 is considered a fever.

✷ To get an accurate reading, the thermometer needs to stay you-know-where for a full three minutes.

✷ Normal resting pulse is 24–40 beats per minute, lowest for fit, athletic horses. Count for fifteen seconds and multiply by 4.

✷ Normal resting respiration rate is 8–12 breaths per minute. Can be as low as 4, or as high as 20. Watch the nostrils or the sides, count for 15 seconds and multiply by 4.

RESOURCES

Breed Associations

American Association of Owners and Breeders of Peruvian Paso Horses
707-544-5807
www.napha.net

American Connemara Pony Society
330-664-0871
www.acps.org

American Gaited Mountain Horse Association
859-842-0270
www.unitedmountainhorse.org

American Gaited Mules Association
info@americangaitedmule.com
www.americangaitedmule.com

American Indian Horse Conservancy
802-888-6623
www.red-road-farm.com

American Miniature Horse Association
817-783-5600
www.amha.org

American Morgan Horse Association
802-985-4944
www.morganhorse.com

American Paint Horse Association
817-834-2742
www.apha.com

American Quarter Horse Association
806-376-4811
www.aqha.com

American Quarter Horse Youth Association
806-376-4811
www.aqhya.com

American Quarter Pony Association
641-675-3669
www.aqpa.com

American Saddlebred Horse Association
859-259-2742
www.asha.net

American Shetland Pony Club
309-263-4044
www.shetlandminiature.com
Manages the American Miniature Horse Registry

American Walking Pony Association
P.O. Box 5282, Macon, GA 31208
478-743-2321

Appaloosa Horse Club
208-882-5578
www.appaloosa.com

Appaloosa Sport Horse Association
334-750-4052
www.apsha.org

Arabian Horse Association
303-696-4500
www.arabianhorses.org

Connemara Pony Breeders Society
+353-0-95-21863
www.cpbs.ie

Foundation Quarter Horse Registry
269-649-1106
www.fqhrregistry.com

International Andalusian and Lusitano Horse Association Registry
205-995-8900
www.ialha.org

International Buckskin Horse Association
219-552-1013
www.ibha.net

International Colored Appaloosa Association
574-238-4280
www.icaainc.com

International Miniature Trotting and Pacing Association
254-853-2806
www.imtpa.com

International Pinto Arabian Registry
615-559-2246
www.pintoarabians.com

International Quarter Pony Association
931-996-3987
www.quarterponyassociation.com

Kentucky Mountain Saddle Horse Association/Spotted Mountain Horse Association
859-225-5674
www.kmsha.com

McCurdy Plantation Horse Registry and Association
903-677-4858
www.mccurdyhorses.com

Missouri Fox Trotter Horse Breeders
Association
417-683-2468
www.mfthba.com

Mountain Pleasure Horse Association
606-768-3847
www.mountainpleasurehorseassociation.
com

National Chincoteague Pony Association
360-671-8338
www.pony-chincoteague.com

National Foundation Quarter Horse
Association
541-426-4403
www.nfqha.com

National Pinto Horse Registry
805-241-5533
www.pintohorseregistry.com

National Spotted Saddle Horse Association
615-890-2864
www.nssha.com

North American Peruvian Horse
Association
707-544-5807
www.napha.net

Norwegian Fjord Horse Registry
303-684-6466
www.nfhr.com

Palomino Horse Breeders of America
918-438-1234
www.palominohba.com

Paso Fino Horse Association
859-825-6005
www.pfha.org

Pintabian Horse Registry
218-689-4439
www.pintabianregistry.com

Pinto Horse Association of America
405-491-0111
www.pinto.org

Pony of the Americas Club
317-788-0107
www.poac.org

Pure Puerto Rican Paso Fino Federation
of America
503-799-9792
http://puertoricanpasofino.org

Racking Horse Breeders Association
of North America
256-353-7225
www.rackinghorse.com

Rocky Mountain Horse Association
859-243-0260
www.rmhorse.com

Single-Footing Horse Owners' & Breeders'
Association
706-969-6224
www.shobaonline.com

Spotted Saddle Horse Breeders and
Exhibitors Association
931-684-7496
www.sshbea.org

Tennessee Walking Horse Breeders
and Exhibitors Association
931-359-1574
www.twhbea.com

Tiger Horse Breed Registry & Members
Association
505-438-2827
www.tigrehorse.org

United Mountain Horse
859-842-0270
www.unitedmountainhorse.org

United States Icelandic Horse Congress
866-929-0009
www.icelandics.org

United States Mangalarga Marchador
Association
480-595-2559

Walkaloosa Horse Association
805-995-1894
www.walkaloosaregistry.com

Walking Horse Owners Association
615-494-8822
www.walkinghorseowners.com

Welsh Pony and Cob Society of America
540-868-7669
www.welshpony.org

RARE BREEDS

The Livestock Breeds Conservancy
919-542-5704
www.livestockconservancy.org

Riding Organizations

Amateur Field Trial Clubs of America
662-223-0126
www.aftca.org

American Competitive Trail Horse
Association
877-992-2842
www.actha.us

American Driving Society
608-237-7382
www.americandrivingsociety.org

American Endurance Ride Conference
866-271-2372
www.aerc.org

American Hunter and Jumper Foundation
859-225-6700
www.ahjf.org

American Junior Rodeo Association
325-277-5824
www.ajra.org

American Polocrosse Association
843-825-2686
www.americanpolocrosse.org

American Riding Instructors Association
239-948-3232
www.riding-instructor.com

American Vaulting Association
323-645-0800
www.AmericanVaulting.org

Back Country Horsemen of America
888-893-5161
www.backcountryhorse.com

Barrel Futurities of America
918-773-5246
www.barrelfuturitiesofamerica.com

Carriage Association of America
859-231-0971
www.caaonline.com

Cowboy Mounted Shooting Association
888-960-0003
www.cowboymountedshooting.com

Fédération Internationale de Horseball
info@fihb.net
www.fihb.net

Gladstone Equestrian Association
908-453-3332
www.gladstonedriving.org

International Hunter Futurity
859-879-3600
www.inthf.org

The Jockey Club
859-224-2700
www.jockeyclub.com

Long Riders' Guild
longriders@thelongridersguild.com
www.thelongridersguild.com

Master of Fox Hounds Association
540-955-5680
www.mfha.com

National Association of Competitive
  Mounted Orienteering
616-675-7342
www.nacmo.org

National Barrel Horse Association
706-722-7223
www.nbha.com

National Cutting Horse Association
817-244-6188
www.nchacutting.com

National High School Rodeo Association
800-466-4772
www.nhsra.com

National Hunter and Jumper Association
540-687-3455
www.nhja.org

National Jousting Association
410-482-2176
www.nationaljousting.com

National Little Britches Rodeo
800-763-3694
www.nlbra.org

National Pony Express Association
785-562-3615
www.xphomestation.com/npea.html

National Reined Cow Horse Association
940-488-1500
www.nrcha.com

National Reining Horse Association
405-946-7400
www.nrha1.com

National Snaffle Bit Association
847-623-6722
www.nsba.com

National Steeplechase Association
410-392-0700
www.nationalsteeplechase.com

North American Junior & Young Riders
  Championships
859-225-6964
www.youngriders.org

North American Ski Joring Association
Northeast: 603-496-3005
West: 406-261-7464
www.nasja.com

North American Trail Ride Conference
303-688-1677
www.natrc.org

Path International
(formerly North American Riding for the
Handicapped Association)
800-369-7433
www.pathintl.org

Performance Horse Registry
859-258-2472
www.usef.org

Ride and Tie Association
contactus@rideandtie.org
www.rideandtie.org

United States Dressage Federation
859-971-2277
www.usdf.org

United States Equestrian Federation
859-258-2472
www.usef.org

United States Eventing Association
703-779-0440
www.eventingusa.com

United States Pony Clubs
859-254-7669
www.ponyclub.org

United States Team Penning Association
817-599-4455
www.ustpa.com

United States Trotting Association
877-800-8782
www.ustrotting.com

Adoption Organizations

American Horse Council
202-296-4031
www.horsecouncil.org

American Standardbred Adoption Program
608-689-2399
www.4thehorses.com

Bureau of Land Management
U. S. Department of the Interior
866-468-7826
www.blm.gov
Manages the National Wild Horse and Burro Program

Communication Alliance to Network Thoroughbred Ex-Racehorses
www.canterusa.org

Equine Angels Rescue Sanctuary
203-733-3576
www.foalrescue.com

Equine Rescue & Adoption Foundation, Inc.
772-220-0150
www.eraf.org

The Exceller Fund
mail@excellerfund.org
www.excellerfund.org

Finger Lakes Thoroughbred Adoption Program, Inc.
585-924-9510
www.fingerlakestap.org

Humane Society of the United States
866-720-2676
www.humanesociety.org

New Vocations Racehorse Adoption Program
937-642-3171
www.horseadoption.com

ReRun, Inc.
859-595-6660
www.rerun.org

Saddlebred Rescue, Inc.
908-605-6032
www.saddlebredrescue.com
Rescues and places Saddlebreds, Hackneys, and Morgans

Thoroughbred Retirement Foundation
518-226-0028
www.trfinc.org

Unwanted Horse Coalition
202-296-4031
www.unwantedhorsecoalition.org

Craft Supplies

Buckaroo Bobbins
928-636-1885
www.buckaroobobbins.com
This is a great source for patterns and accessories for making authentic costume for sports like Cowboy Mounted Shooting.

InteriorMall.com
800-590-5844
www.interiormall.com
English and Western themes

Peak Fabrics
403-242-3537
www.peakfabrics.com

Plaid
800-842-4197
www.plaidonline.com
Craft supplies, including Mod Podge. There are different versions of Mod Podge for outdoor use, paper, and even fabric.

Speedball Art Products Company
800-898-7224
www.speedballart.com

SuitAbility
800-207-0256
www.suitability.com
Patterns for an amazing array of clothing and horse equipment.

Model Horses

Breyer Animal Creations
800-413-3348
www.breyerhorses.com
Breyerfest scheduling and special events, and a wealth of information on model horses, customizing, and showing

Model Horse Guide
www.modelhorseguide.com
Instructions on repainting models using acrylic paints

North American Model Horse Shows Association
recording-secretary@namhsa.org
www.namhsa.org
The sanctioning organization for model horse shows

Rio Rondo Enterprises
620-668-5421
www.riorondo.com
Kits and materials to make your own model horse tack.

Stone Horses
866-581-1370
www.stonehorses.com
Information about model horse events including Stone's own Model Horse Country Fair

Informative Websites

The Clicker Center
kurlanda@crisny.org
www.theclickercenter.com
The website of Alexandra Kurland, who specializes in clicker training for horses

Endurance.Net
www.endurance.net

Jessica Jahiel Holistic Horsemanship
www.jessicajahiel.com

Jessica Jahiel's Horse-Sense
www.horse-sense.org
The official newsletter of Jessica Jahiel's Holistic Horsemanship. The site includes a page featuring true helmet stories from Horse-Sense readers.

Karen Pryor Clicker Training
www.clickertraining.com
The website of Karen Pryor who pioneered clicker training. Her site includes tips and news about training all species, including human.

Art, Photography, and Writing

Crochet Do Dads
http://crochetdodads.com
Patterns for great crocheted accessories for your horse.

Fleishman, Sid. *The Abracadabra Kid: A Writer's Life.* New York: Harper Trophy, 1998.

Groves, Lesli. *Photographing Horses: How to Capture the Perfect Equine Image.* Guilford, CT: Globe Pequot Press, 2006.

Golden Wood Studio
ruth@ruthsanderson.com
www.ruthsanderson.com
Ruth Sanderson's Web site, illustrator of the Horse Diaries series

Kerr, M. E. *Blood on the Forehead: What I Know About Writing.* New York: Harper Teen, 1998.

Mann, Charles. *Photographing and "Videoing" Horses Explained: Digital and Film.* North Pomfret, VT: Trafalgar Square Books, 2007.

Savitt, Sam. *Draw Horses with Sam Savitt.* Boonsboro, MD: Half Halt Press, 1991.

Todd-Daniels, Marilyn. *The Complete Book of Equine Drawing.* Whitewright, TX: Woodsong Institute of Art, 1993.

Ueland, Brenda. *If You Want to Write: A Book About Art, Independence, and Spirit.* St. Paul: Graywolf Press, 1987.

Magazines

Blaze Magazine
800-725-7136
http://blazekids.com

The Draft Horse Journal
319-352-4046
www.drafthorsejournal.com

Rural Heritage
319-362-3027
www.ruralheritage.com

The Trail Rider
866-343-1802
www.equisearch.com/magazines/the-trail-rider

Trailblazer
928-759-7045
www.trailblazermagazine.us

Young Rider
800-888-4640
www.youngrider.com

Youth Beats
United States Trotting Association
877-800-8782
www.hoofbeatsmagazine.com/youthbeats
Magazine for kids 7-14, published as part of *Hoof Beats*

INDEX

Page numbers in **bold** indicate tables; those in *italic* indicate illustrations.

Other Storey Titles You Will Enjoy

Cherry Hill's Horse Care for Kids
The essentials of equine care, from matching the right horse to the rider to handling, grooming, feeding, stabling, and much more.
128 pages. Paper. ISBN 978-1-58017-407-7.

Games on Horseback
by Betty Bennett-Talbot and Steven Bennett
A great collection of more than 50 safe, exciting, and challenging games for horse and rider.
144 pages. Paper. ISBN 978-1-58017-134-2.

Horse Games & Puzzles by Cindy A. Littlefield
Keep young horse lovers busy with more than 100 activities about their favorite animal. For children 8 to 12.
144 pages. Paper. ISBN 978-1-58017-538-8.

Judy Richter's Riding for Kids
A comprehensive handbook to teach young riders the essentials of horsemanship.
144 pages. Paper. ISBN 978-1-58017-510-4.

Jumping for Kids by Lesley Ward
A complete program that provides all the fundamentals of jumping safely and correctly.
144 pages. Paper. ISBN 978-1-58017-672-9.

Pop-Out & Paint Horse Breeds by Cindy A. Littlefield
Using the easy step-by-step instructions and some basic craft supplies, kids ages 8 to 12 can create their own herd of model paper horses.
48 pages plus 20 die-cut cards. Paper. ISBN 978-1-60342-963-4.

These and other books from Storey Publishing are available wherever quality books are sold or by calling 1-800-441-5700.
Visit us at *www.storey.com* or sign up for our newsletter at *www.storey.com/signup*.